THE PEOPLE ADVANTAGE

The People Advantage

Improving Results Through Better Selection and Performance

Neville Bain and Bill Mabey

Ichor Business Books
An Imprint of
Purdue University Press
West Lafayette, Indiana

First Ichor Business Book edition, 1999.

Copyright © 1999 by Neville Bain and Bill Mabey

Published under license from Macmillan Press Ltd, Houndmills, Basingstoke, Hampshire, RG21 6XS

This edition available only in the United States and Canada.

03 02 01 00 99   5 4 3 2 1

Library of Congress Cataloging-in-Publication Data applied for.
ISBN 1–55753–177–3

Printed in Great Britain

For Charles and Mae Bain, Peter and Kathleen Kemp

NEVILLE BAIN

For Trudy, Georgina and Stephanie – always supportive

BILL MABEY

Contents

List of Case Studies and Figures

Foreword

Competition – at the level of the firm or the country – is ferociously tough today. Markets are turbulent places, full of risk and opportunity. Globalization has brought the prospect of massive rewards but it has opened up an unparalleled need for a deeper knowledge of customers and potential customers. And, because a revolution is moving apace in information technology and telecommunications, keeping in touch with what is possible is a challenge companies must get and keep on top of. Innovation and creative thought are needed.

We either achieve or we don't because of our people. They, in the end, differentiate us from our competition. Our strategy is formulated by people, throughout the organization. Our ability to harness technology depends on people. And implementation, so often the key to success or failure, is delivered by people.

Many of the constraints on today's business leaders are legacies of a past where inadequate attention was paid to thinking ahead; we deal with legacy systems, legacy structures and, often worst of all, legacy attitudes. Often, they were put in place by leaders who failed to think ahead and who failed themselves, and their people, by failing to prepare for the future.

Continued development for all is needed but thinking through how to do it is tough. It means thinking hard about people's competencies, their motivation and their needs. For a business, that means thinking hard about the organization's needs. For a country, it means thinking about where its advantages are going to come from.

Neville Bain and Bill Mabey understand all this and, reassuringly, they make it very clear that this book has no simple, single point. In a management book, that is refreshing. It avoids the tedium of one simplistic concept extended to fill a couple of hundred pages. And it will avoid the short life that any one simple notion is destined to have in the changing, complex organizations now needed to win against the world.

This is a book that recognizes complexity and promotes attention to detail. Careful and analytic in its methodologies, it promotes models of competencies which give a lot of material for thought; thought that managers should be putting into understanding the people they have, the people they will need and the way they can continually develop everyone in the organization.

Continual development, constantly and for all, well organized and well led begins at the top. You feel, throughout this book, that the writers practise everything they write about. We can all learn a great deal from it; reading it is one step in ensuring our own development is not neglected. Read it and think about what it means for you and for everyone you lead.

Derek Wanless
Group Chief Executive
NatWest Group

Preface

Putting the right people into the right jobs and encouraging the right development activity will enhance organizational efficiency, productivity and where appropriate, profitability.

This proposition should be self-evident and is indeed supported by a growing volume of research evidence. The management, and indeed macro-economic, implications here are substantial. If this proposition can be shown to be true for a job then it should equally follow for organizations as a whole and indeed for the economy at large. Apart from the general case for increasing productivity through people, we are now operating in a world environment of increasing competition, involving millions of new, well-trained, educated and recent technology supported workers. As organizations reduce numbers to compete, it becomes more critical to ensure that the remaining people are well suited to their roles and properly developed to give optimum performance.

And yet there are real problems in achieving this goal. The fundamental issue is that people are beautifully complex while jobs are multi-faceted and in many cases constantly changing. Understanding the relationship between the two is a daunting proposition. Not only must we deal with an individual's suitability for the key tasks required in the job but we must also cope with their fit to the corporate culture, the departmental culture, the boss, the subordinates, the cross-functional team, the internal clients, the external clients and so on. Then we must deal with the so-called 'paradoxes' of person–job fit – the many cases where ownership of a personal attribute may facilitate one aspect of job performance while obstructing another. Strong independence of mind, for example, may benefit an entrepreneurial role but hinder teamwork.

We have to be able to measure both people and jobs with precision and to be able to interpret the many links and permutations. This is arguably a specialist field for the work and organizational psychologist but as George Miller observed in his Presidential Address to the American Psychological Association some years ago, 'It is time to give Psychology away.' Somehow we have to bring together the psychologist's disciplined understanding of people to interact with the manager's experience and understanding of business goals and objectives. For the most part management requires simple actionable methods. It wants to cut through much of the complexity that the psychologist understands to be inherent in selection and development decision making. If we can manage this move from the complex to the simple, we will make a major contribution to organizational performance.

Across the world organizations have begun over the past decade in particular to come to terms with the measurement and profiling of their human resources and to enhance the development process. There are clear examples of excellence in this respect. Yet there is a long way to go. Many organizations continue to spend more money per capita on tea and coffee for their employees than on assessing their fundamental abilities, personality and motivational characteristics. The interview – with its tendency to quick first impressions – is still excessively used in making the substantial investment that is the recruitment of a key staff member. Boards of companies are still pushing the assessment and development process away from themselves as if it only applies at lower levels of the organization. Top managers still tend to use vastly simplistic theories of occupational behaviour to guide their decision making.

The situation is further exacerbated by the need referred to above for organizations to reduce numbers to operate from a leaner, more competitive base. One of the implications of this reduction for many organizations has been a reduction in the size of the HR department. They have been trained in large numbers and have been developing pools of experience and expertise. Reducing the HR function has put even more pressure on the line managers themselves to be able to understand and use people data. The time that a manager – under increasing resource pressure – will give to developing an HR expertise is inevitably limited. Herein lies even more of an argument for finding new ways and means of bridging the gap between the complexity of the input data and the management goal of having simple, usable outputs.

A further implication of the slimming down of organizations lies in the growing requirement to be able to devolve decision making and empower subordinates to decide and act. If there has been one key lesson from research on empowerment, if has been that it only works if the empowered staff are competent to use their power. Here again the pressure is on to help management to understand the basis of managerial competence – how to identify it and how to develop it.

This book concentrates first on the measurement of people's behaviour at work, for if we cannot properly understand the key elements of the human resource then we cannot properly apply it. It is deliberately not an academic text although it is based on theory and methods which have been academically researched. It attempts to guide managers in a practical, down to earth way in terms of both the assessment and development of staff. For those more interested in the background research a comprehensive bibliography is included as an appendix.

The main theme of the book is that the relationship between people and jobs is necessarily complex and often forces management in some desperation towards simple but unsatisfactory solutions. Yet for those managers who tackle and come to terms with this complex relationship, the potential rewards are substantial. The book contains many practical suggestions to facilitate this process.

There is a secondary theme to the book, which is that the assessment and development of staff is becoming an increasingly internationally focused activity. The problem here is to balance an organizational need for standardization of method and approach with the clear recognition that cultures are different and require a degree of adaptation in assessment and development practice. This book encourages an international perspective where appropriate. It is based in the United Kingdom but it draws on research and opinions from more than 30 specialists in the field of international assessment and development – including most of the world's leading economies. The book is also fortunate to be able to draw on the combined research experience over the past 20 years of the SHL Group plc[1]. The Group is essentially comprised of work and organizational psychologists operating in close to 40 countries world-wide. It is arguably the world's most broadly based organization specializing in assessing and developing staff at work. It has focused on the development of occupational models of behaviour and has extended that research across the many cultures in which it operates. At the same time this is not an SHL book. It draws on other models and the views expressed about optimum practice are those of the authors themselves.

The people advantage within an organization is achieved when the latent capability of the people within it is released, thus enabling it to reach its full potential. This book is intended to have a broad readership appeal. In addition to the Human Resource specialists both within and external to organizations across the whole spectrum of private, public and not-for-profit sectors, it will also have wide application with general managers committed to increasing effectiveness of their organization. Given the practical approach, which is strongly based on empirical evidence and theory, the book is intended to appeal internationally to general managers, to those people studying management on advanced learning courses, as well as being a valuable textbook for those training for the specialized field of Human Resources. We have attempted to write the book in an easy to read style, and the reader can dip backwards and forwards into the topics included in each chapter. The summary at the end of each chapter is intended to provide a convenient refresher of the main points included.

The book is in two parts. Part I is designed to take an overview of the main ways in which an organization can take a competitive advantage through its people. The focus is on providing practical advice for ensuring that the right people are recruited and then subsequently on ensuring that the right development occurs. Part II examines a number of specific issues relating to people, such as motivation, leadership and communication, that we believe to have an important impact on the organization's productivity.

The book does not have a simple point to make. It is full of ideas, models and propositions which should challenge the reader in considering the optimum use of people in the workplace. The book's final thought is for those who put a value to businesses. It is a challenge that now is the time to bring the people factor into that valuation and we have the means to make that happen.

Neville Bain & Bill Mabey

1. Founded by Peter Saville and Roger Holdsworth in 1977

Acknowledgements

It is inevitable that a book of this kind which attempts to cover such a breadth of human performance should draw on the knowledge and experience of many colleagues. It sometimes seems unfair that authorship should be down to two individuals. At least we can record here our sincere appreciation of all those who have contributed in one way or another.

Professor Rick Jacobs of Landy, Jacobs and Associates and of Penn State University was helpful with his insights into demonstrating the real value of good selection practice. His case study is included in Chapter 1. Brian Dive of Unilever went to the trouble of providing the detailed case study for the optimum use of the total people resource in Chapter 5. Mike Hall similarly provided helpful case study experience from The Post Office (UK) relating specifically to the management of knowledge. Valuable case study inputs were also contributed by Marco Kim in Korea, Deborah Negus in New Zealand and Neil Cowieson in Hong Kong as well as several other international members of the SHL Group plc.

Helen Baron and Sue Henley made important contributions to the chapters on motivation and stress management. Professor Christine Farrell made a variety of suggestions in the areas of competency mapping and 360° assessment. John Mahoney-Philips was the stimulus for a useful preparatory discussion on international assessment. All at the time were working within the SHL Group plc. Professor Roger Gill of The Leadership Trust helped us in our consideration of Transformational Leadership.

The management of SHL is due a substantial general vote of thanks for making much of its research and survey data available for this book and allowing access to its specialist staff of psychologists. We hope all those involved will allow an overall note of our appreciation here.

The book went through several drafts. The first draft not surprisingly needed most attention. We are grateful to those who worked their way through it and gave careful comment, including Professor Peter Saville,

Roger Holdsworth and Lisa Cramp of SHL as well as John Roberts and Jerry Cope of The Post Office. Stephen Rutt of Macmillan Business Publishing is experienced in this process and made a number of very valuable suggestions for reshaping the second draft.

The final draft was read by some of the busiest people around but we have valued their comments and have included some of them as a guide to potential readers. Derek Wanless, CEO of National Westminster Group, was kind enough to make the time to review the book in detail and to write the Foreword. We are extremely grateful to him for his interest and help. Valuable review points and comments were also received from Sir Dominic Cadbury, Chairman of Cadbury Schweppes; Tim Melville Ross, Director General of the Institute of Directors; J Adair Turner, CEO of the CBI; Professor Tom Cannon, Chief Executive of the Management and Enterprise Council; Mike Kinski, CEO of Stagecoach and Professor Ivan Robertson of UMIST.

Professor Jeffrey Pfeffer of Stamford University Graduate School of Business is an acknowledged expert in the field of optimizing the output of people at work. We are pleased to have been able to quote his work and are grateful to him for his positive comments on the final draft.

We have tried to broaden the book by making reference to the research and models of selected other authors. We would especially like to thank the following for their permission to use specific material:

- Ann Marie Ryan of Michigan State University who directed the international survey of assessment practice referred to in Chapter 6;
- Professor Paul Evans of INSEAD for his pertinent comment on competencies included in Chapter 2;
- SHL Group plc for the use of the OPQ® Concept Model profile chart, the Inventory of Management Competencies profile chart, The Motivation Questionnaire profile chart and the models of Influencing Style and Potential Work Stressors.

Of course, the production of a book of this kind is not possible without the disciplined hard work of those who type the drafts, make the inserts, do the corrections and then see it all substantially rewritten. Susan Deehenderson bore the brunt of this work and the high standard of her initial production saved us much time. We are very grateful to her and to Pearl McLeod who assisted with the general administration. Finally, our thanks go to Trudy Mabey who had the unenviable 'proofing' job of trying to find some editorial consistency from two different styles and stubborn views on acceptable grammar.

It would not have been practical to list everyone by name who helped in one way or another with this book but we sincerely acknowledge all the contributions. While we fully recognize the input of a wide group of people, the final work is, of course, the responsibility of the authors. If we have been able to use all that assistance to help and encourage organizations to enhance the use of their people, then the project will have been well worthwhile.

Neville Bain
Bill Mabey

Part I
An Overview

Setting the Scene

People power

There are two distinguishing features of the most successful businesses around the world. These are a focus on strategy and a focus on people. Strategy is an essential building block for the commercial organization that wishes to maximize value for its owners. This book is more about people than strategy although we cover strategic thinking as an area of management competency in Chapter 11.

In this chapter where we are setting the scene, we wish to underscore the important truth that people really do make the difference to an organization's performance. Given the forces of competition and the market opportunities that are largely open to any who choose to compete, it is the quality and contribution of the people at all levels that are the key differentiators. This is not a novel thought. It is common good practice for managers to talk about the importance of their people resource, and how they strive to empower them to deliver. Examples from literature and research will also attest to this importance. Take for example the work in the USA of Jeffrey Pfeffer, where he has observed that the top-performing companies in the 20 years 1972–1992 came from deeply competitive industries, such as airlines, retailing, publishing, and food processing. The underlying cause of the performance of these winning companies was down to the people within them.

Michael Porter's now historically famous work on the 'five competitive forces', which were used to differentiate the profitability of an industry, is another example. At the centre of his model is the degree of rivalry among existing firms, and other variables were the threat of new entrants and the threat of substitute products or services, along with the bargaining power of customers and suppliers.

Others have taken the view that people and how they are motivated and managed is, perhaps, more important in today's environment. A major reason supporting this position is that historical factors that have influenced an industry's profitability, and the roles of the competitors within it, have changed significantly over time. Pfeffer observes that changes in fairly recent years demonstrate the decline of some of the non-people elements of competitive advantage. Below is our list of the reasons that support this view:

- Regulated and protected markets have declined significantly, and on a world-wide basis. Industries such as the airline industry are a classic example of this.
- Product life cycles are shorter and new technology is being made redundant at a faster rate each year.
- Access to the required financial resource is not an inhibitor today given the mobility and flexibility of the financial markets.
- Economies of scale are much less important today than even a few years ago. The significant economies are achieved early on the scale, and increasingly the consumer is demanding greater variety without any cost penalty.

Superior service has become increasingly important and this is heavily reliant on the people in the organization for consistent delivery.

There is therefore strong support for the importance of people at all levels in any winning organization. Perhaps some will feel that this is a truism that most would subscribe to and is therefore neither novel nor iconoclastic. This is a fair observation, yet the disturbing reality is that in the great majority of organizations, especially commercial ones, nothing much more than lip-service is paid to the notion that investment behind people is valuable.

As an illustration to support this suggestion, the 1995 research by Neville Bain amongst 150 internationally based general managers, who were deemed to be successful in their roles, indicated that only a small amount of time was devoted to management development and to personal development. The analysis showed that these managers claimed to spend, on average, only 8 per cent of their time on developing the people in their organization, and less than 4 per cent on personal development. These time allocations were estimates rather than accurate measures, and given the propensity to over-claim in these high profile and important areas, the truth is likely to be short of these very modest amounts of time. The conclusion from this and our own observation in practice is that there is a lot more talk than action about developing people!

This book will emphasize the need for accountability in delivering results from people initiatives. It will emphasize the importance of the precise measurement of people and their behaviour in the world of work. As directors and managers we accept the need for careful measurement when it comes to sales, production or financial performance. Yet all too often we shy away from the demands of precise measurement when it comes to assessing our people resources. Many will argue that it is not possible to measure improved performance of an organization's people, for while the costs can be identified, the benefits are not always as precise. Although some will attempt to apply a broad cost benefit analysis, and ask the question in general terms, whether the benefits to the organization are likely at least to equal the costs, we consider it is possible to be more precise in measuring real benefits. This is a theme with which we persist in other chapters too. In setting the scene for this book, we should start by looking at the potential to achieve productivity gains on a measured basis.

Achieving a productivity gain

The preface to this book began with the proposition that by putting the right people into the right jobs and encouraging the right development activity, efficiency, productivity and profitability will be enhanced.

This process starts with the selection of the right people for a particular job or role. The essence of the proposition is that we need to find people with **personal attributes** that are relevant to the tasks and context of the job. Relevance here implies that there is a relationship between having a particular attribute and performance in the job. This correlation itself forms the basis of assessing the validity of any method purporting to predict success in the job. At the outset we observe that simply selecting the right people with the right personal attributes for the job will significantly lift job performance and the productivity of the enterprise. Let us first illustrate this with a simplified theoretical example.

Figure 1.1 on the following page makes a powerful point in terms of getting the initial assessment right.

In this example an organization has taken a sample of current holders of a particular job and assessed their job performance on a scale of low to high value. At the same time the sample has been assessed on a personal attribute which job analysis has suggested to be relevant to the job. Again, high and low scores have been assigned.

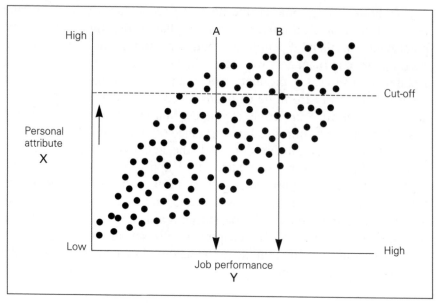

Figure 1.1 Productivity gain when an attribute predicts performance

The distribution of '●' shows the correlation between the two variables. A positive relationship exists. It is not perfect by a long way (that is, not a straight line), but there is a clear tendency for higher scorers on the personal attribute to be higher performers in the job. In this case line 'A' estimates the current average level of job performance.

Knowing that a relationship exists, in future selection the organization reasonably selects applicants who score higher on the personal attribute (say above the given cut-off). The average level of performance expected for the newly selected group is given by line 'B'.

The difference between line 'B' and line 'A' – the difference in average level of performance – gives a measure of the potential increase in productivity from using that attribute measure. This is often referred to as the **utility** of the measure. It should be clear that the stronger the relationship between the attribute score and job performance (the closer the distribution of '●' to a straight line), the greater the productivity gain will be. However, even a weak relationship (a broad ellipse of '●') will still show some productivity gain for a high selection cut-off.

Both theoretical and empirical research have shown that it is perfectly reasonable to expect productivity gains of the order of 10 to 15 per cent – even where the relationship between the attribute measure and job performance is modest. The following are the conditions under which potential productivity gains are maximized:

1 Where the relationship between the attribute measure and job performance is high. In other words it pays to find the best attribute predictors of job success. Avoid assessment procedures that are not related to job success (and be tough in demanding evidence of this).
2 Where the cut-off can be set at a high level. In other words it is advantageous to maximize the applicant pool for any job in the interest of setting a high selection criterion. In short, give yourself more choice.

While these may appear self-evident principles, it continues to surprise us how often jobs are allocated on the basis of procedures whose validity has not been checked and where selection rationalizations are made from an extremely limited choice.

The model above is admittedly a basic one and there are many questions of the level of job performance which is deemed to be acceptable; the impact of training and development on weaker performance; equal opportunity principles and so on. Yet the fundamental tenets hold and the model lies at the heart of more sophisticated utility analysis. We will take the model further in Chapter 3.

The implications here are substantial. If this model holds true for a particular job, then it holds true for a division, for an entire organization and indeed for the economy as a whole. There are serious productivity gains to be made across a country's economy by ensuring that the right people are placed in the right jobs. More than ten years ago, two leading researchers in this field, Hunter and Schmidt – gave examples of productivity gains from the standardized testing of specific job aptitudes of US$18 million p.a. for the Philadelphia Police Department; US$37 million p.a. for programmers in the US Civil Service and US$16 billion p.a. for the total US Civil Service. Even in Japan as we write, the country's competitiveness is under scrutiny and the concept of generalized job rotation is under review. We are beginning to see in Japan a clear move towards the more appropriate placement of graduate entrants against specific areas of activity based on personal attribute analysis. In Case Study 1.1, overleaf, we look at some recent North American experience of the benefits to be gained from improving selection procedures.

CASE STUDY 1.1
North American experience in gaining value from an
investment in people

Professor Rick Jacobs, one of the two founding partners of Landy,
Jacobs and Associates Inc., has wide experience in developing selection procedures for a wide range of jobs from clerical and factory
positions through senior management. His work, in conjunction
with students and colleagues of Penn State University, has clearly
demonstrated that the use of selection procedures not only provides higher quality, more suitable employees, but also that the
investment in this pays off most handsomely.

Take, for example, the selection process Professor Jacobs and
his co-investigators developed for selecting city bus drivers. The
original study was conducted in nine different bus companies
across the USA and Canada. The system includes a battery of
predictors that are easily completed by applicants and quickly
scored to yield suitability ratings. Those rated as highly suitable are
then scheduled for a behavioural interview with ratings completed
by the three-person interview team. In the original study it was
possible to perform a utility analysis to determine the savings that
could be realized by using the system for selecting bus drivers in a
medium size city. If 100 bus drivers are hired per year, it was
shown that savings could amount to approximately US$160,000
p.a. with an investment of less than US$20,000 to establish the
selection system. Obviously, as the number of bus drivers hired
per year increases, the value of the programme grows. As an
example, New York City, a current user of the system, hires as
many as 1100 bus drivers per year. The estimated saving is in
excess of one million dollars annually. This benefit arises because
the selection procedures enable the employers to choose, with
confidence, employees who are less likely to miss work, whether
due to illness or other reasons, and who are more likely to drive in
an accident-free way.

This model is simple and logical. It incorporates a combination of
biographical information, items reflecting temperament, a sense of
timeliness, and personality measures that assess conscientiousness,
openness and attitudes towards safety and authority.

In another area, Landy and Jacobs have worked with a number of
police forces across the country from city departments to state
agencies in an attempt to improve the cost effectiveness of their
personnel programmes. Again, in this case, selecting the right

people with the right characteristics will improve effectiveness that may be measured in reductions in injuries or fatalities to citizens, more effective ratios of arrests to convictions, and/or more effective resolutions of crimes.

Landy and Jacobs believe the utility arguments extend well beyond selection. The logic of looking at HR programmes from a cost/benefit perspective can be applied to technological innovations involving increasing the applicant pool via Internet recruiting, to computerized testing of applicants, to structured feedback to the organization regarding candidates' strengths and weaknesses. Additionally, the utility logic can be applied to HR interventions such as performance appraisal and training. For too many years HR professionals have been silent on the benefits of their various programmes. Clearly looking at enhanced performance, translating that improvement into dollar-based or other relevant outcomes and comparing the results to the organizational dollars expended is an important advancement in thinking and practice.

In addition to looking at the technical basis of selection and other HR practices as well as documenting the cost benefit of these actions, Landy and Jacobs pay particular attention to the interface of HR and the law. In the American context, the employment procedures need also to be seen to meet fully the requirements of equal employment opportunities to avoid future expensive litigation. The requirements of fair employment require close correspondence between HR practices, the relevant statutes and emerging case law.

SOURCE: Landy Jacobs and Associates Inc.

Much work has been done in the area of utility analysis since the 1970s. In Appendix A we look at the statistical model which underpins much of this research and examine the implications for management action. This research has brought industrial psychologists together with accountants to enable estimates to be made of the annual profit contribution to an organization of a good, as opposed to an average, performer. Of course assumptions have to be made in developing models of this kind. However, even taking the most cautious financial impact assumptions on any variable it is possible to show that as a general rule the financial benefits of using a valid initial assessment procedure vastly outweigh the cost of that procedure. The models also show that the pay-off is linearly related to the validity of the assessment procedure. So, if you can double the predictive capability of a selection method you could double your financial pay-off. That ought to cause us to think hard about the efficiency of our selection processes and encourage us to demand accountability from those delivering this service to the organization.

The beautiful complexity of people and jobs

We are arguing that there are large pay-offs to be had in recruiting the right people and that it pays to put any assessment procedure under tight scrutiny in order to evaluate its subsequent relevance to job performance.

However, an examination of a current assessment procedure is no easy matter. There may be political issues. There will almost certainly be practical issues of time, expense and sometimes of just finding enough cases to justify validation analysis. But over and above all this lies the challenging and beautiful complexity of both people and jobs which makes the establishment of simple relationships between attributes and performance so hard to achieve. The problem is that people vary on a multitude of related characteristics while jobs are multi-faceted and increasingly changing with technological and economic developments. The situation is exacerbated by the hard-pressed manager's demand for quick and easy decision making and a mental set which so often works against a detailed appreciation of the person–job match.

Conventional wisdom has it that the right way to assess an individual for a job is first to carry out a careful job analysis covering job objectives, key tasks and context factors from which a person specification for the job can be prepared. A traditional person specification might be structured against the following headings[1]:

  Education/Training
  Work experience
  Abilities
  Personality
  Motivation
  Health
  Personal circumstances

We would hope for a good candidate to satisfy against all seven of these criteria appropriately weighted for the job. We referred above to the job context. The definition of the specification will not only be a function of a careful analysis of the key tasks in the job. It will also take account of the corporate culture, the divisional or departmental culture and the interaction between the individual and his or her boss, subordinates, peers, clients and so on.

To give an example of the issue of the complexity of the person–job fit, let us take just one of the seven headings – that of Personality. In this book we will be referring to a particular well-researched model which currently measures 32 dimensions of occupational personality across three domains: Relating to others; Thinking style; Emotional response. The number of dimensions alone presents some difficulty in defining what it is in personality terms that matters for the job. Yet we will argue that you need a finely discriminated model of personality to do justice to the finely differentiated demands of jobs.

We then find that there are interactions between the dimensions that have to be taken into account. For example, a 'controlling' dimension tells us that an individual likes to be in charge and give direction. However, it is one thing for this to be linked with a low consideration for people and a preference for autocracy. It is quite another to see control linked with a caring and democratic preference in interacting with others. It is not that one is right and the other is wrong. Subordinates, situations, circumstances may require different preferred styles of behaviour.

Permutations of two, three, four or more subsets of personality dimensions in a model of 32 provide enormous scope for differentiating people against jobs. We strongly believe that this is a critical part of reading an individual's job suitability. For example, it is not enough to know that a sales applicant enjoys the process of persuading others. We may also need to understand that he or she is insightful about people, confident in interaction, competitive, achievement driven and so on. It is not enough to know that managers being evaluated as decision makers enjoy making quick decisions. We may also need to know that they are inclined to plan ahead, prefer working with hard facts and data and are not too optimistic in outlook. There are innumerable examples of the need to qualify one piece of personality information with one or several other pieces. It should be no surprise that those being trained in occupational personality assessment value this aspect of linking dimensions as much or more than anything else that they learn.

And then there are the paradoxes of personality – the fact that one end of a dimension may suit one part of a job, while the other end suits another part. High affiliation may suit an easy move into a new team or teamwork in general, yet a need to be an accepted part of a group may be a weakness in some senior jobs where unpopular decisions have to be taken. Some board chairmen and CEOs are characterized by a preparedness to take tough decisions despite the lack of ensuing popularity. High emotional control may suit one part of a job where it is important, say, to keep an anxiety response under control. Yet low emotional control may benefit an emotional expressiveness which can enthuse and whip up an audience. We will all know examples of managers who are unflappable but as dull as ditch-water to deal with. We will also know enthusiasts who can lose their cool in a frustrating or worrying situation.

And then there is the question of balancing horizontal and vertical teams so that the personality mix works. The strongly independent-minded boss may work well with a dependent-minded subordinate. The dependent-minded boss who favours delegation may need independence of mind in a subordinate. Those interested in team theory will know well the reported benefits of matching teams of people so that their personalities bring different benefits to the team operation. We know that there are successful sales organizations who plan very carefully the match of salesperson to specific client representatives.

And still we have to deal with personality fit to the culture and the relationship between personality and motivational factors and other issues as well.

It is the subtlety of the personality fit that is so intriguing and has the potential to make the management of the people resource so stimulating. How dull it would be if it were a matter of an easy judgement on a few dimensions. In the same way that we have struggled over many years to understand how advertising works or political choice is influenced – and where no simple model suffices – so occupational performance will continue to challenge us and defy neat theoretical compartmentalization.

Nor do we need a total solution – an all-encompassing theory. As we have seen, for those who can establish specific links and relationships there are substantial financial gains to be made. If it is possible to find a specific relationship that predicts just part of total success in a job then we know from utility analysis that the 10 per cent productivity gain is a realistic goal. Taken across an organization the financial implications are substantial and as global competitiveness increases it is a card that, in our view, management will have to be able to play.

The danger is that we are not challenged by the complexity of matching people to jobs, but put off by it! We still put too much reliance on the personal interview where judgements are frequently made in the first few minutes. We still hear of personality being referred to as a single attribute – 'the candidate has no personality' – as if they should in some way find one before applying again.

The time has come to bring more structure to the process. We need to understand jobs through analysis albeit in a shifting context of employment needs. We need to define clearly the objectives, the key tasks and context factors and we need to use logical inference to specify required personal attributes. Then we should assess these using a multiple of different methods where each is relevant to a defined part of the person specification. It is not a question of one assessment method being better than another. There are some attributes best assessed by interview, some by standardized tests, some by questionnaires/inventories, some by behavioural simulations and so on. The optimum is a balanced mix of methods.

Job analysis should always be done as a basis for selecting appropriate assessment methods and whenever practicable empirical validation should be completed. This will help refine the selection decision-making process and confirm the justifiability of the various components. It will also allow organizations to assess the financial return on the investment in the selection. It will enable managers to make better investment decisions in the assessment of staff and it will encourage accountability for those organizations selling assessment products and services.

Honing your people resource

In the above sections we have concentrated on the critical initial selection and placement of staff. Of course, once staff have been selected and placed there is much to be gained from an ongoing planned process of training and development. This book is not so much concerned with the specific training and development options available as with the creation of a culture in which all staff recognize that management is serious about seeing that real development occurs and is not just paying comfortable lip-service to a concept of the moment. We will also want to argue that successful development is a function of the precise and accurate assessment of staff and of their motivation to want to develop themselves.

In setting the scene then for this book we would want to argue that provided an organization has a sound business strategy in place (or public sector equivalent), then competitive success will largely be determined through the people who will implement it. Their aptitude, capacity, skill-base, motivation and freedom to decide will all influence their effectiveness. Each of the chapters of this book addresses key areas where a real difference can be made. The emphasis is practical so that the thinking manager can see where to apply time and resource to achieve greater impact. As a taster of things to come, we list in Figure 1.2 some key areas which will help an organization to reach a high level of achievement.

Figure 1.2   Key areas of focus for improved performance

---

1. **Select the right people**
   - Use a recruitment process which attracts appropriate candidates
   - Carry out adequate job analysis
   - Use a mix of appropriate selection procedures
   - Create high expectations in every recruit
   - Monitor the effectiveness of the recruitment process

2. **Train and develop people in the right way**
   - Match skill development to the business needs
   - Each staff member should have a personal development plan
   - Aim to recruit from within if possible

3. **Communicate effectively**
   - Ensure that the mission and strategy are understood at an appropriate level
   - The values must be clearly stated and practised
   - Communicate key messages, including successes, through a structured programme
   - Be clear about performance of the organization and the individual

4. **Everyone must clearly understand their role**
   - Aim for clarity of personal objectives, and assessment of performance against these
   - Impose quality appraisals for all, at least annually

5. **Motivate the employees at all levels**
   - They must feel valued
   - They must be empowered and competent to act
   - Reward systems must be compatible
   - Employee ownership should be encouraged
   - Avoid archaic 'them and us' differentials between managers and others, for example directors' dining rooms, executive toilets

6. **Create a spirit of curiosity in the organization**
   - Always be outward looking
   - Encourage experimentation – there is always a better way

---

Summary

In this chapter, the importance of people power is spelled out. We start with the basic premise that permeates throughout this book that there are two clear distinguishing factors found in most successful businesses around the world: strategy, and increasingly, the power of the people resource. Later, the importance of communication is emphasized which is key to the delivery of the contribution from the people resource and this is dealt with separately in Chapter 10. This chapter sets the scene and emphasizes that it is the quality and contribution of people at all levels that are the key differentiators of companies' performance today.

Most people would recognize this as a truism, and therefore it is doubly disappointing that many managers devote insufficient time and rigour to enhancing this resource. When 'successful managers' spend less than 4 per cent of their time on personal development and only 8 per cent on management development in total there is clearly room for improvement! More effort needs to be spent on the selection of the right people for the prescribed job using helpful tools available rather than judgement alone. The reason is not because of some altruistic benefit to society, but rather because it pays off in a commercial sense. This can be through enhanced productivity, greater creativity or benefits that arise from the commitment of the workforce. We should aim to make our successful managers even more so. The point that will be pursued through our book is that there is a need for accountability in the Human Resources area if it is to have greater influence.

Clear benefits can be obtained by getting the match of the right people in the right job, but we do not pretend that this is easy. It requires effort and it is a complex task. There are, though, good tools to help the evaluation, which we would observe are not used often enough, as many managers rely on judgement alone – but without the full picture before them.

There is a need to hone the people resource beyond the initial job-specific training. A total culture of raising standards and lifting the effectiveness of the people resource is needed. This entails:

- selecting the right people for the forward-looking role, rather than what has historically been done in it;
- training and developing the people to make them more fit to exercise judgement and ensure that they are capable of acquitting their accountabilities;
- a communication programme where people at all levels feel part of the organization, committed to it, with a clear view of their objectives and how these fit within the overall goals of the organization;
- in more detail, everyone must understand their role and their key objectives. They must receive feedback through an appraisal system on how well they are doing.

Many of these topics will be picked up later in the book, but first we need to have a good understanding of competencies and attributes, which is the topic of the next chapter.

---

1. Derived from the work on the 'Seven Point Plan' of Alec Rodger and his colleagues at the former UK 'National Institute of Industrial Psychology'.

2 Competencies and Attributes

The critical role of job analysis

When considering the assessment and development of the human resource there needs to be some conceptual framework against which judgements can be made. In creating such a model the starting point has to be job analysis. If we are to choose appropriate assessment procedures and to find appropriate development dimensions, then we must first understand the precise requirements of the jobs that our people will be required to perform. This is not just a matter of common sense; there are important legal implications here as well. In a number of countries world-wide, assessment procedures have to be demonstrably relevant to the content of the jobs for which they are being used. This may be illustrated by correlational validation studies showing a clear relationship. However, these are not always practicable and an alternative is to use an analytical process to demonstrate the justifiability of the method. In other words, the job is analyzed and logical inferences are drawn about the need for certain personal characteristics and appropriate measures. Even if there is no protective legal structure, it ought to be a matter of morally sound practice that we only use assessment procedures that are clearly relevant to the content of jobs.

There is a secondary benefit to the use of job analysis in that it forces a discipline on managers to think carefully about the jobs they are managing. Job analysis practitioners will know well the response from participants along the lines of 'this has really helped me to clarify the key aspects of this role'. Nor is it unusual for bosses and subordinates reviewing the subordinate job to disagree about what is in the job or what are the priorities. Good job analysis methods force a resolution of these issues.

It is not acceptable to defer job analysis, by arguing that the nature of jobs is changing or that we now need 'generalists'. It is indeed possible and desirable to define core requirements of changing roles through job analysis – for example, the need to be able to analyze complex data under time pressure – and to build these into assessment and development plans. Job analysis methods can also be used on a future conceptual basis even where a job has not yet been created.

In considering job analysis, we need to differentiate the **inputs** from the **outputs**. While many different options have been proposed by practitioners, in our view the key inputs are:

1.   A clear statement of the **objectives** of the job – written in terms that are precise and measurable.
2.   A definition of the main **tasks** or behaviours that are required from an incumbent to ensure that the objectives are properly met.
3.   A description of the **context** within which those tasks are to be completed. This will cover both the psychological context (for example, pressure-related factors) and the physical context (temperature, light, working hours, and so on).

The outputs can be variable and may include written job descriptions, written person specifications, schematically presented ratings on models of competencies, attributes, job evaluation dimensions, training needs, and so on. There is no right or wrong here – it depends on the application need. However, it does pay to have a clear idea in advance of the application of the job analysis data so that an appropriate output can be chosen.

There are many different job analysis methods to choose from, but to simplify the options, we would propose the following classification:

● Training for the job or actually doing it
● Diary recording
● Asking questions personally
● Asking questions via a questionnaire/inventory
● Review of job-related documentation

All these methods have been used over the years but in our experience by far the most common approach involves asking questions of those familiar with a particular job. This may be an incumbent, boss, subordinate, peer, trainer or other knowledgeable person. Questionnaires and inventories are usually detailed and give breadth to the analysis. The quality of personal interviews can be much more variable. As the American job analysis researcher Levine has pointed out, it is important that the process is thorough and systematic. At the same time, there are a number of options open to the interviewer which can be reviewed along two dimensions:

> Individual   –   Group interviews
> Open-ended interviewing   –   Structured interviewing

The individual interview allows much more scope for depth of interviewing. In group interviews, the members tend to prompt each other to think of different aspects of the job and this increases breadth of coverage. However, the input from any one person is likely to be light (for example, six people may be sharing 90 minutes of interviewing).

Open-ended interviewing operates with a few key areas to probe but otherwise can flow into any area of interest. It requires much more interviewer skill than interviewing with structured questions but is valuable where there are critical job components that might not have been foreseen.

As with assessment, the best job analysis approach is probably to use a multiple of methods where each one adds something different to the picture. We have achieved useful information using a mix of open-ended individual interviewing and a structured questionnaire. For example:

Method	**Objective**
1. Open-ended individual interview using Kelly's Repertory Grid method (See Case Study 2.1)	To explore the personal constructs of managers with good experience of the job. It has the benefit of clarifying managers' own perception of key job requirements using dimensions that they generate themselves.
2. Open-ended individual or group interviews using Flanagan's Critical Incidents method (See Case Study 2.1)	To give depth to the analysis by focusing on specific historical incidents where the outcome was particularly critical to the job objectives.
3. Detailed structured questionnaires – The Work Profiling System (See Figure 2.1)	To ensure that all aspects of the job are covered and to bring in the quantitative discipline of numerical ratings.

CASE STUDY 2.1
Assessment centre job analysis

A leading international oil company was in the process of developing an assessment centre to identify the potential to move to senior management positions within the organization. It required formal job analysis to identify a set of competency criteria to be used in the assessment. The job analysis comprised a review of senior management appraisal forms and a job analysis questionnaire together with formal interviews with managers operating at the grade level against which managers were to be assessed. The interviews took the form of Repertory Grid and Critical Incidents interviews.

The Repertory Grid method was originally developed by Kelly as a means of researching the structure of personality. He developed this approach as a way of identifying how an individual construes his or her environment – the outputs being known as 'personal constructs'. In this job analysis study, the researchers' objective was to establish how senior managers construed the management role. In each case, a senior manager was required to consider three other managers whom they knew personally and to 'think of a way in which two are similar and different from the third which is relevant to their management role'. This process continued until the respondent could produce no further constructs.

The Critical Incidents method was devised by Flanagan who used it as a means of job analysis. In essence, it requires those familiar with a particular job to recount past incidents that have occurred whose outcome was relatively important to the job – whether favourable or unfavourable. The incidents are diagnosed and classified. The technique may be used quantitatively but in this case it was used qualitatively to explore a smaller number of particularly critical job incidents in greater depth. Incidents were written up on flip-charts and key competencies listed against each successive part which would have contributed to a successful outcome. The skill of the method lies in the open-ended probing of the responses.

In the final analysis, the following competency criteria emerged as relevant to senior management performance and it was possible to give participants clear definitions and hard evidence and explain their relevance.

Management planning	Communication skills
Decision making	Influence
Complex analytical reasoning	People orientation
Lateral thinking	Energy
Commercial orientation	Emotional control

The Work Profiling System (or WPS) is an example of a computer-based job analysis procedure. At its heart lies a detailed pencil and paper or computer-administered questionnaire. This requires a clear statement of job objectives. This is then followed by a stage of rating many tasks in terms of their importance to meeting job objectives and their percentage share of total job time. In a final stage there is a large set of job context questions which also have benefit for job evaluation purposes. This information is then analyzed and integrated by the computer based on expert system rules and equations. The computer-generated outputs include a job description, a person specification, job-relevant competencies, job-relevant personal attributes, job-relevant assessment methods, caveats for selection, interview questions and so on.

There is only room here to give some ideas on job analysis approaches that we have found to be helpful. The more fundamental point is that, when management is assessing and developing its staff, it should have a thorough, systematically derived understanding of the jobs in question. This applies equally to apprentice selection as to board appointments. Apart from the legal implications in some countries, it is a matter of good sense to ensure that a full consideration has been given to the job and that investment in selection and development is properly based.

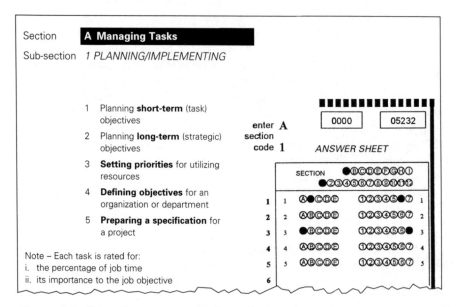

Figure 2.1 Part of a structured job analysis questionnaire

Competencies and attributes

When focusing on assessment and development, it has been common practice over the years for job analysis to generate an output in the form of a person specification – for example, along the lines indicated in Chapter 1. More recently there has been support for the development and application of models of job competence or competencies. Many of these models have been developed by and tailored to individual organizations. There are some more broadly based public models of job-relevant competencies. A particularly well-researched model is that of Boyatzis, based on work done in the USA, which attempted to validate the competencies derived from preliminary job analysis work. Boyatzis' definition of a competency is as follows:

> An underlying characteristic of a person in that it may be a motive, trait, skill, aspect of one's self image or social role, or a body of knowledge.

Not everyone is keen on the competency modelling approach but in our experience it has genuinely helped managers to improve their understanding of success in jobs and to produce more credible development plans.

In our view, the value of competency modelling can be enhanced by a clear distinction between a 'competency' component and a 'personal attributes' component. Existing models of competence – such as that of Boyatzis above – tend to confuse these two elements. However, underlying personal attributes are more complex to understand and can usefully be separated from the more behavioural competencies.

In the model shown in Figure 2.2, 'competencies' are essentially in the manager's domain. They should be behaviourally described in terms that managers can understand and to which they can relate. Concepts used should not require specialized training or knowledge of personal, psychological constructs that one might find, for example, in the area of personality or motivation. In this sense, competencies might include 'making a good formal presentation' or 'writing a relevant strategic plan'.

It is perfectly reasonable for competencies to be hierarchically organized. We know that when running a development centre or workshop, where candidates are being assessed, there is little point in having more than about eight to ten competencies. Any more than this and the assessors find it hard to discriminate and the result is excessive inter-correlation of the competency dimensions. However, when it comes to planning training or development, we need greater discrimination. For example, in terms of competency in 'communication' we need to be clear whether we are looking at written or oral communication, informal interaction or formal presentations, and so on. Models of 30 or 40 competencies may be required. At the other extreme, we have known organizations who have worked at the top with a simple conceptualization of three or four big dimensions. This might include, for example, 'intellectually bright', 'good with people', 'achievement driven'. This might be simplistic but very senior managers will at least remember and utilize such a model and component elements can be built in when necessary. (An example of a behaviourally defined competency model developed by SHL is given below.)

On the other side of the model, 'attributes' are essentially in the specialist's domain – where a specialist is an individual who has been properly trained to understand the subtleties of the models utilized. By 'attributes' here we are referring to the personal characteristics which underpin the behavioural competencies. These characteristics include cognitive abilities and aptitudes, personality variables and motivational elements. So, for example, with the competency of 'making a good formal presentation', the underlying attributes may involve 'understanding difficult questions, emotional control, a planning mentality, sensitivity to the audience, confidence in delivery, and so on'. The point is that the attribute information helps us to diagnose the behaviour. It enables us to take a view as to why someone has performed in the way they have and what kind of development, if any, is going to work.

A model of this kind ensures that managers are behaviourally focused using competency concepts with which they are completely comfortable. However, it proposes that questions of psychological diagnosis and judgements about development pay-off require the assistance of specialists who understand attribute models well and can draw legitimate inferences about future behaviour.

There are those that argue that attribute models do not need to be complex. They might claim that ability can be reduced to a single dimension of intelligence and that personality might be neatly summarized in five dimensions or fewer. It is a fine debate but we would argue strongly in favour of more complex models. It is true that attributes inter-correlate and that summary dimensions can be generated. However, there are many specific attribute interactions which account for tiny proportions of total attribute variance which can be critical in determining a cause of a manager's success or failure. For example, the very precise mix of being independent minded, non-affiliative and uncaring may help us to pinpoint the reason for a failed team intervention, where broader factors would not

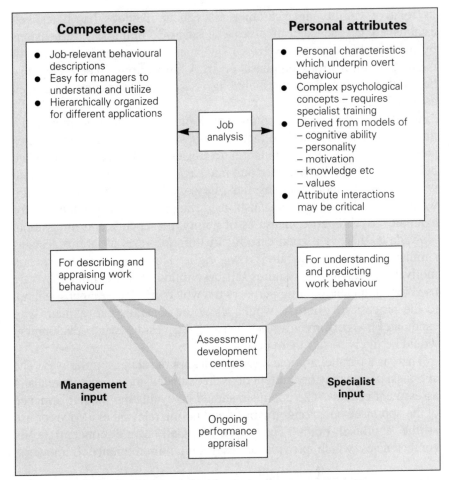

Figure 2.2 Differentiated model – competencies and attributes

discriminate. Users of more complex models in real life do not need convincing on this point and they are ready to invest more time in obtaining the richer data.

Using a differentiated model of competencies and attributes

The assessment centre (or multiple assessment) method has acquired popularity in many parts of the world over the past two decades. This has been well described in numerous textbooks of assessment methods and its relative validity against other assessment methods has been well established. In essence, it involves assessing on a multiple of dimensions by a multiple of assessors (often line managers) using a multiple of methods (with a strong emphasis on work simulations). There may also be a multiple of applications, including assessment for recruitment as well as for ongoing development.

In using a differentiated model of competencies and attributes, the dimensions used by the line manager assessors would be competencies (see Figure 2.3). The simulation exercises would require candidate behaviour that can be analyzed and rated against competency criteria that would be well understood by the assessors. The attribute information would be collected by specialists using appropriate instruments – for example, psychometric measures of ability, personality and motivation. Nowadays, there is a good case for treating job-relevant ability tests as simulation exercises in their own right. However, personality and motivation data usually requires self-description. It would not be directly used for competency-rating purposes but would provide a diagnostic input to the process. In short, it would allow the specialists to explain why candidates had performed as they had and, if necessary, what development would be likely to suit them best.

There is a parallel argument for treating appraisal in a similar way. The appraisal period may be thought of as an extended and ultimately realistic assessment process. The appraiser should be evaluating the performance of the appraisee on an ongoing basis and noting relevant evidence for use at the appraisal point. The appraisal itself would concentrate on competencies which provide an easy common reference framework.

Figure 2.3 Behavioural model of management competencies

Area	Competency	Definition
Managerial Qualities	Leadership	Motivates and empowers others in order to reach organisational goals.
	Planning and Organising	Organises and schedules events, activities and resources. Sets up and monitors timescales and plans.
	Quality Orientation	Shows awareness of goals and standards. Follows through to ensure that quality and productivity standards are met.
	Persuasiveness	Influences, convinces or impresses others in a way that results in acceptance, agreement or behaviour change.

Figure 2.3 *cont'd*

Area	Competency	Definition
Professional Qualities	Specialist Knowledge	Understands technical or professional aspects of work and continually maintains technical knowledge.
	Problem Solving and Analysis	Analyses issues and breaks them down into their component parts. Makes systematic and rational judgements based on relevant information.
	Oral Communication	Speaks clearly, fluently and in a compelling manner to both individuals and groups.
	Written Communication	Writes in a clear and concise manner, using appropriate grammar, style and language for the reader.
Entrepreneurial Qualities	Commercial Awareness	Understands and applies commercial and financial principles. Views issues in terms of costs, profits, markets and added value.
	Creativity and Innovation	Creates new and imaginative approaches to work-related issues. Identifies fresh approaches and shows a willingness to question traditional assumptions.
	Action Orientation	Demonstrates a readiness to make decisions, take the initiative and originate action.
	Strategic	Demonstrates a broad-based view of issues, events and activities and a perception of their longer-term impact or wider implications.
Personal Qualities	Interpersonal Sensitivity	Interacts with others in a sensitive and effective way. Respects and works well with others.
	Flexibility	Successfully adapts to changing demands and conditions.
	Resilience	Maintains effective work behaviour in the face of setbacks or pressure. Remains calm, stable and in control of him or herself.
	Personal Motivation	Commits self to work hard towards goals. Shows enthusiasm and career commitment.

However, there may still be a case for an independent attributes analysis for reasons of understanding the appraisee's behaviour and agreeing appropriate development. In practice this is likely to require the mediation of a specialist trained in attribute measurement – a process which should further enhance management awareness of people issues.

A differentiated model also helps in planning any job analysis. It obviates the danger of obtaining a complex mix of outputs which are difficult to integrate and use. If the requirement is for a weighted set of defined competencies for a job, then this can be specifically built into the process and attributes can be dealt with as a quite separate issue.

The implication of a differentiated model is that life can be made easier for line managers by limiting their contact to a manageable number of competency dimensions with which they can feel comfortable. The further implication is that the more complex questions of diagnosis and development options are best left to those who have undergone specialized training. This does not restrict the application of attributes to psychologists (although their background discipline puts them in a strong position). Specialist HR practitioners who have undergone appropriate training will manage this role with a high degree of success. Furthermore, we believe that they have an important part to play in creating a people-conscious, development culture. Organizations that cut back on this resource in the creation of lean organizations and devolve too much of this responsibility to the line managers themselves are likely to undermine the value of the development process.

Whether competency models are adding value

At the end of a recent international conference on competencies, Professor Paul Evans of the London Business School summed up the current situation as follows:

> Over the last 15 years our understanding of competencies has become increasingly complex. A lot of time and money has been spent on building more and more sophisticated competency models. Competencies are in danger of becoming a meaningless buzz word, the new TQM. Unless companies can see a clear picture of the business benefits to be gained from this approach, it will become discredited.

In our view, part of the complexity and concern has arisen from the confusion of the manifest behaviour with the underlying attributes and this can be resolved as proposed above. When managers are working with a common model of well-defined behavioural concepts, which they understand well, it can only enhance performance management.

At the same time it is true that organizations may find themselves working with different models in different parts of the organization or indeed at different levels. Furthermore, the models may be subject to change as the organization develops and adapts to new demands. Professor Christine Farrell and Neil Thomson working at SHL have introduced the useful concept of **competency mapping** for helping organizations to understand how the competencies applied across an organization relate to one another. The mapping process also has the benefit of providing a dynamic context for understanding how competencies across the organization will change in response to future business priorities and changes in the competitive environment.

The competency map (Figure 2.4) divides competencies into six sectors based on characteristics of the competencies.

● *Culture Specific*   An important aspect of competency models is their ability to communicate the culture of the organization in behavioural terms. Culture-specific competencies form a link between the values of the organization and the behaviours expected of employees, and apply equally to all roles in the organization.

  Competencies which would fall into this area are those such as Empowerment, Customer Focus and Teamwork.

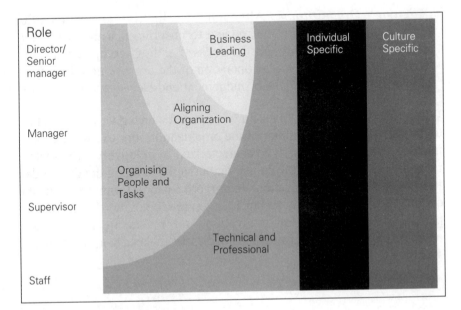

Figure 2.4 SHL competency map

The size of each shaded area shows the relative importance of each competency sector.

- *Individual Specific* These competencies, sometimes referred to as personal competencies, also apply to all roles in the organization and reflect the overt behaviour associated with personal attributes such as Oral Communication, Resilience and Tenacity.

- *Technical and Professional* An element of virtually all jobs are job-specific competencies related to the specialist knowledge and skills required in that position. As can be seen from the map these are a much larger component of staff roles than those further up the organization. This varies from one type of organization to another.

This leaves three areas which are inter-linked by their focus on managing the organization.

- *Business Leading* This is a small group of competencies related to establishing and communicating the vision and strategy of the organization. Typically these are relevant for more senior managers and directors. Examples are Strategic Perspective and External Awareness.

- *Organizing People and Tasks* These competencies relate to operational management of people and tasks on a day-to-day basis. Examples are Motivating Others, Caring for Others and Management Control.

- *Aligning Organization* Although a slightly awkward title, competencies in this area are related to ensuring that the vision and strategy expressed through Business Leading competencies are translated into the day-to-day operation of the organization. Examples are Organizational Awareness, Judgement and Decisiveness.

With a model of this kind, maps may be created which give valuable clues to the current style and culture of the organization. For example, a more traditional organization may be characterized by relatively large sectors reflecting an emphasis on technical output and managing the day-to-day functioning of the organization. In a more visionary organization, the culture-specific sector may be much larger, reflecting more concern with pushing responsibility for innovation and management down the organization and the use of competencies to make a corporate values statement.

Summary

When management is planning the assessment and development of job applicants and current staff, the starting point has to be a thorough understanding of the jobs that the individuals are likely to perform. We reinforce the importance of systematically completed **job analysis** in which job objectives are clarified, job tasks are rated for their importance against objectives, and the background job context is specified. We argue that there is no single current job analysis method – the best approach is a multiple of methods where each one provides a different benefit.

In examining the outputs of job analysis, we believe that models of **competencies** have a useful role to play. However, definitions of competencies can cause confusion and we favour a 'differentiated model' in which competencies are clearly distinguished from underlying psychological **attributes**. In this model competencies are behaviourally defined in language that managers can readily understand and work with. They form the basis of assessment/development centre ratings; they are used in appraisals and they are fundamental to the planning of personal development. The personal psychological attributes underpin the competencies. They require specialist knowledge and training but help to explain why competencies are strong or weak and to define the optimum form of any subsequent development.

Job analysis is not only the logical precursor to sound assessment and development. In a number of countries, it provides a relevant legal defence against challenges to the fairness and justifiability of an assessment process. In our view, it is a moral requirement – as well as a legal one – that organizations should only use assessment methods which are demonstrably relevant against the content of jobs.

Finally, we looked at **competency mapping** as a device which helps us to understand the current style and culture of the organization. Competencies are placed within category sectors. The size and shape of the sectors will vary from one organization to another and form the basis of the current characterization.

3

Selecting the Right People

The management case for examining selection

Training and development investment will not pay the right kind of dividend if the staff involved are essentially inappropriate to their roles. In this chapter we look at the process for ensuring that the initial selection of staff at all levels is as strong as possible. Our first observation is that on a world-wide basis something is going wrong and it has to be put right.

The problem is that the most widely used assessment method – the discursive personal interview – has one of the poorest records of predicting successful job outcomes. The solution is in two parts. First, we need to improve the way interviews are carried out and there is encouraging evidence that bringing a competency-based structure to the process does help. Second, we need to supplement the interview with other methods which have a good predictive record.

This is not just a theoretical proposition: the financial implications for management can be enormous. In Chapter 1 we made the point about the large financial pay-off of good selection practice but consider also the following case. A middle to senior-level manager recruited to an organization may cost US$1 million over a ten-year job tenure, simply to be kept breathing in a covered space. How much information would typically be gathered against this investment decision? All too often it amounts to a self-generated CV, a 40-minute interview or two and possibly an almost valueless reference check. Would management invest in a million dollar computer system on this level of information? The answer is almost certainly 'no' and yet we feel we can do it when it comes to people!

In general, management does not appear to be inclined to embark on an analytical evaluation of the assessment procedures it uses. Mintzberg has suggested it is common in project decisions to pick 'the man instead of the proposal' – in other words, to back the judgement of someone you trust rather than take the proposal to pieces. Latham and Whyte found that experienced managers were more influenced to use a selection method by a psychologist's generalized description of how the method would be validated than by an analytical argument of the financial pay-off from using it.

It is time for management to be much more demanding of the assessment process by which the people, who are going to deliver the results, enter the organization. The implications here are simply too great. If a manager starts with a well-motivated, capable team who fit their roles as well as each other, then he or she is likely to gain a real competitive advantage. Managers need to understand more about assessment and they need to ask some tough questions of those who provide the assessment services and resources. The best providers of assessment services are not frightened of being called to account for the value they add.

The situation is further exacerbated because all methods of assessing people are to some degree flawed. It simply is not possible to make perfect, error-free judgements when we are dealing with people – particularly when they are new to us. This makes it easy for the purist to criticize all assessment methods. However, the recruitment and placement decisions do not go away. We still have to decide who is best for a given role and we still have to optimize our judgement even though we cannot make it perfect. The implication is that we have to evaluate the assessment options on a comparative basis and not against an absolute criterion of predictive certainty. Interviews, tests, simulations and so on will all be error-prone but how do they compare in relative value? How do we combine them to best effect and how do we choose between them? The following sections try to throw some light on these questions.

The right way to select

In Chapter 1 we referred to a conventional wisdom for the right way to select someone for a job. This involves an initial stage of job analysis as described in Chapter 2 in order to prepare a job description and a specification of the requirements of the individual (sometimes referred to as the 'Person Specification'). Apart from the immediately apparent logic of understanding a job well, before we decide if someone is 'right' for it, it reinforces the important concept of **relevance**. In other words, it helps us to ensure that any method we subsequently use in selection decisions can be justified as relevant to the content of the job. This is not only a matter of good sense and ethical practice, but as we have noted, there may be implications for a legal defence of the method should it come under formal challenge.

Armed with a well-supported person specification, it should then be possible by a process of logical inference (sometimes done statistically nowadays by computer) to select assessment methods which are relevant to the job. Here again there is a clear current wisdom which is not that any particular method is generally better than another but that it is best to use a mix of different methods where each one adds something to our overall pool of knowledge.

Any method can be considered at this stage in terms of the criterion of relevance. However, there are two important yardsticks against which any method should be judged before it is allowed to enter the candidate list of methods for recruitment. First, the method should be **reliable**. Although there are various technical definitions of reliability, in essence this means that when used by different people or on different occasions, the conclusions drawn are broadly the same. Incidentally, this is a criterion against which many interviews fall down. Even assuming that similar questions are asked of different candidates, a certain response may be interpreted positively by one interviewer but negatively by another. Second, the method should be **valid**. Again there are varying technical definitions of validity but at the core lies the notion that there should be a relationship between judgements made from the method and subsequent performance in the job.

Unfortunately, not many organizations – when questioned about the reliability and validity of their recruitment methods – can offer evidence of an evaluation in these terms. In most cases, methods would be used on the basis of an implied faith in either the process or possibly an external supplier of a service. Perhaps Mintzberg is right and we would rather put our faith in the advice of a trusted specialist.

We have noted the current wisdom which is to use a mix of different methods. However, the more thorough the process in this regard, the more it is likely to cost. Budgets are finite and herein lies the key management judgement: how to balance the cost of an assessment procedure against the subsequent benefit. But this is where management so often ducks the issue and ends up relying on the personal interview where it feels it can back its judgement. This is not intended as an indictment of the interview method. As we shall see, it can make an excellent input to selection – if it is properly designed. It is also one of the most flexible methods, allowing us to focus on new issues as they occur during the interview session.

It is hard to see how any thorough recruitment exercise could be implemented without an interview. However, there are worrying issues of the speed at which conclusions are drawn about candidates and biases of subjectivity and prejudice when it is used alone. We have seen advice to graduate applicants to have a few good 'white lies' ready when they go to interview. They are told to work out what the interviewer is looking for and then tell them that! We could add that they should get the interviewer talking as much as possible and try a little flattery if they want to cash in on subjectivity bias! In reality we would want to see the interview properly evaluated together with other methods in order to define its best role. Later in this chapter we will look at how it is best carried out.

Cost against benefit

Assessment method costs will of course depend on exactly how they are implemented. Nevertheless, there are some broad rules of thumb to be observed. Application forms and biographical data are relatively inexpensive on a per capita basis, particularly nowadays with options of machine scanning and computerized interpretation. Structured ability tests and personality questionnaires which can be administered on a group basis are also relatively inexpensive on a per capita cost estimate. One-to-one or panel interviews do not require the purchase of carefully researched documentation but the time costs can be substantial, particularly where more senior managers are involved. At the top end of the cost range by some way is the process referred to earlier as the 'assessment centre' method but which is essentially a multi-method approach with a strong emphasis on simulation exercises such as group/committee exercises, in-tray exercises, presentations, decision-making exercises, standardized tests and questionnaires. This method usually requires line managers to be specially trained and involved as assessors working in tandem with trained specialists who can interpret the more complex psychological data.

A perfectly reasonable logic which is being increasingly used nowadays is to use methods sequentially in relation to their cost. For example, initial filtering of several thousand applicants may be completed by a computer-scored application form – perhaps delivered via the Internet. Standardized tests may be group administered for a preliminary assessment. Final assessment of a high potential pool may be completed through a mix of interviews and an assessment centre.

However, once again there is a clear research finding for valid procedures in this area of cost–benefit analysis. This is that whatever the method selected for recruitment, its cost pales into insignificance by comparison with the benefit of finding good as opposed to poor job recruits. Put another way, if you are going to spend a million dollars on someone (or even a tenth of that) before you even start counting what they can make or lose for you in profit terms – then it is largely immaterial whether you spend one dollar or one thousand in ensuring that you optimize that judgement. Or put even more simply, the costs of errors in selection, as a rule, vastly outweigh the cost of the methods, provided they have some validity to them.

In Chapter 1 we showed a simple theoretical example of how a valid assessment method can be used to enhance average job performance. In Appendix A, we work through an example to estimate the dollar return from an assessment method of a given validity and a given cost. Here we take a real example to demonstrate the beneficial impact of a single assessment method.

In the example in Figure 3.1, a major high-street bank identified a group of high- and low-performing managerial staff, in order to validate certain standardized ability tests prior to their use in an assessment programme. Each group consisted of just under 50 people roughly matched for age and experience. The groups were given, amongst others, a test of numerical critical reasoning (that is, a test of the ability to make correct decisions or inferences from numerical data). The total group was then broken down in terms of being high, moderate or low scorers on the test. The figure shows the relationship between their test scores and their performance in the job.

Figure 3.1 Relationship of ability test scores and management performance

Numerical Critical Reasoning		Management Performance Rating	
Test Scores		High	Low
High	(100%)	78%	22%
Moderate	(100%)	55%	45%
Low	(100%)	27%	73%

SOURCE: SHL UK

It can be seen that 78 per cent of the high-scoring test group were high-rated managers against only 27 per cent of the low-scoring test group. The high test scorers were nearly three times as likely as low test scorers to be in the high-performance test group. Put another way, to find 100 high-performing managers, we would expect to have to recruit 128 from a high test scoring group but 370 from a low test scoring group.

This was the best test in the batch but it is not an exceptional example. Research would suggest that this is a typical level of effectiveness for ability tests of this kind.

This example also serves to illustrate another important principle for managers involved in recruitment. A test of the kind shown (or indeed any valid method) will only have pay-off value if it is possible to select high scorers. If our choice is limited so that we have to recruit some moderate or low test scorers, then the benefit will be reduced. The principle here is to achieve a good-sized applicant pool in the interest of setting higher standards on procedures that are valid.

It is not unusual for managers to feel some discomfort with correlational statistics. However, on the whole, managers understand probabilities very well. They like the idea of a 78 per cent probability of success against 27 per cent and as a broad rule of thumb this is achievable where selection methods have correlational validities of around 0.3 to 0.4. This leads to the question of how different selection methods compare in these terms.

Comparative validity of selection methods

For reasons discussed above and in earlier chapters, we would always advocate an investment in establishing the validity of an organization's assessment methods. However, there are theoretical problems which require specialist advice and there are practical problems in setting up such a study. There are two main types of practical problem facing validation studies. First there is the difficulty of establishing large enough sample sizes to give us statistical confidence in the results. For example, statistical confidence begins to grow to satisfactory levels when we have over 100 cases. The second type of problem – and generally even more daunting – is to find a reliable quantitative measure of job performance. Clearly, if we cannot state with precision who is good and who is poor in a particular job, then we cannot ask an assessment method to predict it for us!

This latter point is almost frightening in its enormity. Can it be true that managers are unable to give us a precise statement – with some numerical index – of the job performance value of their subordinates? Yet the research in this area suggests that this is often the case and in Figure 3.2 we give some of the reasons why. This appears to us to be further evidence of many managers' inability to come to terms with the business of understanding their human resource pool and the need to give more time and attention to performance management. We have more to say specifically about performance appraisal in Chapter 4.

Figure 3.2 Reasons for difficulty in assessing staff performance

---

- Poorly defined performance criteria
- Generalizing across criterion ratings (called 'haloing')
- Scaling biases of
  - ⇒ 'leniency'
  - ⇒ 'toughness'
  - ⇒ 'central tendency'
- Political issues (for example, budget protection)
- Over-rating a weak performer that one wants promoted away
- Under-rating a strong performer that one cannot afford to lose
- Over-weighting of recent events (recency bias)
- Impact of external variables (for example, on sales results)
- Personal liking or disliking
- Changing job demands reducing criterion relevance
- Influence of historical academic success
- Semantics (differential understanding of criterion concepts)
- Combination of criteria into a meaningless total
- Prejudice on socio-ethnic grounds
- Interference of pay award/bonus implications

The difficulties of the kind shown in Figure 3.2 can be overcome and should not be a reason for avoiding the completion of local validation studies. However, researchers have given us some assistance here by in effect summarizing many hundreds of validation studies covering thousands of people to give us some general guidelines on the comparative validity of different methods. The technique used is a statistical summarizing technique called 'meta analysis'. Its benefit is that it enables many small sample studies to be combined together in order to reduce the problem of sampling error. At the same time, it allows other sources of error in estimating true validities to be statistically controlled. This would include, for example, the unreliability in the criterion data caused by biases of the kind listed above.

Figure 3.3 gives an example of a 'league table' of the relative validities of a number of methods used in selection. On the scale, '1.0' would represent perfect prediction of job success and it can be seen that no single assessment method comes close to this. The 'assessment centre' or 'multiple assessment method' performs relatively well, as do work-related tests and personality questionnaires. Interviews perform better if they are well structured. References, astrology and graphology have very little to offer.

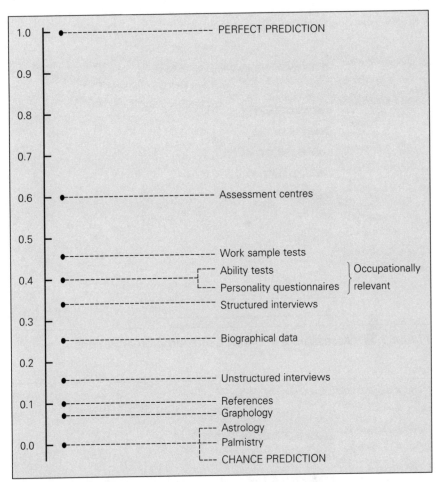

Figure 3.3 Relative validity of assessment methods

Developed by Professor Peter Saville after an idea by Mike Smith – University of Manchester Institute of Science and Technology

Usage of individual methods

In our experience across a number of countries, the past two decades have seen a steady increase in the usage of assessment methods other than the interview. In Chapter 6 we look at international practice in more detail. The data in Figures 3.4a and 3.4b are taken from a UK survey reported in January 1998. The sample was selected on a probability basis to cover large (750+ staff) and medium-sized (500–750) private sector organizations. The definition of usage was 'used seriously on at least ten separate occasions in the past 12 months'.

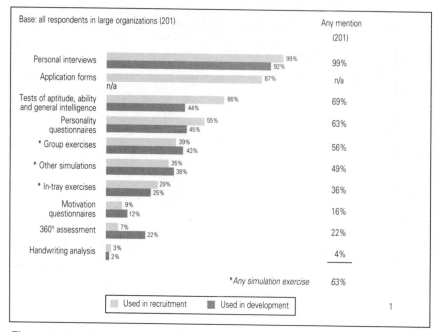

Figure 3.4a   Assessment methods used: large organizations

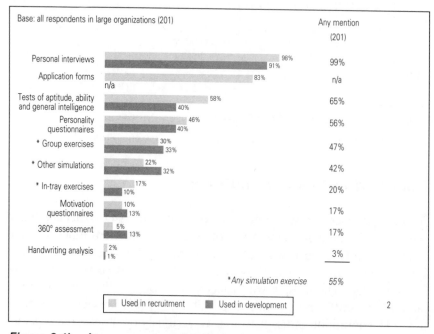

Figure 3.4b   Assessment methods used: medium organizations

Readers are unlikely to be surprised at the high level of usage of the personal interview and indeed may speculate about the 1 per cent not using it. For those familiar with the UK culture, they are also unlikely to be surprised at the low level of usage of handwriting analysis (graphology). Perhaps more interesting is the finding that psychometric tests of ability and personality as well as the broad category of simulation exercises are now clearly majority practice.

One further approach adopted by some senior managers is found in the so-called 'Hunt in Packs' theory. This involves recruiting to a similar role someone who has worked well for a manager in the past. This is sound if the new role clearly equates to the past in terms of the type of task and the context. If there are changes, then there should be an analysis of the new position and a check against the new person specification.

In the rest of this section is a summary in note form of our view of some of the main considerations in using various individual assessment methods. We cannot do justice to the mass of research on these methods. These are broad indications and practical advice that we have found helpful in the past.

Personal interview

- There is a good rational case for its use in exploring areas of a person specification such as education, training, work experience, motivation, health, personal circumstances, and so on.
- It can be effective in integration with other methods such as a personality questionnaire. It is also one of the more flexible methods in terms of following useful 'leads'.
- It is prone to biases of subjectivity and prejudice and there is evidence that judgements may be made very quickly on limited data.
- In an unstructured, loose, discursive form, it has not done well in meta analysis studies of validity. It performs much better in a structured format with questions clearly related to predefined criteria (for example, competencies).
- It tends to be expensive in terms of interviewer time, although this is rarely costed or even considered by many organizations.

Practical Advice

Give the interview a clear structure. Ensure that interviewers have had some training. Check the relevance of the questions being asked. Encourage criterion ratings as a discipline, then check the quality of the

The People Advantage

interviewer evidence and whether there are biases of excessive haloing, and so on. Be careful of any Equal Opportunity issues that might arise from exploring areas such as health and personal circumstances. See Figures 3.5 and 3.6.

Application forms/biodata

● These can be highly cost effective as an initial filter.

	Time Mins
Role – Marketing Manager	
Introduction – Introduce self. Thank candidate. Role of the interview. How it fits the total selection procedure.	3
Background – Points of clarification from education, training, work history.	7
Competencies for interview assessment – Specific questions against each competency:	30

Organizing/Planning

For example:

Strategic Thinking ———	Think for a moment and tell me about the last piece of strategic analysis you carried out.
Creativity	*Probe* What was the strategic objective?
Knowledge of Market Research Methods	What was the outcome? What new information did you need?
Analytical Orientation	Who was it discussed with? What input did others make?
Oral Communication Skill	How would this have improved the company's market position? What if the competition had responded by …?

Conclusion – check issues of health, personal circumstances, and so on. Take any candidate questions. Confirm selection process from here on.	10
Total	$\overline{50}$

Figure 3.5 Competency-based interview structure

| Candidate .... | Date .... |
| Interviewer .... | Position: Marketing Manager |

Criteria	Evidence	Rating*
Organizing/Planning		
Strategic Thinking		
Creativity		
Knowledge of Market Research Methods		
Analytical Orientation		
Oral Communication Skill		
Other Information		

*Scale   5 Well above
              4 A little above
              3 Meets the required standard
              2 A little below
              1 Well below

Figure 3.6 Competency-based interview rating form

- Their reliability and validity can be increased by computer-assisted scoring and interpretation. This should be based on appropriate job analysis and validation.
- Nowadays there is some overlap with personality questionnaires and there are issues of 'faking' or creating a good impression to be countered.
- Well-designed forms can achieve respectable levels of validity.
- It is becoming more common to include Equal Opportunity 'monitoring' questions as well as direct assessment questions.

Practical Advice

Be careful over the selection of questions. These should be based at least on a prior job analysis. A good tip is to look at each question in a form and ask how the answer will be used. If this is not clear and justifiable, then drop the question. This stops questions getting in which look like good application form questions but have no real relevance. Also think carefully about the design of the form. It will be one of the first pieces of documentation that the candidate will see and can influence the image perception of the organization. Include gender, ethnic group and disability monitoring questions.

Ability tests (See also Chapter 7)

- These generally have a good record of validity in world-wide research.
- Group testing is cost effective in time terms and therefore these are often used in a filtering process.
- They can be usefully integrated with information from other methods.
- Test material costs, currently at around US$5 per candidate, are usually insignificant against the utility or pay-off per candidate.
- There has been sensitivity to their use in terms of Equal Opportunity legislation. The technical quality of the tests is, therefore, critical.
- There is an ongoing debate as to whether it is better to measure a general concept of intelligence or specific differential abilities.

Practical Advice

These should only be used by properly trained practitioners. The technical background of the tests should be scrutinized with particular reference to their reliability and validity. We believe that it is best to use ability tests with an occupational content, measuring specific abilities which have been shown in advance by job analysis (and ideally validation) to be relevant to the job in question. Feedback should be offered to all candidates.

Simulation exercises

- These are somewhat similar to ability tests with occupational content but without the same level of discipline in standardization.
- They lie at the heart of the assessment centre method and generally have a good track record of validity. However, this depends on the assessors

being competent and properly trained.

- They have good 'face' validity to back their real validity. For example, if you are recruiting a 'strategic planner' it appears sound to ask candidates to write a strategic plan under controlled conditions.
- They can help candidates understand a bit more about the job and may facilitiate some self-selection.
- They are useful for producing ratings against competency models.
- They can be expensive in terms of time per candidate, particularly where senior line managers are involved in the process as assessors. Management availability to assess candidates is likely to be a practical constraint.

Practical Advice

Check the content of the exercises for relevance to the job. Check the depth of the content also in this respect. For example, a group discussion on the theme 'Discuss this organization in the year 2010' may be too vague to cover all the required competencies. A debate on a specific budget proposal with clearly defined pros and cons together with background data and company context may be more precisely targeted on a competency set. Also, ensure that assessors are properly trained and check the quality of evidence put forward to support criterion ratings. Good exercises should have a supporting technical manual to give assistance.

Personality questionnaires (See also Chapter 7)

- These have seen a resurgence in the 1990s in the USA. They are now recognized as having good levels of validity against occupational performance measures.
- There are issues of 'faking' and responding in a socially desirable way but these can be overcome by appropriate question design and administration method.
- In our view, for use in the world of work, questionnaires should have an occupationally relevant content. Growth in the 1980s and 1990s in Europe as well as the USA has been for questionnaires of this kind.
- Ideally, these should be used in conjunction with other methods such as an interview or simulation exercises.
- Personality questionnaires are generally prone to fewer ethnic group differences than ability tests.

- As with ability tests, material costs at around US$15 per candidate are very low against the utility per candidate. Group testing and computer administration/scoring can make them time effective.
- Occupationally relevant questionnaires will translate well across cultures.

Practical Advice

These should only be used by properly trained practitioners. As with ability tests, the technical background to the questionnaire should be critically evaluated. Professional bodies of psychologists and published reviews can help with this process. The relevance of any scales used should be checked through job analysis/validation. In our view it is much safer to use an occupationally relevant questionnaire where individual items can be justified against job content. Follow administration guidelines carefully and link interpretation to the output of other methods used in the recruitment process. Remember that these questionnaires reflect an underlying inclination or preference, not necessarily ability or competence, although these often go together. Finally, as a matter of ethical procedure, offer all candidates the opportunity of feedback.

The appeal of good assessment

There is a final piece of general advice to offer with regard to the choice and design of an assessment procedure, although to some extent it is related to the economic cycle. It concerns the fact that part of the objective in a good assessment procedure is to select the best candidates. The other part of the objective is for them to select us. In other words, we want the best candidates to accept the job offer once it is made, against other options they may have. Clearly, the job and its terms and conditions will affect this but it is often forgotten that the selection procedure represents a sample of the organization in terms of the management of a project.

We have been in situations where a thorough and highly relevant multiple assessment procedure has been proposed to recruit a key manager or a new graduate intake, and the response has been that this will frighten off good applicants. In fact the reverse is true. Job decisions are important life decisions. Provided the procedure is seen to be relevant, applicants appreciate a thorough test- and simulation-based assessment even if it requires a day or two. Research has shown that the most thorough and time-consuming assessment centre method can enhance the take-up rate to job offers and the retention rates after one and two years of job tenure. Even rejected candidates value a thorough, relevant process. They value it even more if they are given feedback on their performance and, of course, they may well turn out to be tomorrow's customers.

Summary

In this chapter we have re-emphasized the need to bring the right people into the organization at the outset. This is a financial imperative. The cost of an error is too great to tolerate selection methods of low validity. In particular, unstructured, discursive interviews have too little predictive validity against their frequency of use. At the same time, we are not arguing against interviews in selection; they are likely to add value if they are well structured against clearly defined criteria. More importantly, we have argued in favour of a multiple method approach where different assessment processes are combined to cover all aspects of a required person specification. The ultimate objective in selection is to maximize the validity of the process and we have urged readers to be analytically critical of the methods they use. In a selection situation where currently 60 per cent of job incumbents are successful and we can select four in ten new applicants, a relevant multiple assessment approach could be expected to lift the success rate to around 80 per cent. Not perfect but surely a goal worth chasing vigorously.

4 Developing People in the Right Way

The practice of leading companies

The first obvious truth is that the practice varies. This is due in some cases to the size of the company and in others to the degree to which this is an agenda item of the most senior management. We have seen the extremes where at one end the development of people is a high priority and business processes are firmly in place to see that this is addressed on a regular basis. At the other end little is done by the organization, thus leaving the onus on the individual to be proactive. The evidence available is that even in the more successful companies managers spend insufficient time devoted to management development.

Throughout this book we express the view that the full potential of an organization can only be achieved if the power of all of the people is released to the pre-identified common goal. This includes the management as well as the workforce in general. There is then, a strong case to be made for all managers to devote a significant amount of time to finding, developing, and motivating subordinates. This really is a genuine source of competitive advantage. It is an area where the manager can truly add value, even though there may be a time lag between the investment of development resources and the benefits to the bottom line. This time gap is sometimes a major obstacle for myopic managers or indeed for an industry or a company that is under stress as a result of current under-performance. We would accept that in these latter cases, the timing of planned investments in management development may have to be carefully phased. We do not agree with the dated but sometimes still practised view, that 'to train and develop managers is wasteful as it makes them more attractive to our competition' (background research quote). As we move to the future the demands on management will be greater and the gap through differentiation of the best-performing companies when compared with the pack will be larger. Companies today will need to position themselves to be amongst the winners. This is true for all organizations no matter where they participate in the economy and where that economy is physically based.

Continuous learning

This is far from a new concept, and has been practised by the leading companies for 15 years. The proposition is clear. We live in a fast-changing world where the pace is accelerating. Fundamental truths from yesterday will be replaced or at least modified today, and tomorrow those self-same truths may well be ridiculed. Time does not stand still, and our knowledge base depreciates at a faster rate as time goes by. The challenge in these circumstances is to create within the organization an environment that encourages learning and development not only for the individuals but also for the organization itself.

Should there be some who are agnostic about the pace of change and its impact on the world, they should reflect on some of the momentous changes in the past ten years or so. We have seen developments in computing that give individuals affordable power in excess of that of corporations from ten years ago, the rise and use of the Internet, digital information, and the use of biotechnology to clone material, organs and animals. Think also of the changes politically in countries such as China and Hong Kong, the former Soviet Union, and the general decline of communism. There are fundamental changes to values, and an increasing impact of globalization. The list is, of course, much longer than this reminder of a few of the areas of change.

Leaders need to think about the future and to consider the impact of the demands on them if they are to optimize the development of their individuals and the capacity of the organization. Managers will, in the next decade, see:

● faster change;
● more competition, greater customer demands and an increase in the service element as a deliverable;
● complex circumstances with choices that will often call for optimal solutions rather than black or white decision making;
● new technology and processes;
● greater globalization;
● more complex trading arrangements, partnerships, joint ventures and

alliances, which will increase the challenge of working with diverse cultures and managements;

- both greater deregulation and greater regulation in different areas;
- more access to data and information;
- better educated and trained workforces with personal goals that need to be taken into account.

This list is quite a formidable one, but it is not one that will daunt the experienced manager. The management of change is an everyday part of his or her environment, and is therefore best described as normal. Warren Bennis thoughtfully put together a list of the attributes that tomorrow's leaders would need to have if they were to be successful in outperforming their peers. This is still largely relevant today and is summarized in Figure 4.1. We would add to this list:

- a real sense of *drive* and *determination* to *deliver* the vision of the organization;
- a great *thirst for knowledge* that is beyond curiosity. Managers must 'continuously journey, yet never actually arrive'. The fun is in the travelling.

Figure 4.1   Attributes of future leaders

A broad education

Incalculable curiosity

Boundless enthusiasm

Belief in people and in teamwork

Willingness to take risks

Devotion to the long term rather than to short-term growth

Commitment to excellence

Readiness

Virtue

Vision

(Derived from Warren Bennis)

Continuous learning in an organization cannot be commanded in the way that a lever can be pulled to have a train change tracks. It is driven from the top, and embraced by a team that is excited by the challenge, who work together in an open trusting environment and know where the organization is going and what special way they can add value. The features of such organizations are as follows:

- There is a clear vision.
- Individuals are clear about their objectives and personal goals.
- Individuals are encouraged, competent and empowered to perform, and rewarded appropriately when they do.
- The organization learns from being outward-looking and sharing experiences and best practice. Self-improvement is high on the collective agenda.
- There is a high level of communication, including networking as well as the regular channels.

The Human Resources input

This function, or the Personnel function as it used to be known, has been with us since the Industrial Revolution. Today, its role within an organization varies according to the value put on it and also according to the capability of the people that fill it. Some still see their role as the hiring and firing of employees, perhaps with a touch of 'union minding' thrown in. A more comprehensive and valuable role is expected today, embracing the following areas:

- establishing what work needs to be done and getting the right people with the right skills, in the right number;
- ensuring that reward systems are compatible with the objectives, are affordable and motivating;
- establishing and monitoring management development and succession plans, including specific plans of development for senior management, young managers of potential, and fast-track graduate entries;
- thorough involvement in the strategic planning process, ensuring that people and cultural issues are recognized;
- advising on the organization that will give the best chance of achievement of the goals;
- providing input into the internal communication plans;
- attending to the legal, employment administration, and the management of the union relations with the organization.

Increasingly the Human Resources function of today is learning to see that they can best make a contribution to overall success through their influence, as distinct from burdening the organization with a mass of form-filling which was sometimes the criticism of the past. This is welcomed.

Development of managers

There are some key processes that apply in the development of managers. Before we review these, it is helpful to look at a model of where this fits within the totality. This is shown in Figure 4.2.

Most organizations have a well-established process of setting objectives for key managers. There is, however, a considerable variety in the quality of application, and the way that progress is measured against them.

Objective setting is one of the first items on the calendar so that right at the start of the year the people in the organization are clear about the way that they can uniquely add value, and clear on what basis they will be measured at appraisal time. The natural sequence is for the strategic plan to be approved some time before the budget is written, challenged and finally agreed. It is only then that objectives can realistically be set. There will, at the mid-year review, be an opportunity to look formally and briefly at the progress to date against the objectives, and where circumstances warrant, the ability to add to or modify the original objectives. The purpose of this review is to monitor progress and to check if the elapsed time has changed priorities for the individual. It is not a chance to defer or cancel those items that are looking too difficult!

In Figure 4.3 we set out a calendar of business processes that is logical and highlights the natural sequence. For ease of illustration we have assumed that the company concerned has a calendar year for its financial year.

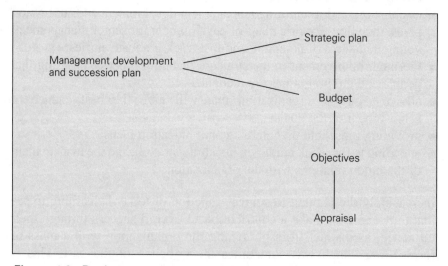

Figure 4.2 Business processes and management development

Figure 4.3 Business process calendar

Process	Process completion date
Strategic Plan ● Management development plan ● Succession plan ● Organizational implications	All, June year 1
Budget	Early December year 1
Objectives	● First draft end December year 1 ● Confirmed at appraisal process end February year 2
Appraisal	● Self-appraisal with manager by early February year 2 ● Appraisal complete end February year 2 ● Personal development plan agreed at the same time
Salary Review	End March year 2
Career Development Review	Before July year 2 (not usually annual)

The appraisal process

This is one of the most important interfaces between a manager and his or her direct reports. It is a two-way process on the assessment of achievements against the agreed objectives. This process is now fairly well embedded in organizations, although the quality is variable, and in some cases the exercise adds little value. The reasons for this are often one or more of the following:

● Objectives are not clear or appropriate, and in some cases not agreed in the proper time frame.
● The appraiser is not straightforward in the process and does not give direct feedback, for fear of either confrontation or demotivation.
● The appraiser has not in advance put in the preparation time needed to make this truly productive, and perhaps in a reactive way only responds to the self-appraisal points of the employee. The best managers gather information for appraisals throughout the year to illustrate with real examples some of the points made during the appraisal.
● Form is followed rather than getting at the very essence of performance. For example, in those cases where performance is graded (with the inevitable link to salary review), all of the tension and focus may well be on the 'grade' rather than the performance.

- There is a belief throughout the organization that the process is less valuable for other than the middle of an organization.

Training of those who need to take part in the appraisal process is a necessary precursor to getting the best value from it. This should include the form of the chosen process for the particular organization under review, as well as the skills that are needed to make the experience positive for both parties. This includes interpersonal skills, covering an understanding of personality types, dealing with conflict, and key elements of motivation. Our experience is that all but the very best organizations spend the great majority of their time on training for the appraisal process based around the documentation to be filled in, rather than the skill-building outlined above.

Much has been written on the form of appraisals, yet this is the least important part. Whatever the form that is chosen (and there is a good case for some degree of standardization in a multi-site company), it is the actual content and style of the process that is more important. Many of the organizations that are more successful with appraisals worry less about the actual fine-looking form and more about the content. However, usually the topics covered in the skeleton of an appraisal are at the core of these. These are shown in Figure 4.4.

Figure 4.4 Key elements of an appraisal

Element	Description
1. Background.	A brief description of the key factors that may have influenced performance, especially those external to the organization.
2. Comments on objectives.	Identifying the key achievements in the review period, and any not achieved.
3. Management development and team building.	This separate focus underlines the absolute importance of this in the manager's priorities.
4. Comments on overall performance.	This is in our view best kept as a commentary on the total performance which encapsulates achievements and areas where shortfalls have occurred.
5. Comments on style and job competencies.	This is often subjective but is a valuable discussion area. Where there is disagreement, then with the help of some good tests/simulations, objectivity can be brought into play. This area allows the two people to

	talk about interpersonal skills, qualities of leadership, allocation of time, and personal attributes, as well as addressing the specific competencies needed to carry out the actual role.
6. Training and development plans.	This follows quite naturally from the discussions and will include specific development areas and opportunities to be pursued. This will be followed up by the Human Resource department during the year, and will also be the basis of a summary, to the governing body, on the organization's competence and need for training to meet the overall goals.
7. Career aspirations.	Where a full career review is suggested or needed this is best done at a different time, to give sufficient opportunity for adequate discussion. This would be an irregular exercise in most cases as the aspirations seldom change annually. The reason for including this here is to look forward for a period, of say five years, and to talk about the manager's aspirations, their realism and the development that needs to take place to turn these into reality.
8. Additional items.	This is the opportunity to raise anything else that either party wishes.

The appraisal document is then prepared, agreed, signed by both parties, and on the 'grandfather principle', read, commented upon and signed by the appraiser's boss. On a confidential basis a copy will go to the Human Resource department for follow-up – especially where further training, development and wider assessment is appropriate.

The development and training of an individual in the organization is a dual responsibility of both the individual and the organization. Too often we have heard the lament that 'my employer is disinterested in my career development, because they haven't suggested a development programme'. This unfortunately may be true, but an individual's personal development is too precious to be left to the employing body! Thoughtful self-analysis based on the individual's strengths and weaknesses, and focused on realistic aspirations, gives the individual the opportunity to be proactive and suggest a development programme that can and will be supported by the employer.

Appraisal practice

The evidence we have is that when two-way feedback is given through a well thought out appraisal process, it does add value in practice. Most managers would intuitively agree with this as a statement, perhaps with the proviso that proper training was applied to ensure that the feedback was given and received in a positive manner. There have been a number of researchers that have tried to measure the uplifted performance that can be ascribed to this process alone. Claims of 20–30 per cent improvement on performance have been made but the case is not a watertight one because other variables cannot be held constant to perfect this measurement.

However, in the UK, SHL has conducted surveys of appraisal practice amongst its clients. In the latest study conducted by Farrell and Perry in 1997, a significant finding is that the appraisal process is the most important contribution to embedding a culture of performance. However, as we have already observed, an effective financial assessment of the Human Resource contribution is quite difficult and something we will return to in the final chapters.

Increasingly, competencies are being used in appraisal with slightly more than half of the UK survey sample now including them. The objectives of using them within the appraisal process are shown in Figure 4.5.

Figure 4.5   Objectives of using competencies within the appraisal process

Objective	% Yes
Identifying training and development needs	95
Influencing salary decisions	14
Influencing promotion	49

SOURCE: SHL 1997 UK Survey of Views on Performance Appraisal

There was another interesting finding from this same piece of research, which highlights culture differences. Almost nine out of ten respondents believe that there are important cultural differences when conducting appraisals which managers need to recognize. This can be seen from Figure 4.6 which ranks cultures perceived to be the most open and honest in giving and receiving feedback.

Figure 4.6 Ranking of cultures in giving and receiving feedback

Ranking	Culture
1. Most open and honest	USA
2.	New Zealand – Australia
3.	UK
4.	Europe
5. Least open and honest	Asia

SOURCE: SHL 1997 UK Survey of Views on Performance Appraisal

Clearly within these major regions there are further significant differences and we would observe that the closer the link to the actual salary review, the greater the propensity for being less open!

Finally, from the list of UK companies in the SHL sample, we can see the array of objectives for the appraisal scheme and the assessment of how well these are currently met (Figure 4.7). The disappointment on the one hand, and the future opportunity on the other, is just how low the success scores are (more than half the total ratings 'adequate' or 'poor').

We believe that at least for the first four objectives, which are at the core of the process, a 'top box' score (which is 'Very Good' in this survey) should be more than 50 per cent and the top two boxes close to 75 per cent. These results are well short of this ideal which means that the **practice** of appraisals needs to be improved.

Figure 4.7 How good is the appraisal scheme at achieving its objectives?

	% Very Good	% Good	% Adequate	% Poor	% Very Poor
Reviewing past performance	13	54	25	3	–
Helping improve current performance	9	49	29	6	1
Assessing training and development needs	6	48	31	8	3
Setting individual performance objectives	19	51	16	3	1
Setting group/team performance objectives	1	10	20	18	5
Determining increases in salary	1	14	16	13	5
Determining one-off bonus payments	–	6	10	10	8
Assessing future potential/promotability	3	18	34	18	3
Assisting career/succession planning decisions	3	21	38	14	4
Motivating employees	–	39	41	6	1
Changing culture	3	16	19	24	9
Other	1	1	–	–	1

(Note: Percentages will not add up to 100 per cent as not all respondents listed every option as being an objective of the scheme)

SOURCE: SHL 1997 UK Survey of Views on Performance Appraisal

Finally, we have one further concern which is really about the difference between the effectiveness of any scheme compared with the norm. Too often we see the well-meaning Human Resource department drafting detailed forms, detailed instructions and training programmes that focus on the procedure, at the expense of the input it makes, or the real value that is added. Form is less important than results; a point made earlier in this chapter.

Management development and succession planning

This is a top-level review that is built up from the many individual actions from the appraisal process. It is done within the wider environment reflecting the trends, opportunities and threats that are likely to affect the organization in the future. This enables the top governing body to get a bird's eye view of the talent within the company and to see the areas of sensitivity and risk, within the setting of the strategic plan for the organization. The key questions to be answered in this exercise are:

1. What are the significant external trends that are likely to have an impact, and what then is the importance of these for future personnel plans?
2. What are the quantitative and qualitative changes needed with the people resource to achieve the preferred strategy?
3. What are the steps being taken first to identify the managers of significant potential and then to develop them, and to motivate them? What are the career steps needed and are they likely to be available?
4. What is happening to the peaked managers, and how will the organization exit those who are blockages?
5. What are the succession issues? This needs to be examined on an emergency basis as well as on the planned approach. Special care must be taken at the top level of the organization or with key roles that go to the very heart of it.

It is of fundamental importance for the effectiveness of this exercise, and more importantly for the health of the organization, that the organization does have in place a reliable way of identifying managers of real potential and those that have the suitability to change roles as a part of their development. Finding this talent is fundamental to the future health of a business or any other organization. The topic should therefore be treated accordingly, with the appropriate allocation of time and resource.

Finding the talent

There is still a lot of subjectivity and trial and error in many, especially larger, organizations as they try to seek out the top talent which they wish to nurture and grow in an accelerated way. This is often due to judgements being made on past achievements of objectives in a particular role that may be quite different to the characteristics that are needed in the future. Unless there is an objective way of identifying this talent for future development that works fairly evenly across the many different sites and cultures in especially global companies, then the search will be sub-optimal. Clearly there are two important dimensions. First is the performance, and here the appraisal process is the first port of call. This will show the level of achievement across the planned, differing roles that the manager has had over a period of time. The second measure is perhaps even more important, and that is the *potential* of the individual. It may well be more important, but the assessment of the potential is often random, subjective and judgemental. This need not be the case as there are well-tried and trusted ways of removing a lot of the uncertainty. We will deal with these in more detail a little later in the chapter. However, many companies are now using specially designed multiple assessment programmes that include specific tests for intellectual capacity, personality, and work/management simulations to measure management behaviour. These are usually run with a combination of external specialists and people internal to the organization for best results. The evidence is that this approach materially enhances the probability of identifying the correct people. It also has the added advantage of objectivity which is positively received within the organization. It is seen to be fair.

We can illustrate in a model the measures of executive potential. This is shown in Figure 4.8.

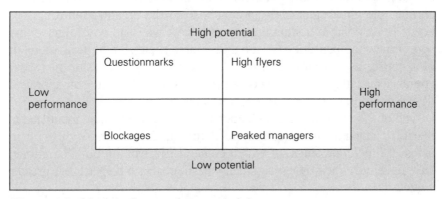

Figure 4.8 Model of executive potential

In this model, the *questionmarks* are the products of low performance yet they are judged to have high potential. There may well be a motivation problem, or a special training need for them to be more effective in their current role. The facts need to be established and corrective action taken. Perhaps the starting point should be that the organization should ask itself why it is that it has failed these people!

The *high flyers* are those people with high potential and high performance. Here the challenge is to find suitable challenging roles that enhance their capacity and therefore their future potential even further. There may need to be some risk-taking with this group in that they may well be put into a position a little earlier than ideal, and with some mentoring and training it is surprising how quickly they close the gap, and get to peak performance in the new role. We reflect on the fact that the really successful managers at senior levels today often owe their current success to the early variety in their experiences, and on the fact that quite early in their careers they were given a role that was extremely stretching – almost too much for them at that time.

Peaked managers are those with high (or sometimes satisfactory) current performance, but with little potential to go beyond the current job in the present organization. These are the great proportion of managers in an organization that are performing well but will not go further. Here the challenge is to find lateral moves for them, to enhance their skills through training, as a way to refresh the manager. Often a number of these managers will be approaching retirement age, which may well limit the opportunities for lateral moves. These managers need to be watched to see that their motivation is retained and that they do not become blockages.

The final group is *blockages*. They are performing at a low level and are judged to have a low potential. They need to be removed from their current role, and realistically, probably from the organization too. This needs to be done in a straightforward honest way and with dignity and appropriate compensation for the individual. There should be no element of surprise, as this should have been the topic of discussion in recent appraisals. Managers that do not address this directly during an appraisal do the individual and their organization an injustice.

One of the most important characteristics that needs to be identified is that of leadership. It is not easy to define, and is therefore difficult to assess. Some companies, of which General Electric[1] in the USA is one, have developed their own assessment questionnaire to help achieve greater objectivity.

We have set aside a separate chapter on leadership (Chapter 9).

Assessing for potential

We have emphasized that it is a key part of the management role to identify future talent and ensure that it is properly developed. The appraisal system is certainly an important part of this process but it does not alone provide the whole story. Even allowing that the organization has a thorough appraisal system in place, it may still be prone to biases of subjectivity, prejudice, personal liking, haloing effect and others. Even more important, it provides an historical perspective. In other words, it evaluates past performance in a current role when the issue may well be the potential of the individual to perform well, in the future, in a substantially different role. Research suggests that managers, who think that they can intuitively infer future performance from the past, all too often get it wrong. We need a procedure that will enable us to make future predictions with more certainty. The cost of over-promoting an inappropriate senior manager merits a thorough initial assessment.

The solution lies in a rigorous multiple assessment method – often referred to as an 'assessment centre' or 'development centre' depending on its orientation. This method draws heavily on management simulation exercises and we saw in Chapter 3 that it is at the top of the league table for assessment validity. Regardless of the statistics, consider the rational case. At the simplest level we may need to know whether in future a manager will be able to write a good strategic plan, chair a tough committee, make a decision on complex commercial data, negotiate a major deal and so on. An assessment centre might require a candidate in a structured and controlled environment to write a strategic plan, chair a tough committee, make a decision from complex data and negotiate a result. The individual's performance would be assessed by a senior line management group who had been specifically trained and would operate with assessment manuals. The psychological attributes of the candidate would be assessed and interpreted by a specialist practitioner.

Research has suggested that where chance prediction would give a 15 per cent probability of management success, adding an appraisal would raise this to around 35 per cent and further adding an assessment centre would raise it to over 70 per cent. Furthermore, there has been a general research finding that those who do not achieve selection or promotion by this method still rate it positively as a fair and objective method. Figure 4.9 shows the predictive potential from an early assessment centre at the AT&T Corporation in which the assessors' predictions were kept secret for a number of years so that they could not 'contaminate' the promotion decisions. Of those entrants predicted at the assessment centre to reach

The People Advantage

Figure 4.9 Predictive potential of assessment centres

Predicted from assessment centre to reach middle management	Achieved middle management at 6–8 year review	
	Yes	No
Yes (103)	42%	58%
No (166)	7%	93%

SOURCE: Data for 269 college and non-college graduates from D.W. Bray and D.L. Grant, *The Assessment Centre in the Measurement of Potential for Business Management*, 1966. Copyright © 1996 by the American Psychological Association. Adapted with permission.

middle management, 42 per cent had done so within 6–8 years. Of those not predicted to reach this level, only 7 per cent had done so at the 6–8 year review.

Much has been written about the technical aspects of assessment centre design and references are provided at the end of the book for those who wish to follow up on this. What follows here are some supportive arguments and practical guidance tips for those considering an implementation of this method.

- It is not unusual for management to be reluctant to adopt this method. There is a feeling that current managers' judgement must be better than an artificial assessment procedure. However, the research evidence is clear: managers' intuition has much less predictive validity than the assessment centre method. Remember that validity is linearly related to the financial pay-off.
- Cost may be a barrier and an assessment centre tends to be hungry for senior-level resources. However, the cost implications should not be judged in isolation but related to the costs of an error in senior-level placement. Without some notice of cost benefit, management will continue to feel 'edgy' in this respect. With a well-developed programme the benefit should vastly outweigh the cost.
- The method may be seen to demand too much senior management time for both initial training and the assessment programme itself. In reality the method can be flexibly designed to economize on senior-level time. However, the issues of succession planning are sufficiently critical to merit a senior-level resource. Furthermore, a senior input helps to create a culture in which thorough assessment and development are seen as key organizational values. Be wary of letting senior managers vote themselves out of the process.
- The important assessment principles remain fairness, objectivity and

relevance. In addition the process should be 'open' so that participants understand the objectives, the content and the follow-up implications.

- Feedback is essential whether the process is assessment or development orientated. Participants should have a clear idea of how they have performed on the assessment criteria and specific feedback on any psychological tests they have completed. Feedback should be as close as possible to the assessment event, though any follow-up developmental debate might occur at a later stage when the individual's line manager can be involved.

- The best assessment centres are characterized by excellent behavioural evidence from the assessors to support their competency ratings. High quality evidence improves the validity of the output and gives credibility to the feedback process. This is not easily achieved. The design of the process will be important but it is particularly important that the assessors are well trained. There may well be an inclination to skimp on this, but it should be avoided. If time absolutely cannot be made available for formal training then expert coaching and colleague shadowing should be considered for new assessors in a real programme.

- Exercises should be thoroughly developed to be realistic, challenging and relevant to the appropriate management level. They should be supported with clear assessor guidelines and scoring procedures. A good test of an exercise is how immersed the participants become, as if they were facing a real problem. Selecting organization-specific as opposed to external exercise content is a matter of individual choice. The former offers more face validity, the latter has less risk of bias for a particular organizational role. Good exercises in terms of a relevant process are likely to discriminate whether the content is organizationally specific or not.

- The advice of an experienced practitioner should be taken in advance in the interest of setting high standards and maximizing the likelihood of the process having predictive validity.

A particularly important choice facing the organization is whether to introduce a programme that is mainly for assessment or mainly for development. There is a broad continuum of options and there is no right or wrong. The method may vary somewhat. For example, at the assessment end, the final discussion and integration session may be extremely short for a weak promotion candidate. In a more developmental process such a candidate may require a particularly lengthy discussion of the development options. Nowadays, there are pure development programmes in which line management assessors are completely removed and the participants learn under professional guidance to assess and feed back to each other. This can create a much more positive developmental atmosphere.

Whatever the positioning of the programme in terms of the degree of assessment and development, there are two important points of guidance. First, it is important to be open and honest with participants. In other words, if it is largely an assessment process then it should not be presented as mainly a 'development centre'. Participants will understand the need for objective assessment and respect the management integrity in a correct statement of objectives. Second, if the programme has a development objective then this must be followed through. We have found that one of the main problems with a so-called 'development culture' is not the initial assessment process but the participants' view that no follow-up development occurred. This is an issue of resourcing and a prevailing culture that communicates to participants that the organization is serious about development.

360° evaluation

As a final point in the review of potential, the past few years have seen much support for the so-called 360° analysis of managers. This involves not only a self-rating from an individual on a relevant model of competencies using a thorough questionnaire but also a parallel set of ratings from bosses, subordinates, peers, colleagues, customers and so on as appropriate. As the name implies, this gives a far more rounded perception of the individual and is based on the most reasonable assumption that no one source observes all of an individual's behaviour and that different work styles can be evaluated.

Professor Christine Farrell and her colleagues Kate Oliver and Andrew Geake at SHL have surveyed the usage of and attitudes towards 360° analysis in a sample of Human Resource practitioners in 216 UK organizations covering both the public and private sectors; 47 per cent of organizations in this 1997 survey were using the 360° approach. (The precise figure may be sample dependent but had shown clear growth over a similar survey two years before.) The main categories of usage are given in Figure 4.10. Other key findings from the survey included:

- seven in ten had been through formal training;
- a strong view that the use of 360° analysis will increase over the next two years (including current non-users);

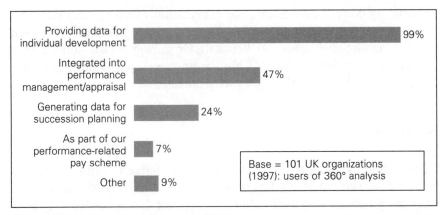

Figure 4.10 Purpose of current 360° use

- a tendency for the method to be used relatively more with middle and senior management groups;
- the method is seen as moderately threatening;
- 'piloting' the method is the best way of overcoming resistance;
- there is a good level of satisfaction with the 360° instruments being used.

Our contact with colleagues world-wide would confirm that 360° analysis and appraisal is here to stay. It is not surprising that there should be some defensiveness about a process of critical personal evaluation. However, users clearly find that the enhanced picture of key staff facilitates the developmental process. Furthermore, it is possible to move directly from a 360° evaluation into a self-managed process of development through the use of computerized or pencil and paper based development resource packs. This renders the entire procedure more practical, less expensive, more open to self-ownership and less directly threatening than a simulation-based development centre. 360° analysis has, therefore, become a serious developmental option. However, as with any method involving the evaluation of people, there are caveats on implementation:

- The competency models should be relevant.
- The 360° questionnaire instruments should be psychometrically sound.
- Users should be properly trained with particular emphasis on managing the feedback process and any developmental debate.

Professor Farrell reinforces the point that organizations need feedback to grow and adapt. We live in a changing world with ongoing shifts in job content, working practices and the expectation of young entrants. She believes that the important issue is to get the dialogue started between those managing businesses and their staff. Organizations will suffer if they fail to take regular feedback – both from their own people and their marketplace – in terms of the way they operate.

Summary

Recognizing the competitive advantage that is derived from the effective use of a workforce at all levels, leading companies enshrine in their business processes and their culture the support that is needed to deliver the maximum benefit from this resource. Regrettably, this approach is far from universal and many employers will need to play 'catch up' to stay competitive. A number of forward-thinking companies are able to create an environment where learning is continuous and valued because it is commercially attractive to the organization.

Leaders need to think about the external trends and to think about the implications for their industry and for their organization and then to develop the competencies and attributes that will meet today's and tomorrow's environment. We reviewed the more detailed attributes of leaders of the future, but especially highlighted the importance of:

- the drive and determination to deliver the organization's vision;
- a great thirst for knowledge that is beyond curiosity.

In order to get the best from people and to develop them in the right way, the appropriate processes must be in place and practised with enthusiasm and expertise. This is similar to the concept of leadership; effective leadership needs more than charisma – it needs the building blocks to deliver the leadership in a practical way. In this chapter, we set the scene of business processes in general but highlight the development of managers. We show first how important the management development and succession plan is and note, incidentally, that it is an area of great importance to the boards of directors of companies.

Within this context, one of the most important interfaces between managers and their direct reports is the appraisal process. While the process is fairly well embedded in most organizations, the implementation is patchy, and the content often superficial. We see many examples of the triumph of form over the real practical matter. Appraisals and objective setting are critically important.

If organizations are to get the best from the pool of talent, they need to have an objective way of locating and stimulating those of above average capability and current performance. We have suggested a model that looks for high flyers, and develops them on an accelerated path, picks up on the questionmarks and gives them the opportunity of becoming high flyers, improves peaked managers and finally provides an exit path for those peaked managers that have become blockages.

Assessing for potential requires time, effort and the right tools. The credibility of an organization is lost if the selection is seen to be arbitrary or on a personal favour basis. Organizations need the right tools and methods which is why we highlight the potential of assessment and development centres. 360° questionnaires are discussed as another credible option for gathering information for competency development purposes.

Developing people in the right way will increase the organization's competitiveness, improve motivation and enhance competitive ability. The positive reputation derived from such an approach will also increase the potential to recruit capable people, thus helping to join up the virtuous circle.

Note

1. See the July/August 1993 issue of *The Chief Executive* magazine, and the summary reproduced by Neville Bain, *Successful Management*, op. cit., pp. 45–47.

5

Optimum Use of the People Resource

The employee's perspective

In our preface we made the point that putting the right people into the right jobs and encouraging the right development activity adds value. We have seen in earlier chapters that there are challenges in the implementation and that more effort and resource are needed in the area of understanding the key tasks of the organization, and the matching of the right people with the right skills to deliver them. In Chapter 4 we pursued the theme of developing people in the right way, recognizing that development is essential, is continuous, is value-adding, but in reality receives insufficient attention. We offered guidance on the implementation of appraisal systems and development centres. Throughout this chapter we will spend most of the time looking from the viewpoint of the organization at the challenge of optimizing the total people resource in the use of these processes.

Before we pursue this agenda, we would like to dwell on the perspective of the employee, to see what insights this will give us. Given the different expectations of those who are managers and those who are front-line employees, we have separated the two categories. Our research and experience show that the factors listed in Figure 5.1 are the most frequently highlighted by the workforce as important factors in deciding overall job satisfaction.

The list of most frequently mentioned attributes of job satisfaction for those in managerial positions is shown in Figure 5.2.

The ranking in both tables is not precise owing to the different sources of data – some from our research, some from observation over the years, and some from the work of others who have published their findings. We can observe that salary or wages is not the first factor in either case and that the higher the income potential of the individual, the more other

Figure 5.1 Factors rated as important to the workforce in deciding overall job satisfaction

Factor	Detail
Security of employment	● Not a job for life, but transferable skills ● An industry with a future
Feedback on performance	● Useful appraisals
Rewards	● Includes deferred (pensions)
Sense of belonging	● Sharing of information ● Open environment (absence of fear) ● Some voice in major decisions ● Opportunity to share in employer's success (bonuses, options)
Job interest	● Utilize full employee potential (multi-skilling) ● Flexibility about how the job is best done ● Self-governing environment ● Opportunity for personal growth and promotion
Social dimension	● Company activities ● Community involvement

Figure 5.2 Attributes of job satisfaction for those in managerial positions

Factor	Detail
Career and personal skill development	● Within a construct where family and community are valued
Reputation of the company	● Highly regarded in the community ● Learning environment ● Open culture ● People truly valued ● Promotion from within where possible ● Development plans for individuals ● Leadership is seen as able
Valued contribution	● New ideas welcomed ● Good feedback on performance (both praise and under-performance)
Rewards	● Competitive salary, significant reward based on results ● Appropriate fringe benefits, with some (for example, car) having emotional significance

factors will take precedence. There is a basic level of income needed to meet the needs of the household and this portion will need to be secured first. Given this proviso, some observations can be made:

- Employment security ranks highest for the workforce. This provides real challenges for industries that are contracting, but this task can be met by ensuring that transferable skills are added to the workforce which will improve productivity in the existing roles and their marketability.
- Development of skills is high on the agenda of managers, who have an eye on their career path. They wish also to be proud of the organization they work for, and therefore have regard for its reputation.
- Both groups want to feel valued, and included within the organization. They need to be consulted, communicated with, and in an open environment told how they are performing.

Many managers will now routinely prepare and update a 'personal life plan' that will formally review their goals over a finite period. This will include their career aspirations, those for personal relationships including where applicable the family, their material expectations, and the personal development plans that might be needed to achieve their multi-faceted goals. The employer must recognize the legitimacy of these goals and have business processes that will address the personal aspirations of the employees.

There is an interesting American study of 115 Harvard MBAs which deals with insights into managers and their economic and psychological needs. This was written up by John Kotter. From this study he observed the following:

1. The criteria for success in business over time have changed significantly so that the career paths of the past that led to success are no longer paying off. However, significant numbers of people are still using the old strategies, usually aided and abetted by the major institutions of big business, government, education and trade unions.
2. Many factors affect the success rate of managers today, but none is more important than the globalization of markets and competition. This is increasing the rate of change, producing more opportunities and threats.
3. Managers who are doing well today are capitalizing on this global trend, and pursuing more dynamic, less linear, career paths, accepting some resultant risk. In many cases they will have had experience in smaller organizations and developed entrepreneurial behaviour.

4. Successful managers will need high personal standards, a strong drive to compete, self-confidence in competitive situations, and a willingness to keep growing and to learn new things.

Again, from this work we can glimpse at insights that are helpful, and compatible with our earlier observations of what is needed to motivate the best contribution from those that work in the organization.

The appraisal is central

While there remain a number of organizations that rely on personal observation of the performance of people within it, this would be neither normal nor acceptable other than in the case of the very small ones where people are known intimately by the one senior manager or owner. We have seen in Chapter 4 that where people are developed in the right way there are clear objectives in a measurable form that tie back to the organization's plans. People need to know what they are required to do, have the skills to achieve these tasks, and be measured objectively against them. The appraisal process is key here. In Chapter 4, we went through the process and reviewed the coverage of it. Here, we wish to focus more on the behavioural aspects of the appraisal. Sometimes, objectives are not fully met despite the best efforts of the individual as external circumstances have materially changed. Even though a number of corrective steps have been taken to get back on course, the external change is of such a magnitude that it cannot be fully offset in the time period under review, by the appraisee. An example of this may be a significant strengthening of the domestic currency of a commercial enterprise, which hurts margins owing to imports being relatively cheaper. In the long run, if the exchange rate is likely to be maintained, production can be shifted off-shore, but this is usually not possible in time to save the shortfall from the objectives. What is important in the actual appraisal process is to look at the individual's behaviour to see how he or she has reacted to the new threat. Equally there should be no surprise, for during the year under review the individual will have been discussing, with the boss, the actions being taken.

Getting the appraisal right and managing the feedback are clearly important. In most organizations managers receive training on how to handle the appraisal process for best effect. Our experience shows that this is often heavy on understanding the methodology and the form-filling, and lighter on the interpersonal skills in making sure that the messages are clear (remembering that this is a two-way process), and that they are received.

Neither is there much thought given to understanding the personality and motivation of the person being appraised, and contrasting that with the manager undertaking the appraisal. If this was a regular part of the preparation for the appraisal, then there is a better chance of the message being put in a way that will be more readily received. The managers that achieve greatest success with the appraisal process will be seen as follows:

- well prepared;
- clear in communication;
- understanding of the different personalities, and aware of potential clash points with his or her own;
- able to first praise and draw out the very positive things, before dwelling on the areas for improvement;
- not fudging difficult issues, and dealing with these with sensitivity where this is needed;
- relying less on personal opinion, and more on factual evidence;
- open, approachable and straightforward, with no 'hidden agenda'.

Some practitioners prefer not to use a numerical scale because it can lead to a mechanistic link with salary increases as opposed to a balanced overall judgement. Others prefer the precision of a rating process, in which case we would recommend the use of an even (say 4 point) scale to avoid the predominant tendency to use a middle scale rating. We would also prefer ratings to be made against specific competencies to maximize subsequent developmental benefit.

As we have already seen, the identification of special training needs is derived from the appraisal and both the manager and the employee need to commit to the plan of action, which will have clearly identified dates for completion. There must be resource available to deliver the training. This may seem obvious, yet as an example it is not always forthcoming in the public sector, as many teachers or municipal employees have found. In the private sector some companies, especially in difficult industries, will raid the training budget as the first stop when times get tough, and the training does not take place. The training plan must be followed up by both parties, as a shared responsibility.

The career review

For a number of people in the organization there will be a request to undertake a career review. The employee will pre-state his or her aspirations, within an indicative time-frame. The first task is to discuss and decide if these aspirations are valid, given the competencies and personal attributes of the individual. These in turn need to be matched against the needs of the organization, and the future role that is envisaged. This is not an easy task for busy managers, and often they are not well prepared for the task as they have inadequate information. In order to do justice to the task, the manager needs to know not only the track record of the individual, but also the competencies and the personal attributes. Managers are probably more comfortable with observing the competencies, because these are in more practical, easy-to-understand terms than the personal attributes that underpin them and are the domain of the industrial psychologist or trained specialist. However, with training, they are relatively easy to assess and understand, and it is therefore surprising that more use is not made of these measures.

If the trouble is taken to identify the core competencies for the role to which the manager aspires and this is compared and contrasted with a profile of the individual, then objective analysis and feedback is possible. Where there is a gap in the manager's skill-base that is vital for success in the role to which he or she aspires, it is then possible to see whether a development plan will close that gap. Certainly the information is available for a direct two-way conversation which can give vital feedback.

In assessing a manager against the job requirements for the role to which he or she aspires, we find it valuable to include an analysis of competencies, verbal and numerical reasoning skills, a personality profile, and a review of the manager's recent track record. In our view the development centre is an ideal way of gathering this information, where the manager is in a realistic situation and operating with others under time pressure.

On some occasions the manager will have realistic goals which are well supported by the skills, competencies, experiences and personality that he or she has. Despite this, it may not be possible for the organization to meet these legitimate expectations, because a succession plan is already in place with a different preferred candidate identified. We strongly believe that in such a case, total honesty must be maintained by first supporting the individual's aspirations, but indicating that they are unlikely to be realized in the time-frame chosen. This gives the opportunity to talk of other alternatives for such a valued employee, even if one cannot be precise about a role. We have seen in many examples of this kind, where the employee's worth is recognized, and ongoing development is maintained and directed to their aspirations, that the individual stays motivated and highly performing. This is based on trust in the organization and the possibility that some, perhaps unexpected, change in the organization will present new opportunities of interest.

Identifying the talent

If we are to select people to receive accelerated development we had better be sure that we pick those who are genuinely people of high potential, and who have the personal attributes needed to match the future needs of the business. It is an erroneous assumption to think that one can rely on past performance alone, so a process is needed to help gain a better understanding of the people that are nominated. It is usual for the first sieving process to be based on the information from the appraisal and career review, so that candidates can be more formally assessed at development centres. If the organization already has knowledge of candidates' preferred style of working and their personal attributes, preferably using a common across-the-company methodology, this will provide valuable additional data to help the initial selection. It will be clear that this is a selective process, and there will be many good managers not judged to be exceptional that will not be selected for accelerated development. To maintain their morale and commitment is a challenge, but this is managed by the many organizations that follow a selective approach. Those people that are selected for the development centre will all receive feedback on the event, including a personal development programme. It is inevitable that some of those who were initially accepted will not stay on the fast development track, as the analysis of results will show that there are areas of doubt, or further developmental tasks that are needed before they can be reconsidered. The review of results with the individual needs to be very supportive, providing opportunity for personal growth through a personal development plan, and holding out the opportunity to revisit the 'fast track' in the future. Again the challenge is to maintain morale and commitment.

The most successful operators of career development centres use a mix of appropriately qualified and senior managers from the organization, and specialists with the appropriate technical knowledge. Credibility is sometimes enhanced if support from the very top of the organization is seen, with the participation as an assessor of the chief executive. The individuals attending need to be comfortable with this presence, so that their performance is not impaired.

Development centres are especially valuable in three separate circumstances, where the content is adjusted for each: (1) the selection of senior managers of potential where it is judged that within five years they have the ability to rise to the top level; (2) the identification of young managers of potential, who may be capable within three to five years of significantly greater responsibility, perhaps involving a change of geography or function; (3) the selection of university graduates, who will be put on an intensive, usually two-year, course of learning and development, during which time they will not contribute at a rate equal to the total cost of training them. This is about investing for the future, and given the high costs of recruitment and development and a turnover which quite often reaches 50 per cent over three years, there is a need to be more successful in identifying the right people. There is also a need not to create false expectations, and to model the intake numbers to the ability of the business to absorb them. To do otherwise is to train people at high cost for the benefit of others, or sometimes to the disadvantage of the individuals that are misplaced in the role for which they have been recruited.

One of the great benefits that an individual organization utilizing experienced external help has here is access to the large data bank of individuals that have been through similar tests and exercises over the years, and the positioning of their candidates within this. There is then knowledge in detail about the individuals, and also how they stack up against appropriate norms.

Making managers accountable for their people

First, the development of people needs to be imbued within the culture of the organization – not just in the words, but lived out in the actions at all levels, and especially at the top. The board must regularly review the management development and succession plans, and set the example in ensuring that learning takes place. The board should appraise its own performance and plan the development of each of the directors, including the independent ones.

Next, it should be a requirement for every person who supervises or manages people to have a very specific, measurable objective on people development. The best appraisals will have a heading on 'development of people', ensuring that this receives individual attention.

Another sign of a genuine organizational commitment to development is the 'Learning Account'. The organization might make, say, $300 to $400 available to individuals per annum to pursue personal development interests. Not only does this reinforce the idea of real organizational support but it leads to serious accountability for the individual to show how the money has been invested.

Many organizations are now utilizing periodic, 360° assessments of managers, with good effect. This need not be an annual exercise, but it does provide new insights for managers who may have had blind spots, or been less attentive to their impact on those that report to them.

Increasing use is made of employee attitudes through surveys that are conducted by third parties. Such an approach was used at Coats Viyella plc on an international basis, as a way of involving the workforce and improving employment practices. When they started this, most of the almost 180 companies within the group at that time had confrontational employee relations. They constructed a model called 'the employment practices clock'. This was divided into four quadrants, with the lowest being 'antagonistic employee relations', then an 'uneasy alliance with employees', followed by 'consultative relations with employees', and the top measure of 'co-operative and participative employee relations'. An individual programme was agreed, with union involvement, to move to a minimum of quadrant three in under five years. Real progress was made, as it was clear that this measurable objective then had top management's attention and high visibility within the group.

There is a danger that development might be rather narrowly focused on certain sectors of the organization. In particular, there is a danger that it is seen to fall within the management domain to the exclusion of other staff. One way of overcoming this is to bring development into a 'Partnership Agreement' with the Trades Unions. This can overcome barriers and suspicions and ensure that development becomes part of the total organizational culture.

Making development bite

In this chapter we have made a number of suggestions in the interest of optimizing the use of the people resource. However, there is an overriding concern that senior management in particular may only pay lip-service to the criticality of staff development. It is a concern born from a perception among some managers that development is something done to 'other' people; that there are 'more pressing budgetary demands' and that in the final analysis 'people do not really change anyway'. Well, people can and do change provided that the conditions are right. We have laid down some of the specific requirements in this chapter but we would like to conclude by proposing a model designed to give us the best chance of making development bite in the real world.

There was a time when we used to congratulate ourselves if we had implemented a good quality 'development centre' for an organization, which reliably identified development needs. We would subsequently be brought back to earth if the organization reported – one or two years later – a sense of no real development occurring. This forced us to focus on the totality of the development process. It also forced us to realize that our goal was not the implementation of a good 'development centre', but rather the change of behaviour within the organization with the net effect of increasing the likelihood of meeting organization goals. Our research and analysis suggested that there were four conditions that needed to be met for successful behaviour change to occur. Furthermore, if any one of these conditions were not met it would seriously jeopardize the meeting of the overall behaviour change goal. The four conditions are shown in Figure 5.3.

The starting point has to be the reliable assessment of the individual. We simply have to know a person's relative strengths and limitations if we are going to build on the former and develop the latter. In this book we have argued for objective multiple assessment using simulation exercises to create future scenarios for evaluation. Similarly, we have argued that there needs to be a good competency model in place that is relevant to future demands on the individual. Furthermore, these competencies should link to the appraisal process which provides the basis for ongoing review and development planning. The role of the appraisal is key. As we have suggested, all development plans should have review points which can be included within this process.

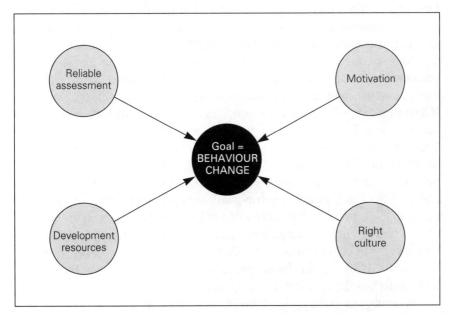

Figure 5.3 Conditions for ensuring that development is achieved

However, even at this stage things can go wrong. If a 'development centre' is perceived by participants as essentially an assessment programme for succession planning, then it will be seen as no more than a career hurdle to be overcome and any development messages will be lost. There has to be a genuine management commitment to a development outcome and this can reasonably dovetail with succession planning objectives. There should be a briefing statement for all participants which openly states the objectives of the centre and what will happen afterwards. If assessment for succession planning is to be part of the process it should be honestly stated and participants will recognise the case and respect the admission. At the same time the developmental follow-up should be reinforced. A suggested set of headings for the briefing statement is as follows:

- What is the Management Development Centre (MDC)?
- Why do we have MDCs?
- Who goes on an MDC?
- What happens at the MDC?
- What happens after the MDC?
- What does the company get out of it?
- What does your management get out of it?
- What do you get out of it?

One organization has usefully facilitated the meeting of twin assessment and development objectives by splitting the competency set into two parts. One part was utilized for assessment. It reflected underlying attributes such as 'Analytical Reasoning' and 'Drive' which were seen as relevant to performance but not easily developable. The other part reflected competencies which were much more experience based, such as 'Customer Focus'. These were concerned with how well developed was the individual's thinking and were manifestly open to improvement. Feedback was split between an assessment review focused on part one and development focused on part two. Other organizations have started the development process within the centre itself, for example by giving mid-exercise feedback to assist subsequent improvement. Others again have opted to use a process that is completely developmental, even to the point of excluding line management assessors and training participants specifically to cross-assess each other. There is good evidence from the UK and the USA that this latter approach takes the threat out of the process and reinforces the development objective.

This brings us to the issue of motivation which we examine as a specific concept in more detail in Chapter 8. Motivation is undoubtedly the key to new learning. If staff are not motivated to want to change or improve their behaviour then it is unlikely that they will do so. This is a self-evident truth to parents who have tried to develop new skills in their children. Not surprisingly, motivation is importantly linked to the prevailing culture as we implied in the section above. We need to look at both these aspects of the model together.

In our experience, people will not strive to achieve development goals that are not in line with organization values. In one particular case, a retail bank wanted to reinforce a sales competency amongst its branch managers and implemented a high quality sales training course. A number of managers were manifestly not giving enough commitment to this training process. As they explained it, what really affected their appraisals and career progress were branch inspections and their perceived control in branch administration. The penalty for missing a 'sale' was, in their minds, tantamount to zero. They knew their priorities when they got back to their branches, and they were not sales related. For the development to work the bank had first to reinforce the importance of 'sales' to the bank and how this would be manifest in career development terms.

There also needs to be a clear perception within the organization that development really does matter to senior management. In the case of one large insurance company, a single executive director believed strongly in the concept of development centres and development planning. Despite much scepticism around him, a development centre was implemented from the top. The centre worked well and senior managers became persuaded of the objectivity of the process. However, the ongoing success of this implementation was not due to the consultants who built the centre. It was due to the leadership of that individual and his management development team who succeeded in building a development culture. At the heart lay a management development committee, with high-level representation, who ensured an integrated approach to development covering training, appraisals, succession planning and continuous progress review. They succeeded in persuading the company at large that development really mattered and even created a demand to join the assessment process.

As with other aspects of the management of culture, the chief executive is a key player. In a major organization in the power sector, a new development centre programme for high-potential managers was followed shortly afterwards by a senior management team meeting to discuss the developmental implications. The meeting lasted the best part of a day and the managing director attended throughout. His presence, given his work-load, was a more powerful communication of the importance of the process than any number of policy statements. In a German oil company, the chief executive let it be known that 'assessors' in a similar process could only be excused from an allocated assessment by direct reference to him – and that he would generally say 'no'. In his view the identification and development of the company's future directors was a high-priority demand for top-level time. In the case of a major UK transport company, the managing director sought the agreement of his top management team to introduce a new development centre programme. He then proposed that the process should start with himself and the top team who duly completed the exercises and took personal feedback of their own strengths and limitations, as well as setting up their own personal development plans.

When chief executives behave as those above, their example makes verbal statements of commitment almost redundant. Their people know that their interest and involvement are deep and sincere and the impact on motivation is as expected. We started this chapter with aspects of motivation and we build on the concept later on. At this stage we want to reinforce the point that all managers should be thinking about the particular sources of motivation for each of their staff. This may vary substantially from one individual to another, but if managers can come to understand motivation then they are more likely to be able to shape developmental planning so that it provides the necessary satisfaction and reinforces the desired behaviour. Managers should be clear that their staff want specific development to occur and that they will be stimulated by the particular method of the learning process. There are questionnaires available which help us to understand an individual's preferred style of learning, whether by training, reading, direct experience or some other means.

The final part of the model requires that the organization has the resources in place to support agreed development plans. At one level this refers to physical training and development resources such as courses, books, videos, equipment and the like. However, the concept of resourcing within this model has a broader implication. It is not uncommon for development plans to require some cross-organizational job movement in the interest of broadening experience. When organizations are downsizing and learning to operate from a lean base, these opportunities reduce. Organizations feel uncomfortable about building additional responsibilities into a role and at the same time using it for developmental learning. Of course, such an appointee may add real value to the role but the feeling of initial discomfort provides the obstacle. In situations of serious downsizing, cross-organizational 'mentoring' may be a partial substitute to facilitate new learning.

In recent years, we have seen the emergence of high quality self-development packs. These provide a basis for the individual to drive their own development by offering a structure for self-appraisal which then leads to specific related development options, most of which can be accessed by the individual him or herself.

A model of the kind shown in Figure 5.3 is relatively straightforward and may well be open to further refinement. We feel that it covers four major components of successful development and our point is that they *all* need consideration in an organization's development planning; failure in any one area would lead to failure overall. As a conceptual exercise, we have in the past argued that if this process is not managed and there is a chance probability (0.5) that the situation in each area is acceptable, then the probability of serious behaviour change occurring would be the multiple of the four probabilities $(0.5 \times 0.5 \times 0.5 \times 0.5)$ – or about six times in one hundred. Perhaps this helps explain why there remains a strong element of feeling in some organizations that people do not really change. (In fact, one bank actually reported to us a 1 in 20 development success rate.)

It is worth reiterating our position which is that if the development process is properly planned, structured and managed against defined objectives – with genuine commitment from the top – then serious change in people will occur and a development culture will be created.

An effective organization

It is hard for even the best people to be effective if they are constrained by an ineffective organization. This is not a novel thought and recent history shows that organizations have swung from centralized to decentralized, from hierarchical to a more devolved decision-making process, and from functional to business streams. Each approach seems to have had its turn in the vanguard of popularity. We have also seen that the business focus of the time will also influence the choice of organization and the competencies of the people that work there. Cost reduction and downsizing may well call for a different structure to one that supports the geographical expansion of an existing product range which has international potential.

We do not propose to review organizational design in depth here but we would observe that the selection of the right organizational structure is an amalgam of the best practice at the time and utilizing the strengths of the key players. If we are to unleash the power of the people in an enterprise we need to ensure that the organizational design positively assists this to take place. Businesses and not-for-profit organizations share in common the need for a structure that delivers the optimum use of the total people resource.

As we reflect on some of the important trends that affect business today, we can recognize the importance of speed of decision making and support for the imperative of pushing the decision making as close as possible to the point of impact. To achieve this, many companies have significantly reduced the layers of management, not just as a cost saving idea, but as a way of speeding up decisions and enriching managers' work experience. Such a company is Unilever plc, a truly global company that accepted the challenge of getting the optimum use of the people resource. (See the Case Study 5.1 provided by Brian Dive, Senior Vice President Remuneration, of Unilever.) It is clear that without this compression of layers and the re-evaluation of the organization, the accountability and the ability to manage the change programme would be significantly reduced.

CASE STUDY 5.1
Unilever – Optimum use of the total people resource

Unilever is one example of a company trying to make the optimum use of its total people resource on a global basis. This has led to the introduction, in 1998, of its Integrated Human Resource Approach to Achieve Outstanding Performance.

Unilever has been transforming its business through the 1990s. Firstly, the corporate strategy has been refocused, which has led for example to the divestment of its chemicals companies. The role of the Corporate Centre has been redefined. In 1996, the total concern was reorganized, a smaller Board was introduced to lead global strategy and the business was divided into Regional Business Groups. The previously diffuse matrix was simplified and sharpened with clearer single point accountability. The purpose was to achieve outstanding performance (defined in relation to competitors) under the umbrella of a newly defined corporate purpose.

The first key point about the human resource changes is that they have been integrated into the business strategy. Their primary purpose was to enhance the performance for all key stakeholders (consumers, customers, employees, shareholders), thereby achieving outstanding performance overall. Secondly, the human resource initiatives have been driven by a new set of principles which serve to integrate conceptually all of the main human resource activities. This underlying logic is the unique Work Level Model which is the result of ten years' empirical work.

All organization leaders want to ensure they have the right number of employees, highly challenged, motivated, close to their customers and suppliers, making rapid value adding decisions in flat organizations, achieving high levels of innovation and performance. **But, it is not clear** *how* **to achieve this.** As a result, many initiatives to re-engineer work, enrich jobs and empower people become devalued in practice and unsuccessful.

In the late 1980s, Brian Dive, then Head of Organization at Unilever, was grappling with these issues in an attempt to identify the framework for a healthy global organization. A critical dilemma was 'how do you know when an organization is too flat'? It seemed clear that the vertical hierarchy of accountability in organizations, whether in the public, private or military sectors, could be likened to the human spine. One vertebra too few or one too many was equally likely to cause the body to malfunction. Rowbottom and Billis' work provided an insight into a possible solution.

Since 1988, Billis and Dive conducted extensive fieldwork throughout Unilever, covering all geographies and businesses in the concern, including the research laboratories and the Corporate Centre. They distilled and developed a totally new Work Level Model which could operate on a global basis.

The essence of the Work Level logic is that it ensures job holders take decisions that cannot be taken at a lower level and which need not be taken at a higher level. In short, it is a map of accountability and empowerment. Six qualitatively different levels of work were identified in Unilever below the International Board. They provide a robust intellectual framework identifying value-added work in the organization. This in turn provides an underlying logic which can drive organization design (because only one layer of management is required in each Work Level above the front line). As a measure of responsibility, the Work Levels can be aligned with pay in different markets around the world. They can also provide a framework for recruitment, individual development and ultimately career planning. The impact of this integrated approach to HR is summarized in Figure 5.4.

Management pay scales around the world have been calibrated in Work Levels; 11 competencies developed by the then Head of Training, Dr D Jones, together with Hay McBer, have been aligned to Work Levels. Unilever uses its competencies to assess potential as a basis for career planning. Thus as illustrated in the figure, a person for example

Figure 5.4   The Unilever Work Level Model

Work Level	Nature of Contribution	Management Layer	Pay Scale	Potential Lists (*)
6	Strategic	V	£	
5		IV		6
4		III	$	5
3		II		4
2		I	¥	3
1	Operational			2

(*) The Potential Lists identify people capable of reaching a higher Work Level within five years

in Work Level 2 with potential to move to Work Level 3 within five years would be placed on Potential List 3. As a result of the new approach to reward and recognition, Unilever has done away with its performance categories of the past and appraisal now focuses more explicitly on an individual's development. This revamped appraisal approach, known within Unilever as the Personal Development Plan, focuses on the development of competencies together with ten professional skills and a raft of general skills that have been identified throughout the business.

It is believed in Unilever that the thrust of these changes moves the company further in the direction of a genuinely healthy organization. Empowerment now means having the right number of jobs with the right people in them at the right Work Levels. The new approach is more transparent, easier to administer and communicate and enables greater line management involvement and ownership. It is also less easy to manipulate and less forgiving of substandard performance. It helps ensure effective organization design, affords well-defined psychological space for achievement and recognition, and provides a clear basis for personal development while facilitating sound career planning. This results ultimately in better individual, group and corporate performance.

SOURCE: Brian Dive, Unilever

Summary

The fundamental message is clear. If we are to make the optimum use of the people resource, we need to do the following things:

- Put the right people into the right jobs, based on objective assessment.
- Encourage a climate where people are valued and developed so that the organization gets the best from them. The halo effect from this is that when people feel valued, stimulated and encouraged, they are also motivated to perform at a much higher level.
- To get the best results, inform people of what is expected of them and how they are performing. The appraisal is a critical process that deserves a full investment of time from managers and employees to get the best results.
- Ensure that the organizational design frees up people to deliver to their full potential.
- The appraisal process will also identify the need for a career review for a number of people. Separate this from the appraisal process and make it an open and honest two-way discussion, rather than accepting at face value aspirations that may be unrealistic.
- Find through objective means the talent that is in every organization and identify those that will be chosen for accelerated development. Development centres are a very helpful way of finding the right people to receive accelerated advancement.
- Make managers accountable for their people and their development needs, so that this becomes imbued in the culture of the organization. Certainly every manager's set of objectives should include a management development facet which can be expressed in a measurable way. Many companies will routinely use 360° assessments of managers which will leave them in no doubt about their performance in this area.

6

An International Perspective

The cross-cultural context

We live in interesting times when organizations are having to take an increasingly international perspective in planning the assessment and development of their people. Commercial organizations, under ongoing pressure to grow their profits and frequently under challenge from external competition, are turning in greater numbers to the international market-place. Governments plan to facilitate their action through the creation of trading partnerships, fiscal incentives, advisory support, trade delegations and the like. Service and support organizations necessarily follow this trend. There are many human resource implications from this move towards international business, including some substantial practical and motivational issues of managing pay and benefits on an equitable international basis. However, in this chapter our objective is to touch on some of the main assessment and development issues for organizations required to take an international perspective. Inevitably, we will have to restrict ourselves to the more substantial issues. Trying to deal with the many variations in assessment and development practice around the world is beyond the scope of this chapter.

We run the risk of sailing into some difficult water here. International cross-cultural differences in the behaviour of people at work are un-doubtedly substantial and are implicitly interesting. It would be easy to be sucked into a fine debate of the differences between one national or ethnic group and another. Researchers such as Hofstede and Trompenaars have provided useful and empirically based models (Figure 6.1) of cross-cultural differences and our own experience confirms the need for management to be cross-culturally aware. However, we will try to retain a practical focus with an emphasis on action rather than interesting differences.

Figure 6.1 Models of cultural differences

Model	Very briefly*
Geert Hofstede	
1. Power-Distance Dimension	1. Concerns the extent to which those who are less powerful accept an unequal distribution of power. High P-D equates to more paternalistic management with less consultation.
2. Individualism versus Collectivism	2. Individualism reflects more self-reliance in society as opposed to group loyalty and interdependence.
3. Masculinity versus Femininity	3. Shows a value preference in society, for example masculine values of heroism, achievement and assertiveness – feminine values of empathy, relationships and quality of life.
4. Uncertainty Avoidance Dimension	4. Reflects the extent to which those in society feel able to tolerate uncertainty and ambiguity.
5. Long-Term versus Short-Term Orientation	5. Concerns a way of thinking that is focused on either short-term, quick results or longer-term perseverance with a preparedness to plan and adapt for the future.
Fons Trompenaars	
1. Universalism versus Particularism	1. Whether rules and procedures are applied universally to ensure consistency or whether flexibility is encouraged through adaptation to particular situations.
2. Individualism versus Collectivism	2. Whether the focus is primarily on members of society as individuals or as part of a group.
3. Neutral or Emotional	3. Whether society accepts and reinforces the expression of emotion and personality.
4. Specific versus Diffuse	4. Whether members of society involve others in specific areas of life (say work only) or more diffusely in multiple areas (say work and leisure).
5. Achievement versus Ascription	5. Whether status is based on achievement and record or is attributed on a broader basis of birth, gender, age, education, connections, and so on.
6. Attitudes to Time	6. Reflects variations in attitudes to time and the differential importance attached to the past and the future.
7. Attitudes to the Environment	7. Reflects variations in attitudes to the environment. Some cultures are more inclined to protect and be in harmony with the environment.

* The models are quite complex for brief descriptions and reference to the source texts is recommended.

How then can we help the manager who is required to take an inter-national perspective? Broadly, there are two categories of situation. First, there is the requirement to select and develop managers and technicians who are going to work in another country or on a cross-national basis. Second, there is the requirement to bring some standardization to the organization's assessment and development policy/practice world-wide. This in turn serves the purpose of ensuring that management is better informed about its world-wide human resource pool in terms that it can understand (and in which it can have some faith). It also encourages a process of the international movement of key staff in order to ensure an optimum fit of resources to objectives.

The international operator

Research has indicated (for example, Hogan and Godson among others) that the failure rate in foreign assignments may be as high as 40 per cent. The direct cost implication, let alone the motivational impact, is substantial. This is clearly an area in which we need to sharpen our practice.

The fundamental principles for selecting an individual to work on an international basis are the same as those that apply to any intra-national job. In other words, the job should be analyzed; a clear description should be written; a person specification should be prepared; assessment methods that are demonstrably relevant to the various components of the specification should be utilized. It is likely that a large part of the output of this process will be determined by the particular task requirements of the job, for example marketing manager, petroleum engineer or whatever. However, the international context will certainly add a layer of complication and raise additional criteria to be met.

There is no single assessment blueprint for the international component. In Figure 6.2, we offer a structure for designing a relevant person specification in the interest of maximizing a local fit.

The competencies and personality check would be completed as for any job. However, issues of health and personal circumstances may raise particular issues for the international operator. There may be a requirement for large amounts of travel across time zones and into areas where comfort and hygiene are highly variable factors. It is an area to check; there can be no absolute guideline here. Another critical area concerns the role of the international operator's partner (and indeed other family members), whether travelling to a new location or not. In our experience a major

---

Figure 6.2 Maximizing an international job fit

Check:

● Individual competencies relevant to the job tasks
● Personality factors related to adapting to the new environment, for example:
  – Emotional stability
  – Enjoyment of change
  – Interest in the behaviour of others
  – Optimism
  – Self-sufficiency and adaptability
● Health and personal circumstances (for example, family related)
● Fit to the local work group/team
● Fit to the divisional/organizational culture
● Fit to the country culture

---

contributor to failure in an overseas posting has been the difficulty faced by the partner in adapting to a new and often highly pressured environment. At the same time, there appears to be a reluctance to bring the partner properly into the assessment process. Our advice would be to think carefully about the role of the partner and build this as openly and as objectively as possible into the assessment process. If it is a relevant factor, it should be fairly and sensitively taken into account.

The other factors in Figure 6.2 are likely to be interrelated. We have separated them to make the point that fit to a country culture alone is insufficient in a diagnosis of overall international fit. Of course we need to consider whether a new appointee's style of operation is likely to match the way that the Japanese or the Belgians or the Americans typically think and behave. However, the organization may well have a distinct culture of its own which may even run counter to the national model. Furthermore, local bosses, peers and subordinates may have particularly distinctive styles of their own. A national culture fit would be no guarantee of harmony in these respects. This is an important point. Banks and Waisfisz are experienced trainers in the area of inter-cultural operation. They have recognized the value of understanding inter-cultural differences but they also point out that models identify only central tendencies in societies. They cannot be used to identify or describe the characteristics of individuals and any attempt to use them mechanistically is likely to lead to error. They recognize the importance of what they call the 'specifics of the situation'.

This raises the question as to whether there is a set of specific personal attributes which make an individual particularly well suited to an international role. In our experience, certain individuals have shown themselves better able to adapt to an international assignment than others. We have referred to this in terms of a broad attribute of **cultural adaptability** although we have identified several important sub-attributes. Perhaps most important is a sensitivity to the likelihood that cultures will think and behave in different ways and a preparedness to adapt one's own behaviour accordingly. It is a matter of thinking in an international context about why those with whom we interact are behaving as they do and what the impact of our own behaviour is likely to be. If an individual does not progress through this analytical thinking stage then it is unlikely that behavioural adaptation will follow. There then has to be a motivation to want to optimize the behaviour required in any situation. There are other factors which are relevant here. For example, an appropriate ability factor might be the learning of foreign languages which can facilitate the communication process. Also relevant is that part of emotional intelligence which is concerned with reading facial cues, body language and other emotional signals of satisfaction, dissatisfaction, frustration and the like. Interest in cross-cultural differences may also play a part insofar as it encourages reading and discussion to broaden the individual's frame of reference. Finally, there is a need for emotional stability in order to cope with unusual pressure or frustration.

Lombardo and Eichinger have differentiated two types of learning. Learning I is concerned with the raw intelligence associated with the acquisition of school, college or technical knowledge. Learning II is more akin to common sense and is concerned with learning from experience how to deal with new or changing situations. They argue that Learning II is generally more predictive of long-term potential or performance. This also seems to us to be a neat way of summarizing what it is that essentially differentiates the more successful from the less successful international operator. The essential requirement is to be open to new learning and experience; an inclination to seek feedback in any new situation and then a preparedness to act on the basis of the new information. To operate successfully in an international context does not just require an understanding of broad inter-cultural differences (although this will help). It requires a mentality that never stops thinking about and reviewing the impact of a chosen line of behaviour and a preparedness to adapt as a continuing process. It is no surprise that this also works within a home culture. It just becomes that much more pressing in an international context.

At the same time there is a clear role for cross-cultural training as a means of development. Models such as those in Figure 6.1 have been thoroughly researched and provide a rich context for learning behavioural adaptation. Organizations with whom we have been in contact in Europe in particular have found that formal cross-cultural training has not only enhanced individual adaptation but has itself helped to reinforce an internationally aware corporate culture.

Of course, care must be taken in the implementation of inter-cultural training. There is a danger that it may be seen as a quick solution to problems in international interaction. Banks and Waisfisz raise the following points of caution in planning to implement inter-cultural training:

- Remember that culture is too complex for quick-fix solutions.
- Training will not work by simply giving information about another culture. The process of cross-cultural interaction must be understood.
- Implementation requires commitment – and ideally attendance – from the top.
- Training needs breadth of cover to achieve a critical mass for effect and a common language. Training at least half the cross-cultural operators is given as a guideline objective.
- Half a day is too short – two days are probably a realistic minimum.

When it comes to assessing candidates for an international role, there is unlikely to be a single neat formula or blueprint. Each case will require a process that is tailored to the requirements of the specific situation; as for example indicated in the structure of Figure 6.2. The following example raises some of the issues to be covered.

The implementation of an international assessment process

Mabey and Thompson have described the case of a multinational oil company operating across 14 European countries with its head office in Brussels. At the time of the report, the company was employing about 15 000 staff and had been through a restructuring process as preparation for the Single European Market. As a result of the restructuring, the company was seeking to identify its future senior managers from across Europe and to enhance its development planning for these future key players. The company had extensive experience of the assessment centre method – mainly through its operations in the UK and Germany. The objective was to set up a new European assessment and development programme which would enable:

1. the **organization** to identify objectively the strengths, limitations and development needs of managers already identified as having potential for special development planning;
2. the **individuals** to increase their self-awareness and encourage them to take responsibility for their own skills development.

There were two international contextual factors to be considered in the design of the programme. First, positive steps had been taken to encourage a new culture which emphasized the empowerment of personal development. As part of this culture change, a formal 'Inter-Cultural Management Training Course' had been introduced to encourage cross-cultural awareness. This drew heavily on Hofstede's research.

Secondly, the design and implementation of the new programme occurred at a time of severe economic recession and when a cost-cutting programme was in hand. There were issues of the ownership of the new programme and concerns about its potential to be fair and objective to all country participants. In short, if there had been serious doubts about the relevance and fairness of the programme then it might well have been cut. From the outset, therefore, the objective was to develop a procedure which was:

- relevant to the likely management behaviour required at several grades above the current participant level;
- culturally fair in the sense of minimizing cultural bias and removing unjustifiable adverse impact.

The programme was designed against a set of ten senior management competencies. These were based on separate job analysis studies that had been completed in individual countries. The studies were reviewed by an international steering committee who agreed the final list for international use and agreed the competency definitions. In addition, the steering committee included a competency of 'Cross-Cultural Adaptability' which was designed to overlay the other competencies as an essential requirement. It focused very much on the capacity to adapt behaviour for a multi-cultural operation and a natural inclination to want to understand people from a different culture. The competency set was limited to ten in terms of the potential of assessors to discriminate the assessment criteria. The full set in summary terms was:

1. Cross-Cultural Adaptability   3. Influencing Others
2. Communication   4. People Orientation

5. Open Thinking
6. Intellect
7. Planning Ability

8. Bias for Action
9. Decision Making
10. Business Sense

The assessment programme itself was designed for batches of 12 participants and lasted for four days. Two and a half days were required for the assessment process as indicated in Figure 6.3 with one and a half days for the integration of results and a developmental discussion. In many respects this was a conventional development centre approach but the point of interest here is the steps that were taken to maximize cross-cultural fairness.

Figure 6.3 Components of an international assessment and development centre

	Exercise Time (Minutes)
Simulation Exercises	
A management in-tray exercise (Individual)	180
A co-operative group exercise (A) (Groups of 4)	45
An assigned role group exercise (B) (Groups of 6)	50
A presentation on a business topic (Individual to participants and assessors)	5 per candidate (Total session 75)
A fact-finding and decision-making exercise (Individual to an assistant)	60
A coaching and developing exercise (Individual)	45
Standardized Tests	
A test of verbal analytical reasoning (Individual)	25
A test of numerical analytical reasoning (Individual)	35
A test of productive (creative) thinking (Individual)	32

In addition, two components of the programme were used for developmental/diagnostic purposes and play no direct part in participant assessment.

A career development interview (One to one with a Senior European Manager)	45
The Occupational Personality Questionnaire (OPQ®)	50

The decision was taken that the simulation exercises should be in English. This was because English is the organization's business language and future senior managers would have to hold their own with native English speakers. However, this added to the concern over cultural fairness and led to the following specific actions designed to maximize fairness:

1. The exercises were reviewed by the 'Inter-Cultural Management' trainer and his recommendations were incorporated.
2. Multinational assessors were used – all of whom had been inter-culturally trained.
3. Basic tests of reasoning ability – as opposed to management simulation exercises – were in almost every case completed in the participants' own first language.
4. Participants were given pre-centre practice in a business exercise in order to sharpen their language skills.
5. Participants were briefed pre-centre to be aware of language issues. A particular problem here is that social language can be so fluent that an assumption is made wrongly about business language fluency.
6. By comparison with previous internal assessment and development programmes, there were more individual exercises and small group exercises (four participants). Experience had shown that in larger groups (six participants) language skills are more critical.
7. The substantial in-tray exercise had a follow-up interview to check on comprehension and language difficulties.
8. Preparation time for exercises was extended. For example, group meeting exercises were prepared the evening before they took place.
9. Exercises were designed which required contributions via role plays. In other words, participants could not opt out or effectively withdraw from any exercise.
10. Exercises were set in a variety of European country contexts. Each exercise contained a glossary to explain any unusual terms. In general, simple language was used and verbal information was set at a realistic minimum.
11. The 'Steering Committee' responsible for the procedure and exercise design was itself multinational.

Mabey and Thompson reported on the first 24 participants comprising ten British, six German, three French, one Danish, one Turkish, one Portuguese, one Swedish and one Swiss. These had been assessed by six senior managers comprising two German, one Dutch, one French, one Swiss and one British. The participants rated the process completely anonymously and the ratings were generally favourable on the question of personal value and fairness. For example, 83 per cent felt they personally got something useful from the process; 71 per cent felt the assessment of themselves was about right; 79 per cent felt the feedback report was helpful. There were very few directly negative comments although a minority were uncertain on the cultural fairness issue. The competency dimension ratings in this case – albeit on a small sample – showed a minimally better performance from the British on seven competency criteria and a more substantially better performance on the competencies of:

- Influencing Others
- People Orientation
- Open Thinking

This study serves as an example of the practical action that can be taken to enhance cross-cultural fairness in assessment. The outcome was a procedure which had a large degree of acceptance by assessors and participants. At the same time, there were certainly individual cases where a young manager ostensibly performing well in his or her own culture performed weakly in an international context. Furthermore, the British tended to outperform their European colleagues. The differences were not that large and were not altogether surprising given the criticality of the English language in the high-level simulations. Some organizations still prefer to run their assessment and development centres on a 'within culture' basis. Our view is that if managers are going to have to meet with, negotiate with, sell to, supervise – and so on – individuals from a multitude of cultures, then it is appropriate for them to be assessed in such a context. Ultimately, it is no different from other assessment projects in that we have to ask whether the process is relevant to the future requirements of the job and whether we have taken all reasonable action to minimize adverse cultural impact. A manager may be excellent on home ground in, say, Turkey or France but if the organization's business language is English and they cannot handle a reasonably paced English language meeting then they have a clear area of limitation and possibly a developmental need. This now takes us to the issue of standardizing inter-cultural assessment.

Standardizing international assessment

Differences in practice

The issue for this section is the balancing of the requirement for a reasonably standardized international approach to assessment with the requirement to adapt any such assessment to local conditions and expectations. The issue is further complicated because cultural norms in assessment are themselves steadily changing.

There can be no doubt that assessment practice varies quite substantially across countries. The survey referred to in Figure 6.4 was directed by Ryan from Michigan State University and covered 834 organizations randomly selected across 21 countries. It was interesting that 59 per cent of these organizations operated in multiple countries.

Figure 6.4 shows that there are clear differences in the international usage of cognitive ability tests and personality or workstyle tests. The same survey also showed that, for management assessment, graphology has a disproportionately high level of use in France; panel interviews are particularly strong in the UK and Australia; biodata has a strong following in Greece; job trialling is particularly popular in Poland; and medical screening has a relatively high frequency of use in Germany.

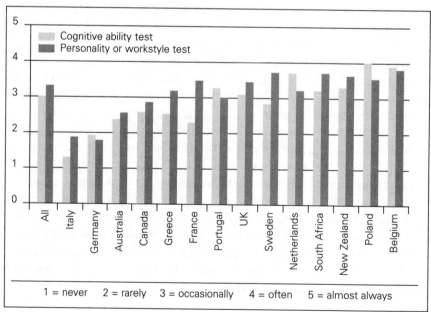

Figure 6.4 Test use (for management) by country

Graphology – or handwriting analysis – is a particularly intriguing case. Two prominent researchers in international assessment, Shackleton and Newell, have produced survey data to show that, while 3 per cent of companies in the UK use handwriting analysis, just a handful of miles away across the English Channel, 77 per cent of French companies use it! The British Psychological Society has produced a formal paper which in effect cautions against its use, while in France, the very level of its use indicates broad public acceptance of its legitimacy. In our view, the popularity of graphology in France has something to do with its apparent potential to give in-depth insight to the persona and much to do with its relative inexpensiveness vis-à-vis other methods. Nonetheless, the point here is that differences in candidate expectation across countries clearly exist and need to be taken into account.

Our own experience and discussion with colleagues working across the world reinforce the notion of large differences in current assessment practices. Points of difference which help to explain some of the findings in Figure 6.4 include:

- differential importance of Equal Opportunity legislation which affects the level of usage of formal job analysis and certain assessment techniques. The survey by Ryan noted particular influence from legal considerations in Australia, the UK, New Zealand and South Africa. Historically this has also been a major issue in the USA;
- differential attitudes towards the role of educational qualifications which in some countries is seen to reduce the need to test abilities;
- the existence of Industrial or Occupational Psychology courses at university level;
- the existence and philosophy of professional bodies of psychologists and Human Resource practitioners;
- organizational preference for the professional outsourcing of recruitment and assessment as opposed to the demand for self-sufficiency;
- the perceived expensiveness of different methods of assessment;
- a preference for more clinical assessment as opposed to more objective, psychometrically orientated approaches;
- the differential requirement for objectivity. For example, in some cultures nepotism and favouritism may be tacitly accepted;
- differential Government support. For example, subsidized training for HR managers in ability test use in one country compared with restricting it to psychologists in another;
- differential acceptance of the computer as a medium for assessment method administration and interpretation;

- many specific cultural issues which affect the value that is placed on the output of individual methods.

However, it would be wrong to assume that current levels of usage of various assessment techniques will necessarily reflect future practice. Change is occurring in world-wide assessment. Surveys in the UK in the 1970s put psychometric test usage at around 20 per cent of large organizations – today it is around 75 per cent. In the 1970s and 1980s, personality questionnaires were out of favour in the USA. Today, they are enjoying a strong resurgence of interest as more appropriate validation studies are being published. In Germany, the educational preference of psychologists towards the clinical and educational fields is shifting markedly towards the industrial/organizational field. In parts of the Far East, new psychology courses are being introduced where none existed before. In Japan, the interview is being increasingly supported by psychometric tests with computer-assisted interpretation. Organizations supplying assessment methods are completing new research and making methods more available on a broad international basis.

Furthermore, the countries themselves are changing. In Eastern Europe, the move away from communism is creating new generations who are more widely travelled, possibly educated overseas, more acquisitive of high status jobs and more prepared to challenge a status quo. New emerging economies bring with them a determination to compete by, amongst other things, adopting recognized world best practice. Even in major economies like that of Japan, change is under way. The pressure to compete is forcing Japanese companies to think hard about jobs for life and a generalized process of job rotation. Five years ago there were not enough graduates for jobs and now there are too many, making selection more critical. Local commentators are noting more careful assessment of new entrants so that they can be properly placed into appropriate jobs. Ability tests and personality questionnaires are much more commonly used. Examples of how two major organizations are bringing their experience to bear in Asia Pacific are given in Case Study 6.1.

Standardization versus adaptation

Our best advice is to be aware of the inter-cultural differences; to be prepared to adapt practice from one culture to another but ultimately to remember to apply the key principles of fairness, objectivity and relevance to the required occupational behaviour. In our view, most modern methods

CASE STUDY 6.1
Changing assessment in Asia Pacific

The following examples show how organizations are changing their practice to improve the effectiveness of staff selection.

● A global banking organization wanted to expand retail banking and customer service standards across Asia. They built a competency model using the Work Profiling System, the Repertory Grid and the Critical Incidents method. This was then used to develop a structured application form (biodata) for the purpose of an initial sift of applicants. This was followed by tailored tests and questionnaires for customer service as well as competency-based interviewing. A completed utility study has estimated a gain of close to US$3 million in the first year of operation through increased business.

● An international oil company was utilizing a large number of expatriates in China who were very expensive to the business. With the objective of localization, the company wanted to identify high flyers internally as well as high-calibre external candidates. Assessment centres were implemented in Chinese with trained Chinese assessors. In a market where nepotism and favouritism can bias selection, the new process helped the company identify those with genuine potential for management. These people then went on to a costly two-year management programme.

SOURCE: SHL Hong Kong Ltd

of assessment can be applied in most countries. However, there will be a need to manage the expectations of candidates in different countries and some modification may be required without affecting the principles described above. For example, in assessing a simulation exercise, it may be necessary to focus the scoring system on the outcome in terms of 'objectives' rather than the 'means' which could legitimately vary from one culture to another. Or again, competency model definitions may require tailoring for relevance to and acceptance in a particular culture.

On the specific issue of standardization within the testing field, we would have to say that the SHL group is in a unique position in terms of its research investment in producing standardized assessment materials across more than 35 countries. At one extreme, it has adapted, translated and created norms for tests of verbal and numerical reasoning ability as well as a 30-dimension model of occupational personality for use in well over 30 countries, including the USA, Canada, Japan, Australia, New

Zealand, most of Europe, the Middle East and much of Asia Pacific. Many of these countries also operate with standard methods of job analysis, competency assessment and 360° analysis.

The experience of this company has been that some adaptation of methods for a particular culture will always be necessary. For example, the personality concept of 'independence of mind' differs in Japan from the United Kingdom. A personal construct of 'planning ability' is not identical across continents and so on. However, SHL has found that standardization is less problematical where the content of the test or questionnaire is occupationally relevant. Concepts such as attention to detail, anxiety in presentation, data orientation and the like are easier to translate and adapt than, say, socio-religious concepts. Norms will vary somewhat. For example, Nyfield *et al.* (1993) report the following differences, based on large samples, between US and UK managers:

US managers are more:	UK managers are more:
Persuasive	Independent
Controlling	Forward planning
Socially confident	Critical
Innovative	
Optimistic	
Active	
Achieving	
Decisive	

However, the differences in average scores for the two groups were not so large that they would hinder comparative analysis of individuals. They represent a small contextual factor to be borne in mind when utilizing an individual output and in an international comparison.

For the future, computer assistance in administration and interpretation will facilitate the international usage of tests and questionnaires. It is now possible to seat a multi-cultural group in a single room in front of a set of computers and for each individual to be assessed in their own mother tongue. The practical problems of doing this by a pencil and paper method would be substantial. Furthermore, the resulting ability and personality scores can be integrated by the same computers and an expert system report produced in any of about a dozen prime languages. In a 1995 survey, SHL Group country managers were asked to rate the importance of a set of factors to current test users. Computer administration and interpretation were close to the top of this international poll (Figure 6.5).

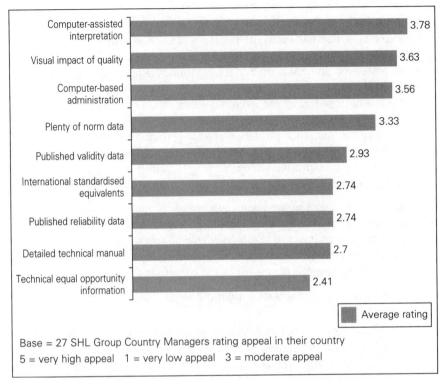

Figure 6.5 International rating of the appeal of test factors

Country variations

Individual countries will raise their own particular problems for the objective assessment of people in the world of work. It is beyond the scope of this book to survey and report all the specific variations in expectations and practice that occur from one culture to another world-wide. The country experience reported in Case Study 6.2 just gives a flavour of the kind of specific considerations that can apply.

Our overall advice to the managers planning international assessment is that standardization of approach is a perfectly reasonable goal to be sought. The structure of interviews and assessment centre programmes can be largely standardized for international application and steps can be taken to make them fair across cultures. In addition, there are tests and question-naires which allow largely similar abilities and personality characteristics to be assessed across many countries of the world. Absolute standard-ization is probably not possible. There will always be fine points of

CASE STUDY 6.2
Country-specific assessment issues – New Zealand

- The increased emphasis on Equal Opportunity and cultural issues within NZ organizations, especially within the public sector, has affected both selection procedures and selection decisions. Affirmative action policies may be seen to conflict with results of objective assessments and have an impact upon the face validity of selection procedures. Objective assessment may also be seen by significant ethnic groups within NZ to ignore important elements such as 'mana' (prestige or standing in the Maori community).

- New Zealand assessment issues are greatly influenced by international market forces since a large proportion of the economy relies on foreign input of some sort. This affects the type of assessments carried out (for example, assessment centres for restructuring and outplacement rather than for selection).

- An increase in international appointments to local positions affects a number of issues:

  – Possible incompatibility of Privacy, Employment Contracts Act and Human Rights Legislation or Psychological Society Codes of Ethics between countries. These Acts have precise laws regarding gaining and holding information, confidentiality, personal access to information, grievances regarding assessments, etc. These may not be compatible with other countries and issues may arise regarding, for example, feedback or retention of information.

  – The level of co-ordination and time required extends the selection process and raises security issues when transferring information (for example, when using e-mail).

SOURCE: SHL New Zealand

interpretation rooted in a particular culture and it is unlikely that identical samples for norm referencing will be achieved. However, to a large degree, it will be possible to make reliable comparative judgements using substantially similar methods and assessment criteria.

The key is to be alert to potential cultural differences and to be prepared to take them into account. It may be the acceptance of ability testing in France or the appropriateness of 360° peer review in Asia or the problem of giving direct negative feedback in Japan or any of dozens of other points of variability. Many of these issues can be overcome. The best advice is to take specialized local advice or advice from those who have assessed widely within the culture. As we have emphasized before, it is important that the assessees feel that they have been assessed in a fair and objective way which is relevant to the roles they would be required to perform.

Summary

We have attempted in this chapter to take an international perspective on assessment for selection and development. We have looked at two main issues – the assessment of potential to be an international operator and the cross-cultural standardization of assessment projects. The general trend towards international business management is pushing these issues to prominence on the HR management agenda.

In terms of identifying the international operator, we restated the need for job analysis and a clear specification. The specification is likely to call for a fit to the local cultures of operation and to emphasize the importance of health and personal circumstances. The existence of a partner will be a critical factor and, in our view, this should be sensitively but objectively brought into the assessment process. We believe that certain individuals are better suited than others to working in an international context and we have described the components of this broad attribute of cultural adaptability. These include a sensitivity to cross-cultural differences; an aptitude for foreign languages; the ability to read behavioural cues; the preparedness to adapt behaviour; and a general interest in understanding new cultures. We support the concept of inter-cultural training.

On the second issue of international assessment projects, it is now possible to bring a high degree of cross-cultural standardization into the assessment process. There are clearly international differences in the acceptance and usage of specific assessment methods. These need to be taken into account but we make the point that methods of high job relevance can achieve substantial standardization. The computer is having an increasingly important role to play in international assessment. Not only does it facilitate multi-culture administration of an assessment method but it can help to standardize descriptive reporting and prescriptive decision making.

The concept of standardization is discussed further in Chapter 7.

Part II
Specific Issues

7

The Testing of Abilities and Personality

Growth in psychometric testing

In the first part of this book we emphasized the need to write a clear specification of the competencies or attributes required for a particular role. With regard to assessment, we acknowledged that the interview will always have a role to play but we agreed that it should be well structured against the specification and ideally supported by other methods. We noted the criticality of maximizing the validity of the total assessment method in terms of giving the organization a financial pay-back and that the research evidence supports the use of a multiple of methods in this respect as opposed to any one alone.

Two of the main areas in which the interview can be usefully supported concern the measurement of abilities and personality. Without reference to the research literature, it should be self-evident that an interview will not easily measure the ability, say, to reason quickly with numerical data. Furthermore, there simply is not time enough in an interview to gather personality information in a reliable way against current models of 30 or more work-relevant dimensions. As a result, we have seen considerable world-wide growth in the past decade in the use of standardized tests of ability and personality to help fill the gap. These are often referred to as 'psychometric tests'.

Psychometric testing has been the subject of considerable research by industrial and organizational psychologists for many years. It will not be possible here to do justice to the many fine points of debate which surround the technical issues of measuring quite complex psychological concepts. Our purpose here is to describe the main types of test, to describe some of the main issues facing users and to offer some practical guidance in the use of these methods.

The organizational penetration of psychometric testing has increased to a point where it is now common practice in many leading economies. Surveys of test use in the UK in the 1970s showed usage levels at around 20 per cent of large organizations. The most recent surveys are showing usage of ability tests at over 70 per cent of large companies and usage of personality questionnaires at well over 50 per cent. Testing has therefore become established as a majority practice in large UK organizations. Levels of usage world-wide are variable depending on a number of professional and cultural factors but the general trend is towards increased usage. It is not unusual for tests to provoke anxiety amongst candidates and there are practical issues of cost and training for them to be properly implemented. We need to understand more about why there has been sharp growth in their usage and the extent to which they can add value to an organization's assessment procedures.

It is possible to differentiate several broad categories of test but we have chosen to focus on the two main areas of application. Measures of 'ability' are correctly described as 'tests'. There are right and wrong answers; the objective is to achieve a maximum score and they provide information as to how well the individual can perform certain defined tasks. Measures of 'personality' are better described through their medium of information collection. Terms such as 'inventory' or 'questionnaire' would be more appropriate. These methods tell us how an individual typically thinks, feels, behaves towards others and so on. They do not directly measure ability although their scores may well be related to occupational performance.

Testing for abilities

The concept

The concept itself is not new. We can trace testing back to Ancient China where the selection of civil servants was undertaken by written tests, including one where candidates had to show verbal creativity by completing rhyming couplets. Plato in *The Republic* called for the testing of the 'Philosopher Rulers' and defined both cognitive abilities and relevant personality characteristics. In the seventeenth century, Samuel Pepys, on becoming Clerk of the Acts of the King's Ships, introduced tests of mathematics and navigation for prospective lieutenants in the British Navy. This effectively reduced the impact of nepotism and favouritism and had a significant impact in strengthening the British Navy.

Pencil and paper testing as we know it today is usually credited to Binet in France in 1905 looking at the educational attainment of young children. However, it was the impact of the world wars and the need to classify and utilize large numbers of people in a short time that led to serious growth in the use of occupational tests. This trend carried on into the fields of commerce and industry, particularly after the Second World War.

Nowadays, tests of ability are used for all types and levels of job selection – from chief executives down to young apprentice technicians. They have been more commonly used in large organizations where their cost effectiveness in filtering large applicant numbers can really bite. It is probably also true that the larger organizations have more readily appreciated the potential of ability tests to support and reinforce the more subjective interview procedure.

Definitions and descriptions

In an area in which there is potentially confusing jargon, we had better define our terms. We use the term 'ability' to cover a range of more specific concepts such as attainment, aptitude and IQ. It is concerned with how well an individual can perform a certain task and Figure 7.1 indicates the types of ability which are more commonly found in an occupational assessment.

It is not uncommon nowadays for managers to be faced with a choice of tests which measure specific abilities of the type described in Figure 7.1 or tests which measure a general concept of 'intelligence'. The more generalized tests of intelligence may have a number of sub-tests but are designed to give a broad indication of cognitive ability. The main argument in favour of these broader-based tests is that they are more appropriate where an organization is looking for generalists who can work across different job areas and apply different abilities as required.

Research shows that both approaches have predictive validity but we would strongly recommend a process of careful job analysis followed by the utilization of specific ability tests which can be shown to be relevant to the job content. Even in the case of the so-called 'generalist' job, it is still possible after analysis to identify specific abilities that are core requirements for different roles. For example, the specific ability of a manager to understand and reason from written reports under some pressure of time is common to a wide range of roles.

The model which emphasizes the measurement of specific abilities is known as the 'Differential Model'. It is our view that by following such an approach, validity is likely to be maximized and the fairness of the

Figure 7.1 Main categories of occupational ability tests

Category	Description
Verbal	Covering attainment tests of spelling and grammar for clerical jobs to tests of verbal critical reasoning for managers and graduates.
Numerical	From basic tests of simple arithmetic calculations for process workers to numerical critical reasoning tests where inferences need to be drawn from business data.
Diagrammatic	Tests of logical reasoning ability presented in the form of abstract shapes and diagrams. Found to be useful in occupations like data processing.
Mechanical	Presents a series of mechanical problems, usually in pictorial form, which need to be solved by the candidate. Useful for a wide range of apprentice and engineering occupations.
Spatial	Assesses the ability to imagine the rotation of shapes in space. Relevant to design and any occupations which require an understanding of how parts of equipment fit together.
Clerical	Measuring speed and accuracy in checking for errors in lists, computer printouts, and so on. Also covers certain filing and classification skills.
Dexterity	Measures hand speed and fine precision skills for process and assembly workers. They also include co-ordination tests used in areas like pilot selection.
Sensory	Measures near or far visual acuity, sound or colour discrimination, particularly relevant to jobs requiring the operation of apparatus, for example in military contexts.

(From SHL Occupational Testing Course Manual)

procedure is likely to be enhanced. This latter point is particularly important in countries where there is strong fairness/Equal Opportunities legislation and where there may be a legal requirement to demonstrate the relevance of specific test questions to the content of the particular job. The problem with some general intelligence tests is that while some of the sub-tests are part of a general reasoning capability, they are hard to justify in terms of job relevance. In one particular test, for example, there is a requirement to put together a jigsaw of an elephant on a timed basis of assessment. It would not be surprising if candidate managers failed to see the logic of being asked to do this. Professor Peter Saville of SHL uses a sports analogy to make the fundamental point. He argues, for example, that the selector of an Olympics javelin team should properly be more concerned with a candidate's ability to throw a long missile than with assessing their general fitness and physical co-ordination.

This leads us to the definition of what we mean by a 'test'. Lee Cronbach, a leading researcher in the area, has offered the following definition:

> a standardized sample of behaviour which can be described by a numerical scale or category system

In our view the concept of a test as a standardized sample of behaviour is an important one. The notion of a test as a sample reinforces the point that the test should be relevant to the occupational behaviour that it is supposed to predict. It also helps to reinforce the logic of the test to the person taking it. Take the case of the applicant for a marketing executive role to whom one might say, 'As part of this role you will be required to analyze tables of data under some pressure of time. In this test we are going to ask you to analyze and draw inferences from tables of data under pressure of time.'

The standardization of the test as a sample of occupational behaviour is also important. It helps to ensure that as far as possible all those tested answer the same questions with the same instructions with the same time allowed in similar conditions. Furthermore, the same scoring system is used and applicants' scores (for a particular job) would be interpreted against the same norm or comparison group. The standardization of the process is a critical contributor to a test's objectivity and fairness. As a discipline it enhances the test's validity and hence its potential pay-off to the user.

The specific content of tests in a differential ability model may be highly variable. Figure 7.2 is an illustration of the kinds of questions or items you might come across in a managerial assessment where numerical reasoning and logical systems design are known to be parts of the job.

Overview of ability testing

Most independent commentators would confirm the sharp growth in the usage of ability tests. This has been sustained for long enough to confirm that tests must be delivering organizational value. Furthermore, in countries where testing is more prominent, local professional bodies are likely to have taken a view on 'testing' and may even have published good practice guidelines and specific test reviews. (See for example the British Psychological Society's 'Review of Ability Tests'). Of course, there are good tests and poor tests available for purchase and care must be exercised in making the right choice. Our comments here about ability testing in

Numerical

Answer the questions below using the figures presented in the table. For each question you are given five possible answers to choose from. Only one answer is correct in each case.

Factory Production Costs	
Production (Units/hour)	Cost ($/Unit)
5	4.65
6	4.56
7	4.52
8	4.53

1. Units produced are sold for $12 each. What is the maximum gross profit per unit?

A	B	C	D	E
$4.65	$7.48	$4.52	$7.44	$7.35

2. Labour currently costs $15 per hour. At a production rate of 6 per hour, what will the unit production cost be if labour costs rise to $18 per hour?

A	B	C	D	E
$7.56	$5.02	$7.52	$4.65	$5.06

Diagrammatic

In these questions, there is a series of diagrams which follow a logical sequence on the left of the page. From each row one diagram has been left out. You are to choose the diagram which will complete the sequence from the five options provided on the right of each row.

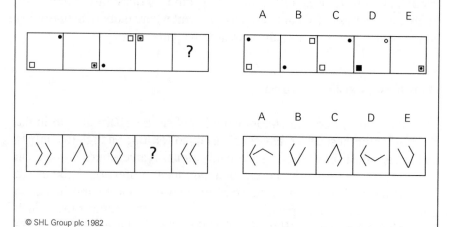

© SHL Group plc 1982

Figure 7.2 Example items for a management-level ability test

general apply only to occupationally relevant tests produced by reputable publishers.

The first point is that ability tests have established a good record of being relatively reliable and have achieved encouraging levels of validity. On a performance index where 1.0 would be perfect prediction and a lengthy multiple assessment procedure might reach 0.6, it is not unusual for single tests of ability – lasting perhaps 20 or 30 minutes – to achieve validities of around 0.4 against good criteria. In other words, with the right selection conditions, they could deliver 15 per cent or higher gains in productivity from those selected.[1] Even more encouraging has been the research work into the concept of validity generalization which has shown that valid tests tend to be valid across a range of job applications. That is, validity is generalizable from one situation to another.

The most important consideration is that ability tests should be chosen carefully to be relevant to the job in question – or, in Cronbach's terms, to be good 'samples' of the appropriate behaviour. This will certainly enhance the validity of the selected tests and hence the pay-back on the investment. However, there is an equally important issue of fairness in selection. As noted above, in countries which have Equal Opportunity legislation, there may well be a legal requirement for the test user to show that the test is fair to all protected groups. However, this should not just be an issue for countries in which such legislation has been enacted. It should be an ethical requirement of any user of any selection method in any country to be able to show under scrutiny that the method is fair. Those concerned with the administration of tests in countries where legislation applies should pay particular attention to the local law and the guidance of appropriate professional bodies. We will restrict our comments to the main points of principle.

Where legislation exists it generally dictates against direct discrimination against a particular gender, ethnic, religious or other group. However, indirect discrimination is more difficult to deal with. This is a situation in which a particular criterion or score is set such that proportionately fewer members of one group in society are able to meet it than is the case for another group. The fact of indirect discrimination may not in itself be illegal or morally unjust. If a particular group has less of an ability which is needed in a particular job, then a lower level of representation may be fair. The key issue is whether the criterion is 'justifiable' against the content of the job. It would clearly be wrong for a test or any measure, with indirect discrimination, to be used for a job where its content could not be justified against the role content.

There is another issue related to fairness and social justice for management to consider in applying ability tests. This concerns the 'cut-off' score which is set as the criterion for selection as opposed to rejection. In order to maximize the utility of the test – that is, in effect, the financial return on the investment in the test – a 'top-down' selection procedure is optimum. This approach selects people from the highest scorer downwards until sufficient people have been selected. However, if the test has a 'disparate impact' for a particular group (that is, it discriminates indirectly) the effect will be maximized by this particular strategy. The alternative is to use a minimum standard to cut out the weakest applicants and then use some other selection criterion. However, this strategy is likely to reduce the financial utility of the test. The management judgement on strategy will depend on a number of job- and test-related factors but underlying these may well be a hard choice between maximizing a financial benefit and meeting criteria for social balance in employment. The balancing on this judgement will be a policy matter for each individual organization.

The need for professional standards

There is no doubt that ability tests will add value to many selection procedures provided they are carefully selected, implemented and interpreted. Reputable publishers rightly make it a purchase requirement that users have been well trained and in several countries collaborate in setting user standards. Local professional bodies may also publish ethics and guidelines to ensure proper use and in the UK the British Psychological Society has gone as far as offering a registration system for users who can show they have met a required set of competencies.

It is also important that user organizations formulate a clear set of policy guidelines to ensure that tests are properly utilized. Figure 7.3 shows a set of policy headings recommended by one test publishing organization which can serve as a management checklist.

With a sound policy in place, there is a much reduced risk of the gross misuse or abuse of ability tests. Among the worst cases would be the use of irrelevant tests, poor administration practice and incorrect interpretation or usage of results. However, the policy document should also reduce the likelihood of less obvious sources of bad practice. For example, we have known of cases where valid tests have been well administered and correctly interpreted against relevant norm groups and then the results have been completely ignored in favour of an interview judgement. It is particularly galling when subsequent job failures are then blamed on the test 'not working'. In a particular case, an organization completed a local

---

Figure 7.3   Topics for test policy guidelines

- Mission statement – short general statement of aims in using tests
- Overall responsibility for testing standards
- Who should use tests?
- When should tests be used?
- Test choice
- 'Equal Opportunities' issues – Race, Gender, Religion, Disability
- Use of test scores
- Confidentiality and storage of results
- Responsibility to test takers
- Re-testing and time period of score validity
- Monitoring
- Access to materials
- Copyright

SOURCE: SHL – Best Practice in the Management of Psychometric Tests: Guidelines for Developing Policy

validation study which showed good predictive validity against new graduate performance after one year of employment. However, in future recruitment the test scores of graduate applicants were only referred to if the interviewers could not agree on a candidate on the basis of the interview alone.

Of course, ability tests are not perfect. As with any means of measuring 'people' attributes, some error in measurement is likely to be present. Administration procedure, practice effects and test strategy effects (for example, deciding to double-check answers) are examples of where error may creep in. The reputable suppliers of tests will show research to indicate the degree of precision or reliability in their tests and will train users to take this into account when interpreting test scores.

The acknowledgement and measurement of error in ability testing is a strength of the method, where for other methods it is only tacitly accepted and rarely taken into account. We are reminded of the case of the professional survey researcher who correctly pointed out to his client the sampling error associated with his estimates. The client responded that he had not realized that he was paying for 'error-prone estimates'! As a general rule, the degree of error associated with thoroughly developed tests is small but it is a matter of professional good practice that the user management should know about it.

Future prospects

For the future we expect to see the international use of ability tests continue to grow. Organizations are becoming increasingly aware of the need to use valid assessment procedures to find the best people. Ability tests have a good record in this respect and, because they are capable of being group administered, they add a high degree of cost efficiency. They are particularly suitable for filtering down large numbers where an ability element matters to job success. However, they also have a key role in smaller-scale management assessment – for example, as a supplement to the simulation exercises of an assessment centre.

At present the vast majority of testing is completed by pencil and paper method but good research has now been done on the equivalence and relative benefits of computer-based testing. As computers become more available and more portable, we can expect to see growth in computer-based testing. Not only will there be advantages in administration, scoring and data interpretation/retention but the tests themselves will benefit from multimedia item capabilities.

In terms of international assessment it is our view that abilities should be assessed in a candidate's native language. If foreign language skill is to be assessed, that should require a specific ability test in its own right. We can expect to see more standardization of professional tests across the world supported by good developmental data covering the tests' reliability and validity and providing local norm groups for comparison.

Testing for abilities is here to stay. Management should not be deterred by the technical aspects of test implementation. The principles are straightforward and specialist advice can be made available from trained individuals inside the organization or directly from the test publishers. In the final analysis, ability tests are a defensible and cost-effective weapon in the assessment armoury.

Measuring personality

The concept

The measurement of personality in an occupational context has always been surrounded by a degree of cynicism and disbelief. Sir Frederick Bartlett illustrated the scepticism surrounding the use of personality questionnaires when he said, 'I don't know – they may be alright – they always seem to me to overestimate the self-knowledge of the subject and to underestimate his sense of humour.' However, personality questionnaires are now used by the majority of large UK organizations, have become a key part of graduate recruitment in Japan and are enjoying a resurgence of interest in the USA and other leading economies.

There is a logic here that runs along the following lines. First, do we believe that personality attributes matter in job performance? The answer is almost certainly 'yes' and, without us referring to empirical research, the reader might reflect on cases where they know someone who has failed in a job and consider how much of this depended on a personality factor as opposed to, say, job experience or attained knowledge.

Second, if we believe that personality matters then, of course, it makes sense to assess it at the point of staff recruitment or promotion. This is where the problem lies because all methods of assessing personality are to some degree flawed or unsatisfactory. We cannot and should not judge them in absolute terms. We need to understand the relative strengths and limitations of the various options and ensure that we select the best single approach, or mix of approaches, to suit our assessment purpose.

In this section we will touch briefly on the various options and then focus on the personality questionnaire, a method which brings real benefit to an assessment process. We will describe this benefit but we will also cover the limitations and the potential pitfalls in application. We believe indeed that the best users of the personality questionnaire are those who understand best what they cannot do and hence provide a more balanced appreciation of their contribution.

Definitions and descriptions

We ought to begin with a neat definition of what is 'personality'. However, this is not so easy. It rather depends on the theoretical position you take and over the years psychologists have taken some widely different positions in defining and describing personality. For example, the 'psychoanalytic' school typified by Sigmund Freud would emphasize the importance of the subconscious and the developmental influences of the id, ego and superego. The 'social learning' theorists have concentrated on the role of observation and imitation in the development of personality while those supporting the 'humanistic' view have been more concerned with the concept and development of the 'self', higher human motives, acquisition of knowledge, understanding and aesthetics.

To some extent, we can duck the issue here because we are more interested in the process of measurement of personality at a point in time than in trying to understand its derivation. To this end, we are sympathetic to the definition of Cattell – one of the leading early researchers in the field – who described personality as being something which 'enables us to predict what a person will do in real life situations'. The emphasis on measurement rather than derivation of personality has been described as the 'psychometric' view and has led to a growth in the use of question-naires as a relatively reliable measurement device. The questionnaires that have emerged over the past few decades have been based on various theoretical models. However, our focus will be the medium for measurement rather than the model.

Another way of looking at the issue of definition is to take some of the more common questions asked by managers about personality when they are considering that part of a person specification. In offering answers to these questions, we have tried to reflect some common themes that run across the various theoretical positions.

Q: Does personality change or is it fixed with adulthood?

Behind this question lies the manager's interest in whether you can do anything about it, particularly if an individual is not currently suited in personality terms to the requirements of a specific role. The answer is that personality can and does change although the process tends to be slow. Cross-sectional studies suggest that there are some general ageing trends towards more conservatism, less achievement drive and less need for status and recognition but specific life-cycle or situational influences can also create long-term changes in personality. For example, working with a new boss who regularly encourages every piece of lateral thinking and rewards every example of innovation can lead to an habitual tendency to think creatively when faced with a problem. The reverse is also true.

Q: We often behave in different ways: do we have more than one personality?

Back in the 1960s a researcher by the name of Mischel proposed that behaviour is explained more by differences in situations than differences in people. This was worrying because it implied that there was no consistent personality within us to be measured. Nowadays, the research evidence points to a relatively high degree of consistency in our behaviour that makes it worthwhile trying to measure. In other words, an anxious introvert, say, tends to manifest related behaviour in a fairly general way. At the same time, there is some variability in our behaviour across situations and there is some support for the idea that we have more than one 'persona'. Our 'parent' persona may be different from our 'work' persona and this is one reason why we recommend that personality measures should be focused on a work context. To put this another way, we believe they should be occupationally relevant.

Q: What are 'types' and what are 'traits'?

Type theories generally classify people into certain type categories which show particular combinations of personal characteristics. The Myers-Briggs Type Indicator based on Jung's theory of types is an example of a widely used and internationally applied type inventory. They tend to be favoured for their relative simplicity and the developmental applications that can be linked to the type assessment.

Trait models tend to focus more on individual differences. Traits are well-established, relatively habitual individual characteristics and tend to offer more flexibility of description. Fewer people will have a similar combination of traits than fall into a particular type. The OPQ® model shown below is an example of an occupationally relevant trait-based model.

Q: How does personality relate to ability?

Personality is concerned with how we typically think, feel, relate to others; it tends to concentrate on our attitudes, inclinations and preferences. Personality does not directly measure occupational ability but it is related to it. For example, if a manager feels confident in more formal social situations then it is likely that he or she will handle those situations better. At the same time, it is possible to develop an ability where no natural inclination exists. For example, a manager may hate the routine attention to points of detail but may learn the ability to proof read and check written work to a high standard. Of course, there is a motivational point here about requiring an individual to perform tasks for which there is no natural personality fit.

Q: Are models of personality stable across cultures?

We believe that there is more stability in models of occupational personality across cultures than might be the case in more general models covering socio-religious behaviour. In effect we are saying that there is a high degree of consistency in the world of work across cultures. The concept of detail-mindedness, say, would be similar in Asia and in Europe. The experience of SHL has been that it is possible to work meaningfully with a standardized model of occupational personality developed into more than 30 cultures. This has been a great help in the process of cross-national assessment and development. Of course, within the model there may be cross-cultural differences in the precise interpretation of the concepts and some differences in average scores. For example, the Japanese concepts of 'independence of mind' and 'achievement drive' are somewhat different from those in the West and questionnaire content needs to be carefully adapted.

Q: How many dimensions should be measured in occupational personality assessment?

This is an area in which there are some clear differences of opinion between practitioners. Figure 7.4 shows the trait model of the Occupational Personality Questionnaire (OPQ® – Saville *et al.,* 1984) which currently has 32 dimensions based on many years of careful research into behavioural differences across a wide range of jobs. At the other extreme, there is a body of opinion that underlying models of a so-called Big Five (or Big Six) dimensions are efficient in accounting for interpersonal differences. In effect, there is a choice in the degree of summarizing that one is prepared to accept in the interest of reducing the time and cost of questionnaire administration, interpretation and feedback. Options are also available that will measure personality at a variety of levels between five and 30 or more.

In an earlier chapter we made our own view clear that, in the case of managerial assessment, we prefer the added discrimination of a more detailed model. It takes about 50 minutes to gather information on a 32-dimension model with a questionnaire. We believe that the criticality of personality fit is too substantial to argue that this is an excessive assessment time allocation.

Figure 7.4   Occupational Personality Questionnaire – OPQ®

Low Score	CONCEPT MODEL	High Score
INFLUENCE		
rarely pressures others to change their views, dislikes selling, less comfortable using negotiation	**Persuasive**	enjoys selling, comfortable using negotiation, likes to change other people's views
happy to let others take charge, dislikes telling people what to do, unlikely to take the lead	**Controlling**	likes to be in charge, takes the lead, tells others what to do, takes control
holds back from criticising others, may not express own views, unprepared to put forward own opinions	**Outspoken**	freely expresses opinions, makes disagreement clear, prepared to criticise others
accepts majority decisions, prepared to follow the consensus	**Independent minded**	prefers to follow own approach, prepared to disregard majority decisions
SOCIABILITY		
quiet and reserved in groups, dislikes being centre of attention	**Outgoing**	lively and animated in groups, talkative, enjoys attention
comfortable spending time away from people, values time spent alone, seldom misses the company of others	**Affiliative**	enjoys others' company, likes to be around people, can miss the company of others
feels more comfortable in less formal situations, can feel awkward when first meeting people	**Socially confident**	feels comfortable when first meeting people, at ease in formal situations
EMPATHY		
makes strengths and achievements known, talks about personal success	**Modest**	dislikes discussing achievements, keeps quiet about personal success
prepared to make decisions without consultation, prefers to make decisions alone	**Democratic**	consults widely, involves others in decision making, less likely to make decisions alone
selective with sympathy and support, remains detached from others' personal problems	**Caring**	sympathetic and considerate towards others, helpful and supportive, gets involved in others' problems

Low Score	CONCEPT MODEL	High Score
ANALYSIS		
prefers dealing with opinions and feelings rather than facts and figures, likely to avoid using statistics	**Data rational**	likes working with numbers, enjoys analysing statistical information, bases decisions on facts and figures
does not focus on potential limitations, dislikes critically analysing information, rarely looks for errors or mistakes	**Evaluative**	critically evaluates information, looks for potential limitations, focuses upon errors
does not question the reasons for people's behaviour, tends not to analyse people	**Behavioural**	tries to understand motives and behaviour, enjoys analysing people
CREATIVITY AND CHANGE		
favours changes to work methods, prefers new approaches, less conventional	**Conventional**	prefers well established methods, favours a more conventional approach
prefers to deal with practical rather than theoretical issues, dislikes dealing with abstract concepts	**Conceptual**	interested in theories, enjoys discussing abstract concepts
more likely to build on than generate ideas, less inclined to be creative and inventive	**Innovative**	generates new ideas, enjoys being creative, thinks of original solutions
prefers routine, is prepared to do repetitive work, does not seek variety	**Variety seeking**	prefers variety, tries out new things, likes changes to regular routine, can become bored by repetitive work
behaves consistently across situations, unlikely to behave differently with different people	**Adaptable**	changes behaviour to suit the situation, adapts approach to different people
STRUCTURE		
more likely to focus upon immediate than long-term issues, less likely to take a strategic perspective	**Forward thinking**	takes a long-term view, sets goals for the future, more likely to take a strategic perspective

Low Score	CONCEPT MODEL	High Score
unlikely to become pre-occupied with detail, less organised and systematic, dislikes tasks involving detail	**Detail conscious**	focuses on detail, likes to be methodical, organised and systematic, may become preoccupied with detail
sees deadlines as flexible, prepared to leave some tasks unfinished	**Conscientious**	focuses on getting things, finished, persists until the job is done
not restricted by rules and procedures, prepared to break rules, tends to dislike bureaucracy	**Rule following**	follows rules and regula-tions, prefers clear guide-lines, finds it difficult to break rules
EMOTION		
tends to feel tense, finds it difficult to relax, can find it hard to unwind after work	**Relaxed**	finds it easy to relax, rarely feels tense, generally calm and untroubled
feels calm before important occasions, less affected by key events, free from worry	**Worrying**	feels nervous before important occasions, worries about things going wrong
sensitive, easily hurt by criticism, upset by unfair comments or insults	**Tough minded**	not easily offended, can ignore insults, may be insensitive to personal criticism
concerned about the future, expects things to go wrong, focuses on negative aspects of a situation	**Optimistic**	expects things will turn out well, looks to the positive aspects of a situation, has an optimistic view of the future
wary of others' intentions, finds it difficult to trust others, unlikely to be fooled by people	**Trusting**	trusts people, sees others as reliable and honest, believes what others say
openly expresses feelings, finds it difficult to conceal feelings, displays emotion clearly	**Emotionally controlled**	can conceal feelings from others, rarely displays emotion
DYNAMISM		
likes to take things at a steady pace, dislikes excessive work demands	**Vigorous**	thrives on activity, likes to be busy, enjoys having a lot to do

Low Score	CONCEPT MODEL	High Score
dislikes competing with others, feels that taking part is more important than winning	**Competitive**	has a need to win, enjoys competitive activities, dislikes losing
sees career progression as less important, looks for achievable rather than highly ambitious targets	**Achieving**	ambitious and career-centred, likes to work to demanding goals and targets
tends to be cautious when making decisions, likes to take time to reach conclusions	**Decisive**	makes fast decisions, reaches conclusions quickly, less cautious
has been more self-critical in responses, is less concerned to make a good impression	**Social desirability**	has been less self-critical in responses, is more concerned to make a good impression
has responded less consistently across the questionnaire	**Consistency**	has responded more consistently across the questionnaire

Q: How does personality relate to motivation?

Motivation is such an important area of occupational performance that we have made it the subject of a separate chapter. However, personality is importantly related to motivation and it cannot be dealt with as if it were a single dimension. Figure 7.5 shows the OPQ® model of personality which has three domains and shows motivational energy as deriving from all three areas. For example, in the 'relating' domain there may be motivational energy from wanting to be included in team activity; in the 'thinking' domain energy may be derived from an interest in creativity or theoretical analysis; in the 'feeling' domain anxiety to avoid failure may be a key motivator. In the next chapter we will show how a more thorough model of occupational motivation has been developed but a detailed personality questionnaire can go a good way to identifying key areas of motivation for an individual.

Q: Is personality inherited?

There is a continuing debate among psychologists over the relative importance of genetic and environmental influences on

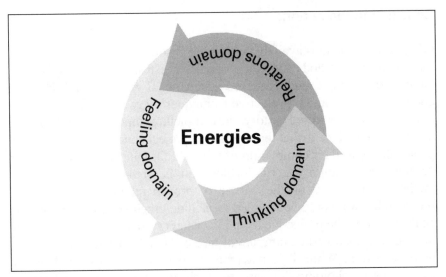

Figure 7.5   OPQ® model of personality

personality. It is difficult to separate the two since those who inherit similar genes from their parents tend to experience similar environmental influences. However, studies involving identical twins, separated near to birth and brought up in different homes, suggest that there is quite a strong inherited component to personality. Perhaps more important than trying to establish the precise mix of heredity and environment is the realization that cultural and educational influences are also important and that we should be encouraged to develop our personalities to maximize the occupational benefit.

The fundamental assessment problem

Earlier on we made the point that personality is sufficiently important in determining work success for it to be well worth measuring at times of recruitment or internal development. We cannot afford to ignore personality assessment in terms of competency development, team building, client match, leadership style, enhancing selling or customer service and many other areas of activity. However, none of the options available to us is perfect. They are all error prone to some degree and we have to make a relative judgement of the best method to suit our needs.

Considering the options

Of the various options available we would absolutely rule out some of the more extreme methods such as phrenology, astrology and palmistry as having no thorough research-based occupational validity at all. In some countries, the so-called 'projective techniques' have found favour. These require candidates to tell a story, draw a picture, interpret an ink-blot or the like and the idea is that the candidates project something of their own personality into their completion of the task. Despite attempts to tighten up the interpretation process, which can be rather subjective, these methods tend to fail on the criteria of proven reliability and validity. Incidentally, we would be inclined to include graphology or handwriting analysis within the projective technique category since it assumes that an individual projects something about him or herself through the medium of handwriting. While it is not unusual to hear anecdotal evidence in support of graphology, the hard research evidence is clear. Levels of reliability are relatively weak and there is very little statistical evidence of occupational validity. As we have noted, the British Psychological Society has published a paper summarizing current research with the clear implication that graphology has little value.

By far the most commonly used way of assessing personality is by means of the personal interview. As we have noted earlier, there are certain aspects of a person specification for which the interview is well suited. However, it faces several major drawbacks when used alone as a device for personality assessment. First, the questions usually lack the structured discipline that leads to the generation of reliable data. Second, there is normally insufficient time to cover the breadth of occupational personality. Third, there is a tendency to subjectivity and to the drawing of fast conclusions on limited evidence. There is a good case for using the interview in conjunction with other methods to explore in a more qualitative way various aspects of personality. On its own, research has shown that the interview tends to be unreliable and to lack validity – particularly in its normal discursive form.

If there is an ideal method of assessing occupational personality then we might argue that it lies in well-constructed and relevant simulation exercises. The benefit of simulation is that we can see the behavioural manifestation of personality. The logic is along these lines. If you want to assess candidates' leadership then ask them to lead a difficult group to a defined business goal. If your objective is to assess candidates' creativity, then ask them to generate original solutions to a set occupational problem. Careful analysis of the resulting behaviour should provide good information for predicting how these aspects of their personality will affect future performance in similar situations. Indeed, simulation exercises do have a good track record of being both reliable and predicting occupational performance.

The case for questionnaire-based assessment

However, there is a problem with simulations in that they are extremely time consuming and expensive to utilize in order to cover the many relevant dimensions of occupational personality. Herein lies the strength of the personality questionnaire. In about 50 minutes it is possible to elicit around 400 pieces of personality-based information to cover the breadth of occupational personality. Questionnaires provide structure and discipline in the construction of their items so that they are objective and reliable. They are based on self-report and therefore have the added advantage that they can cover feelings, thoughts and opinions which might not be open to elicitation from an analysis of overt behaviour alone. Furthermore, it has been argued that the fact of self-report means that we are gathering information from the source best placed to know what the individual is thinking, feeling, worried about, interested in and the like. Finally, the per capita assessment cost is small in relation to other methods.

At the same time, we must remember that we are talking here of self-reported questionnaire data and there may well be biases in action with the potential to limit the validity of the method. For this reason we would not advocate the use of personality questionnaires on their own. We would want to see them used in conjunction with a probing individual interview and if possible within a multiple assessment programme including some simulation of key behaviours. In addition and because of the somewhat sensitive nature of personality information, we would always recommend that candidates are offered a feedback of the personality data collected.

The issue of faking

From management's point of view, there has always been a good degree of scepticism surrounding the use of personality questionnaires. Much of this has to do with the quite commonly held belief that it is not too difficult to create a self-picture that one would feel to be appropriate for a particular role. This takes the lovely technical name of 'impression management' or more bluntly 'lying'. In reality this is a misconception. First, researchers have noted that the incidence of deliberate faking in real-life assessments is a relatively rare phenomenon. Second, it is known that the impact of faking is substantially reduced when the questionnaire is professionally administered and there is supporting evidence for comparison. For example, the candidate may be told 'we shall be giving you feedback on your questionnaire results and at that time we will be comparing what you have said with other information we have about you'. Declaring in a questionnaire that one 'always takes the lead in meetings' becomes more problematical if one has just sat quietly through a difficult budget planning group simulation exercise. Then again, with more complex models of occupational personality, it becomes less easy to see where the right answers lie. Where would managers want to position themselves in terms of being optimistic, theoretical, critical, people dependent, emotionally inexpressive and so on?

The research of a leading practitioner in the field, Leaetta Hough, has shown that intentional distortion in real-life applicant settings does not affect the performance-related validity of personality questionnaires. However, if management remains concerned, then nowadays there are versions of occupational personality questionnaires available which are designed to control to a large degree any intentional distortion on the part of the respondent. This is essentially by forcing the respondent to choose between answer options in the questionnaire which are matched for their perceived desirability. How, for example, would a prospective trainee manager answer the following question: 'Which of these statements is more like you – taking the lead in meetings OR having creative ideas to solve problems?' There are some technical scaling issues surrounding the choice of questionnaire model that a well-trained user would understand but the point that we want to reinforce here is that faking personality questionnaires is nothing like the problem it is sometimes assumed to be.

A current overview

On the face of it then, personality questionnaires are cost and time effective; the structure and standardization of the questions lead to good levels of reliability and the bias of socially desirable responding can be largely controlled. This leads to the question of their track record in terms of validity in the occupational field. In fact, personality questionnaires got off to a bad start in early usage in the USA. At the same time that Mischel was questioning the consistency of behaviour across different situations and arguing against the measurement of traits, questionnaires were being used for occupational purposes that were never intended for such an application. The result was that candidates were likely to be asked inappropriate questions on dimensions that were irrelevant to the world of work. This was exacerbated by the concurrent sensitivity to issues of fairness in assessment for those protected under the federal Civil Rights Act of 1964. Add in some methodological problems concerning the definition of criterion performance measures and the conclusion at the time was that personality questionnaires did not have much to offer.

Now the situation has changed with what has been referred to by leading researchers as the 'rebirth' of the personality questionnaire. The measurement of 'traits' is back in vogue. Modern questionnaires have been designed to contain occupationally relevant questions that are much less susceptible to charges of unfair discrimination. Validation studies have concentrated on linking specific sets of personality characteristics to relevant competencies rather than vague overall measures of job performance. There has been a substantial investment in the proper training of practitioners. The result is that American studies are now showing good levels of validity for questionnaires in predicting management potential, sales and customer service performance and generalized integrity/dependability. In the UK, SHL has been a major contributor to the pool of validation research. Using large-scale validation samples, SHL has been able to link specific sets of OPQ scales to pre-hypothesized management competencies. For example, in one large cross-validation exercise, a correlation in excess of 0.4 was obtained for three OPQ scales and a measure of Creativity competence.[2] Furthermore, the Creativity measure was not well predicted by analytical reasoning tests and is notoriously difficult to assess by simulation exercises.

From an Equal Opportunity perspective, recent research in both the USA and the UK has shown that personality questionnaires are much less prone than ability tests to create adverse impact for different gender and ethnic groups. So while growing evidence of the validity of personality questionnaires is increasing the perceived justifiability of their use, the relatively small gender and ethnic group differences in achieved scores are enhancing their apparent fairness as an assessment device.

Gaining acceptance for personality measurement

In the Preface to this book, we commented on the beautiful complexity of matching people to jobs and in Chapter 1 we asserted that this is particularly true of the process of assessing personality against the varied requirements of a particular job. We noted that there are many personality attributes to be considered. We proposed that there are subtle but important links between them. We argued that personality profiles cannot be judged in isolation but should be assessed in interaction with other members of work units or teams. Our plea here is that management should not be put off by this inherent complexity and should be alert to the consequences of getting personality 'wrong' – whether at board level or on the factory floor. We are talking here of poorly performing teams, enhanced stress, inadequate job competence, inappropriate leadership, a misfit with the prevailing culture, reduced motivational commitment and the like.

Of course there are dangers from poor practice in personality assessment. The usage of inappropriate instruments, badly administered and interpreted, can be harmful to candidates and damaging to an organization's public image. This is an area in which practitioners should be thoroughly trained in the usage of a particular questionnaire. With thorough training from a reputable source, those using questionnaires should understand the limitations and areas of risk at the same time as being able to complete a thorough interpretation taking into account the complexity outlined above. Reputable publishers of questionnaires will reinforce this process by establishing codes of good practice to protect their own interests and by releasing questionnaire materials only to those who have met rigorous training standards.

It will not be a surprise for senior management at a stage removed from such training to retain some scepticism about the potential contribution of the personality questionnaire. In Figure 7.6 we list some of the more common objections and some means of overcoming them.

In the final analysis, it is our view that personality questionnaires will come to demonstrate their worth by the perceived outcome of their many areas of application. Apart from competency assessment, they have the potential to be used in team building, stress management, self-development planning, motivation analysis, leadership development, culture fit and other areas. We will look at a number of these in the chapters ahead and we will discuss the increasing role of the computer in the facilitation of both administration and interpretation. Of all the options open to us, they have the benefit of being relatively reliable and valid measurement devices combined with a low per capita cost of assessment. Having experienced a rebirth, they are now poised for a period of international maturation.

Figure 7.6 Personality questionnaires – management objections and solutions

Objection	Solution
● They are fakeable.	While this is true to some degree for many assessment methods, it is a relatively small problem in practice for good personality questionnaires. Invite publishers to demonstrate a thorough administration and take a feedback interview.
● They will undermine the interview.	The questionnaire should supplement the interview. Both are vulnerable alone. In combination they can produce rich insights to personality. Try using a questionnaire in advance to set specific probing areas for the interview.
● We have experienced/ heard of obtrusive, irrelevant questions.	This may indeed have occurred where non-occupational questionnaires have been used and in our view this is indefensible. Look at questionnaires whose content has been developed or at least reviewed for occupational relevance.
● They are expensive to use.	On a comparative basis, vis-à-vis other options, this is simply not true. There may be an initial investment in training an internal user and some instruments are licensed. Volume of usage is a factor. Ask a publisher to give you a full per capita cost estimate at a given volume over several years.
● We are not convinced they work better than our interview judgement.	This is an issue of the relative validity of different approaches. Call for publishers to show you their validation data. Separately, enquiries can be made of independent specialists of professional bodies. In the UK, the British Psychological Society publishes an objective review of the more common questionnaires.
● Candidates may be put off by personality assessment.	Any form of testing can be threatening to candidates. The solution lies in good administration and the provision of feedback. There are explanatory leaflets to be sent in advance; administration should be thorough and sympathetic; feedback should be accurate and relevant. In our experience, even rejected candidates have valued the professional usage of a relevant questionnaire.
● Management loses ownership of the decision-making process.	The overall objective is to gather information against a clear 'person specification' for the job. The personality questionnaire is just one input. It should be kept in perspective against other issues of ability, technical competence and experience, relevant training, personal circumstances and the like. Decision making on a balanced input basis remains management's prerogative.

Summary

The past decade has seen substantial international growth in the use of psychometric tests of ability and personality. In this chapter we have tried to describe and evaluate the contribution they make.

Ability tests have right and wrong answers and the objective is to achieve a maximum score. There is a range of occupational categories of test which are designed to tell us how well an individual is likely to perform certain 'thinking' and 'moving' aspects of a job. The benefits of ability tests are that they are relatively reliable and valid in predicting success. When group-administered they can also be highly cost effective and are often, but not solely, used as a filtering device. Ability tests may be subject to 'adverse impact' for certain ethnic or gender groups. There are technical issues in their usage that need to be well understood and we offer guidelines on creating a test use policy.

Much work has been done to standardize certain tests internationally. We are also seeing an increasing application of the computer in facilitating administration, data storage and interpretation.

Personality questionnaires or inventories have been generating strong occupational interest in many countries and are enjoying what has been described as a 'rebirth' in the USA. These are not strictly tests as there are no right or wrong answers as such. They describe how individuals typically think, feel and relate to other people.

Validation data and our own experience tell us that an individual's personality is critical to his or her work success. Unfortunately there is no perfect way of measuring it. Simulation exercises are good for measuring the expression of personality attributes in behavioural terms. However, they can be time consuming and expensive to undertake. We examine a range of options and conclude that the strength of the questionnaire lies in its potential to provide reliable and valid information on a highly cost-effective basis. For example, several hundred pieces of work-relevant information can be gathered in less than an hour for about the cost of a modest lunch.

It is often assumed that the faking of a personality questionnaire is a relatively easy matter. We argue that faking is much less common in real practice than often suspected and that there are administration and technical design devices that can overcome it.

Personality questionnaires are less open to ethnic group bias and if their content is occupational they can be transferred across cultures.

At the same time, they are not perfect and we caution that they should be used in conjunction with other methods, that feedback should always be given and that they should only be used by properly trained practitioners. Their information may be complex to interpret but this is not a challenge to be ducked. We cannot leave a proper evaluation of personality out of the assessment and development picture. We will return to the application of personality questionnaire data in later chapters.

Notes

1. See Chapter 1 for the rationale.
2. See validity league table of Chapter 2.

8

Motivation

The case for motivation analysis

Leaders know that there is great power in motivation. This is true in commercial organizations and indeed in any goal-oriented one. There are countless examples from sporting life that show how team performance is lifted when motivation is high. Because of this we have devoted a chapter to this important area.

Research has clearly established a relationship between ability and occupational performance. We are seeing new evidence that personality is also importantly related to occupational success. Motivation is a critical area for us to consider that goes beyond ability and personality although it is related to both of them. We are talking here of the drive and energy that is so important to the meeting of goals and objectives. Whatever the stock of competencies within an organization, it is a key part of management's role to influence the energy with which tasks are undertaken. We are aware of teams in many areas of human endeavour who have performed beyond any reasonable level of expectation. Commitment, drive and energy are frequently given as the reasons for their success and in our view these are vital concepts to be applied in the world of work.

This chapter is concerned with both the measurement and development of motivation. By motivation we mean not only that which energizes behaviour but also what channels and directs behaviour as well as sustaining it. There are a number of ways in which it is important for management to be able to understand and utilize the concept.

Motivation matters in selection because we want people who are not only suited to a role in terms of their underlying attributes but who are energized to perform within it. We know that if motivation is low, even for an able and experienced performer, then there is a good chance that we will lose that person. We have made reference earlier to the finding that thorough simulation-based assessment procedures enhance the graduate take-up rate of job offers and the retention rate at the end of years one and two of employment. Our experience is that the quality of the assessment process itself enhances the motivation of the individual to want to join the organization. Furthermore, organizations using this kind of approach also work hard at the early training and development of the new graduate intake, which increases the motivation to stay.

Motivation affects internal appointments, particularly towards the top of the organization. We know, for example, that there is an ageing factor in motivation and for some managers their drive and energy dissipate as the years advance. Of course, this is not always the case and for some managers the reverse is true as life circumstances change. However, it is a key issue for board appointments and should be on the agenda for candidate review. The fact of an historical track record of attaining goals and outperforming expectations may not be matched by a similar future level of performance if the motivational edge has gone. This transition can happen quickly. The energy and drive levels need assessing before key roles at the top of the organization are assigned – and need reviewing as part of regular appraisal. What is more, this needs to be done thoroughly because separate agenda may be in operation which do not allow the individual to admit a loss of drive.

Motivation is a key aspect of leadership. In Chapter 9, we describe our views of inspirational leadership. Recent models of so-called 'Transformational Leadership' (for example, Bass) concentrate on the potential of leaders to encourage subordinates to perform beyond normal levels of expectation. The idea is that a transformational leader can motivate followers to operate beyond their self-interests for the good of the group or organization. Various factors have been proposed to identify the transformational leader, including:

- charisma – the display of confident conviction; the communication of purpose and commitment; the emphasis on trust;
- intellectual stimulation – the questioning of assumptions; the stimulation of new perspectives;
- individual consideration – the recognition and consideration of individual needs, abilities and aspirations;
- inspirational motivation – the preparedness to challenge followers; the display of enthusiastic optimism; the provision of encouragement towards an appealing vision of the future.

We are not so sure about the differentiation of charisma and inspirational motivation but we can see that personal enthusiasm and energy are key factors in these attributes. Researchers in this field have noted among identified charismatic leaders an extraordinary determination and generally high levels of activity and energy. There is an almost infectious quality to energy linked with self-confidence and optimism that has a motivational impact on those associated with it.

Roger Holdsworth, co-founder of SHL, reinforces the importance of motivation in general and believes it is more appropriate to think of motivation as having a 'multiplier' effect. In terms of a simple model, this is the idea that performance is a function of ability **times** motivation. His experience suggests to him that this is more likely to be true than a summation model. Of course, there are many other elements which affect performance and make this a difficult hypothesis to test.

Motivation is also vitally important to the successful development of staff. Developmental action is only likely to succeed if the individual wants it to happen. Any parent will recognize the difficulty of trying to develop skills and characteristics in children where the children are not motivated to achieve the desired outcome. In aggregate, levels of motivation can affect team morale and beyond that it can influence the culture of a division or indeed the organization as a whole. Managing within an organization that lacks that general spark of dynamism and focus on action is unlikely to be easy. Furthermore, changing such a culture is not achieved overnight.

The reading of motivation

Good managers should be able to motivate their staff. The first step in this process is to be able to understand what it is that motivates a particular individual. However, this is not so easy because individual motivators can vary substantially and some of them are quite complex to understand. Managers who show no interest in trying to understand the motivation of their staff – as in the concept of individualized consideration above – are unlikely to achieve the status of transformational leadership. They are unlikely to take the right action at the right time which is needed by a particular individual to boost their performance.

This reading of motivation is an important skill. It was first recognized several decades ago within the concept of so-called 'social intelligence'. It was built upon more recently by Gardner who reinforced the notion of multiple intelligences to get away from an over-reliance on IQ in understanding successful performance. Gardner's concept of 'interpersonal intelligence' emphasizes the ability to understand other people and what motivates them. This concept has been built into a broader notion of 'emotional intelligence' which is concerned with the understanding, development and personal management of the total emotional aspects of an individual's make-up. While the concept of emotional intelligence is still relatively under-researched by comparison with a cognitive-based IQ, researchers are beginning to put together evidence that the impact of understanding and managing the more emotional aspects of our lives is substantial in determining how successful we are in our day-to-day activities. At the other extreme, we are also aware of the damaging effect on performance of depression within an individual.

The Motivation Questionnaire

The requirement, therefore, is for a model of occupational motivation that managers can understand and utilize in coming to terms with their own and others' individual profiles of motivation. Over the past 50 years, many models and theories have been proposed but none of them alone has been able to cover the breadth and complexity of motivation in the world of work. In the early 1990s, two researchers at SHL, Baron and Henley, set about integrating the available research and theoretical contributions in order to produce an occupational model with the emphasis on practicability. In effect their objective was to produce a broadly based model with the emphasis on measurement with a reasonable time cost and applicability in terms of management decision making. They were less interested in universal motivators than in identifying dimensions which could demonstrate individual differences in patterns of motivation.

In our view Baron and Henley have taken us a long way forward in being able to work with a concept that we all recognize as important and yet we have never quite had the framework to comprehend. It is worth looking at their eclectic process and the final model they produced.

The researchers began with a review of past theory and research. For those unfamiliar with this area, some of the more influential models they considered – together with their brief descriptions[1] – were as follows.

Need theories

Murray (1938), one of the earliest researchers into occupational motivation, worked on the basis of the intensive study of individuals to develop a model of 20 major needs. Among the more psychological needs were autonomy, deference, aggression, dominance, power, achievement and affiliation.

Maslow (1954) proposed a set of five universal, innate needs ordered in a hierarchy from the most basic physiological needs, through those for safety, belongingness and love to the need for self-esteem and, at the top, the need for self-actualization, that is, the realization of one's full potential.

Herzberg (1966) distinguished two sets of needs. The first set were called **motivators** and were linked to the concept of self-actualization. These included 'need' concepts such as achievement, recognition, responsibility and advancement, where satisfaction can be achieved only through events directly linked to job activities. The second set, called **hygiene** factors, were based on an individual's need to avoid pain and were concerned with job context factors such as the work environment, pay and benefits. They can only reduce pain but not in themselves lead to positive satisfaction.

Intrinsic Motivation Theorists (for example, Deci 1972) assumed motivation to be essentially based on innate needs for competence and self-determination. The main motivational goal is to be able to improve one's skills and to accomplish tasks more effectively. This leads to high levels of task involvement emphasizing the intrinsic nature of task satisfaction as opposed to external rewards and benefits. Individuals are seen to differ in terms of the extent to which they are motivated by the more intrinsic task-related factors as opposed to more extrinsic factors such as pay and conditions.

McClelland (1987) emphasized the development of needs 'learned' through experience and which motivate the pursuit of particular goals. In particular, McClelland is associated with acquired needs for achievement, affiliation and power.

Reinforcement theories

Hull (1943) and Skinner (1953) proposed that behaviour is fundamentally controlled by the consequences or rewards associated with it. They have helped us in the process of analyzing the factors which direct and maintain behaviour.

Cognitive theories

Equity Theory (for example, Adams 1963) considers the judgements and comparisons people make regarding 'inputs' to and 'outcomes' from jobs.

Inputs are concerned with what the individual brings to the job; outcomes include pay and other benefits of the job such as status and interest. The theory assumes that individuals generate a weighted aggregate of inputs and outcomes for a job. Motivation depends on the ratio of the two and equity is said to exist if the two are equal. The individual seeks to reduce any inequity by changing one or more of the elements of the input:outcome ratio.

Expectancy Theory (for example, Vroom 1964) makes the basic proposition that people's beliefs and expectations regarding future reinforcements provide the main motivational impetus for behaviour. People select among various courses of action those anticipated to be maximally advantageous to them. In Vroom's theory, motivation is seen as a function of the probability of a particular outcome; the belief that a particular activity will lead to a particular outcome and the attractiveness of the outcome to the individual. It tends to emphasize motivation as a rational cognitive process.

An integrated model

Baron and Henley recognized the complexity of occupational motivation and supported a position which sees motivation as an interactive function of the characteristics of the **individual**, the nature of the **job** and the prevailing **culture** of the organization. All the above theories had something to add to the picture but none could account for the many subtleties of motivation in real life. They decided to focus primarily on the development of a systematic questionnaire procedure for assessing individual differences in motivational patterns. Their research extended over several years and included substantial empirical data gathering. The broad steps of the process are summarized briefly here.

An initial review of existing research was combined with empirical work with managers who were asked to list conditions and situations which tended to increase or decrease their motivation. With some pruning for redundancy or irrelevance to the world of work, they generated a set of 32 motivational constructs on which individuals were likely to vary. Questions or items were then generated to measure these constructs and a detailed iterative process was undertaken to refine the model using a combination of factor analysis and statistical procedures for testing the properties of individual questions and total scales. The result was a model of 18 scales of occupational motivation within four broad summary factors of energy-dynamism, synergy, intrinsic and extrinsic considerations. The full model is shown in Figure 8.1.

Figure 8.1   Motivation Questionnaire scales

Motivation	Description
Energy & Dynamism	
Level of Activity*	Invests energy readily and thrives on time pressure. Always on the go and pushing to get things done.
Achievement	Needs to achieve targets and overcome challenges. Enjoys striving to complete difficult projects.
Competition*	Motivated by trying to do better than others. Comparison often spurs performance.
Fear of Failure*	Needs to succeed to maintain self-esteem. The possibility of failure spurs activity.
Power	Motivated when given responsibility and able to exercise authority. Demotivated by lack of opportunity to exert influence.
Immersion*	Thrives on feeling involved with job. Prepared to work extended hours and invest much energy in job.
Commercial Outlook*	Orientation towards creating wealth and profits. Demotivated when work does not relate to results in cash terms.
Synergy	
Affiliation	Thrives on meeting people, team work and helping others. Likely to feel demotivated by conflict in relationships.
Recognition	Likes to have good work noticed and achievements recognised. Becomes demotivated without support.
Personal Principles	Needs to feel that the organization's work is sound. Demotivated when asked to compromise ethical standards.
Ease and Security	Needs to feel secure about job and position. Does not easily tolerate unpleasant or inconvenient conditions.
Personal Growth	Is motivated by work which provides opportunities for development, learning and acquisition of new skills.
Intrinsic	
Interest	Values stimulating and varied work. Enjoys working creatively. Demotivated by too many run of the mill tasks.
Flexibility*	Favours a fluid environment without imposed structure. High tolerance of ambiguity.
Autonomy	Prefers working independently without close supervision. Demotivated when not allowed to organise own approach to work and timescales.
Extrinsic	
Material Reward	Links salary to success. Values perks and bonuses. Demotivated when remuneration package is poor or perceived as unfair.
Progression	Career progress, rate of promotion and just advancement are motivating.
Status	Concerned with position and status. Demotivated by lack of respect from others.

* More extreme bipolar scales – see text

SOURCE: Manual for SHL Motivation Questionnaire

An interesting feature of the Baron and Henley research was that some of the motivational scales emerged as uni-polar and some as bipolar. For example, with the 'Recognition' scale everybody in the research study reported finding recognition or praise motivating to some degree but some more so than others. By comparison, with the 'Flexibility' scale, when the conditions suggested by the scale are present, some individuals experience a drop in motivation. However, other individuals experience an increase in motivation when their jobs have this aspect of flexibility. The more extreme bipolar motivational scales are indicated in Figure 8.1.

The consequence of this research is that we now have a credible model of occupational motivation for which there is a well-developed questionnaire which can be completed within 20–25 minutes. It is known as the 'Motivation Questionnaire'. Various norm groups are available for comparison and there are adaptations into a number of languages. It is possible for managers to achieve a much better understanding of motivational profiles and the authors report that a particular benefit has been the clarification for management that the motivation factors for other people are often different from their own. We are often guilty of assuming that others will see things the same way that we do ourselves.

Applications of motivation analysis

Like most conceptual innovations in management, there will only be value if it is possible to apply the new thinking and see some genuine benefit accrue. The final part of this chapter therefore focuses on the practical applications of a better understanding of motivation. It should, however, be noted that the Motivation Questionnaire is in many respects like a personality questionnaire. It should only be administered and interpreted by trained individuals. There is a responsibility to give feedback and ideally it should be used in conjunction with other methods such as an interview or simulation exercises. However, if it is professionally applied, it has a variety of uses for management.

In terms of selection and promotion the Motivation Questionnaire can help us to ensure an optimum match at the point of decision making as well as providing a basis for managing the new appointee on an ongoing basis. The questionnaire cannot be used in isolation. It will not, by itself, provide some magic yes–no solution to the motivational question. The issue that we must be able to deal with at the time of appointment is:

Will this individual be motivated in this particular job in this particular culture?

The implication is that our initial job analysis must be able to provide a specification of the motivational pattern which is best suited to the role. If the job is in a fluid environment with a minimum of imposed structure, then we can infer that 'Flexibility' is a key motivational factor. This alone is not enough. We must then examine the culture of the organization. If the culture values independent working with a minimum of close supervision then we can infer that 'Autonomy' is a relevant motivational factor. Armed with information of this kind, we can then review the individual's personal profile of motivation.

Of course, the above question is essentially concerned with a recruitment decision and the degree of person–job match at the time of selection. However, both at the time of appointment and later on, managers have the scope to affect the degree of person–job match. The management question then becomes:

How can I influence the motivation of this individual in this particular job and culture?

From a motivational point of view, the management options are substantial. Managers can certainly influence the values that underpin their local culture and they may well have it within their scope to vary the content of jobs to increase the motivational impact. If a job holder is demotivated by the flexibility of a job, then consider giving it more structure. If he or she is strongly motivated by affiliation, then consider building the teamwork element and so on. There are also implications for the content of management communication in everyday interaction. If the individual is motivated by competition, then the manager can emphasize the competitive nature of the job tasks and objectives and give feedback in these terms. The overall objective is for the manager to keep in mind the individual's profile of motivation and continually ask, 'How do I draw on the motivational strengths?'; 'How do I structure tasks to capitalize on the particular sources of motivation?'

Jobs, individuals and managers can change and it is important to maintain a watching brief on motivational factors. However, it is in our view a fundamental point of good management that a manager should understand the motivation of his or her staff and take the appropriate steps to raise and keep motivation at a high level. If managers are to optimize their people management, they have to know whether there is a current need for more or less flexibility, autonomy, recognition, reassurance on ethics, commercial rationale and so on.

A general theme of this book has been that management should not be frightened away from the complexity of people and jobs but should do more to try to understand them. We cannot make human motivation simple although we can provide models, tools and advice to help managers deal with the complexity. Take the case of an individual who has a high 'fear of failure'. If we understand this and we can also recognize that the job entails a high risk of failure, the individual lacks self-confidence in personality terms and the organizational culture is severely punitive of failure, then we know we have a problem to resolve. Solutions may be found at the individual, job or organizational level.

Motivational analysis, therefore, also has implications for organizational development. It can be used to audit the motivational factors at work within the organization and to create more flexible means for management to get the motivational equation right. Important as pay and benefits may be, motivational analysis can open management's eyes to other action which may be more effective without such an immediate direct cost. Shifting the culture is a macro option which is becoming more common in organizational planning. We would want to emphasize the many micro options that models such as the one above open up for individual supervisors and managers. Case Study 8.1 gives an example of the use of the Motivation Questionnaire in analyzing individual and team motivation.

CASE STUDY 8.1
Motivation profiles of a management team

This case study concerns a small but successful medical supplies company. It was a comfortable and friendly workplace with a stable workforce. A newly appointed MD was concerned that the Management Team should adopt a more active and sophisticated approach to management in order to meet the challenges of a changing health sector. He instigated a development review for the Management Team including the Motivation Questionnaire (MQ) and a range of other personality and 360° instruments.

The MQ profiles revealed the sources of energy of the team (see Figure 8.2). They were all quite strongly motivated by Commercial Outlook. They liked seeing how their work benefited the business and this, together with their above average scores on Personal Principles, was the source of their great commitment to the company. However, in other respects energies were moderate and more typical of lower-level than senior managers. Although striving to meet objectives would energize the group, they were not motivated by competition and there

Figure 8.2　MQ Profiles of Management Team

	Low 1	2	3	4	5	6	7	8	9	High 10	Scale
Energy and Dynamism		○		○		○		● ○			Level of Activity
					● ○	○	○ ○				Achievement
				○ ○	○	●	○				Competition
			○○ ○				● ○				Fear of Failure
			● ○		○	○	○				Power
			● ○		○	○	○				Immersion
						●○ ○○	○				Commercial Outlook
Synergy		●		○		○	○			○	Affiliation
			○			● ○○		○			Recognition
					●	○ ○	○ ○				Personal Principals
				○ ○			○	●		○	Ease and Security
		●			○ ○	○	○				Personal Growth
Intrinsic				○	○	● ○		○			Interest
				○	●			○	○		Flexibility
				● ○○		○	○				Autonomy
Extrinsic			○	○			○ ○			●	Material Reward
			● ○		○	○	○				Progression
			○	○ ○		○	●				Status

John ●　　Other Management Team Members ○

See Figure 8.1 for definitions

was a tendency to give in relatively easily in the face of a more difficult challenge (low Fear of Failure). Only one was particularly motivated by opportunities to exercise power and influence. There was also a rather low tolerance of work encroaching onto private life.

John, perhaps the most able of the group, was typical of this pattern. In charge of finance, he had little need for power or control. He did not have much personal ambition (low need for Progression) and thus resisted the MD's suggestions that he change his style. Although often the first to diagnose a problem and suggest a solution, he made little effort to persuade the team to adopt it. He had a very low need for Affiliation and would return to work alone on his figures rather than trying to influence policy in what he perceived was the right direction. He had a high need for Material Reward and for Ease and Security. Therefore, he avoided taking risks, particularly if these could affect his financial security.

The review helped the MD to understand his team much better. Their motivational structures were perfectly attuned to the stable quality of the business to date. He realized that the changes he was trying to introduce were going to be difficult for the team, although other evidence from 360° analysis showed they had the capacity to cope with it. The proactivity and assertiveness he was trying to generate did not come naturally and they would not respond to being played off, one against another. He would need to support them in learning these new ways of working together. The profiles also showed the key to energizing the group. Their will for the commercial success of the enterprise would be a real source of motivation in meeting the challenges of the future.

The ongoing monitoring of motivation is appropriate for the ongoing planning of training and development. As such it also has a part to play in the planning of the appraisal process. For example, following a series of promotions, the need for power may be largely satisfied and become less of a driving force for an individual; increasing family responsibilities, on the other hand, may increase needs for flexibility and security. We should be trying to pre-empt situations of shifting motivation. It may be too late when the letter of resignation arrives or the local culture has been influenced by disaffection. We have argued the case for ongoing development as part of appraisal. Motivation should be a prime consideration within this process.

For new graduates entering the organization as trainees with a range of career development options, motivational analysis is particularly appropriate. Not only are perspectives on working life open to rapid change in the early part of a career but decisions at this stage can have a critical impact on the level of satisfaction derived and energy spent in the years to follow. Arguably, this process of analysis should begin at the latter stages of education. Recent research by SHL has indicated that more than a third of new graduates in the UK have left their first organization within three years. While this costly turnover may be understandable in terms of the changing and shorter-term nature of work and the need for breadth of experience, we would expect part of the reason to be due to motivational factors of initial mismatch or the poor management of subsequent motivation.

Motivational implications for the organization as a whole

On a world-wide basis there is a growing concern about organizations' capability to retain their top talent. In a survey completed by The Conference Board amongst members of its human resource councils in the USA and Europe, nearly 90 per cent acknowledged difficulties with retention in certain parts of their business and 65 per cent believed their companies needed to improve their strategy. In terms of reasons for unwanted turnover, 'insufficient attention to non-monetary rewards/ recognition' ranked third after issues of uncertainty in the work environment and limited career opportunities. 'Non competitive compensation and benefits' ranked fifth. However, when it came to the action taken to improve retention, monetary compensation was by far the most frequently mentioned option. It suggests a failure to appreciate the nature of job motivation. The survey report makes some useful recommendations to pre-empt the turnover of key talent. These include:

- having a comprehensive system for identifying key players;
- taking a long-term view in the selection of employees;
- promoting the organization internally to generate employee pride in affiliation;
- focus on retention incentives that go beyond compensation;
- developing and refining instruments that provide early warning signals about potential retention problems.

The need to develop a better understanding of work motivation is reinforced in a separate report from The Conference Board based on research by Finck, Timmers and Mennes at Erasmus University,

Rotterdam. The authors report on research which essentially showed that conventional employee satisfaction questionnaires do relatively little to help us understand about employee motivation. From their research they estimate that factors in satisfaction questionnaires only cover about 40–50 per cent of all factors contributing to employee satisfaction. They also note that these questionnaires rarely cover issues such as:

- person and personality-related factors (capacities, competencies, stress and coping behaviour);
- employee recognition, trust and respect towards management;
- work procedures;
- human dynamics (personal evaluation of one's own leadership style, performance appraisal, communication style, decision and responsibility taking, and personal experience of trust, dignity and respect).

The report concludes that organizations should begin to concentrate more on the specifics of motivation, to understand the motivation process better and to learn how problems can be overcome.

In Figure 8.3, we offer a checklist of applications of motivational analysis, all of which are designed to ensure that the organization is going beyond the assessment of ability, personality and experience in order to capitalize on the energy factor. While this chapter has focused on individual motivation, note that there is also a case for monitoring total employee motivation as part of an ongoing measure of corporate climate. This is likely to be based on attitudinal survey work and can provide important signals of an impending downturn in productivity.

In our comments above on motivation, we have tried to be objective and analytical about the process of motivation from an individual perspective. In closing this chapter, we would like to offer our own view of some general prerequisites of a 'well motivated' organization. We see this as most likely to occur where:

- the staff know and understand the mission, objectives and values of the organization;
- the right people are selected for the right roles;
- there is respect for people as individuals throughout the organization;
- there is a commitment to development based on individual understanding and feedback;
- excellent communications are in place;
- there is a large degree of interest in the jobs to be done and pride in the workplace;

Figure 8.3   Management checklist for motivational analysis

Use	*Objective*
● Organizational Climate	Maintain a regular check of the overall level of motivation within the organization. Use this to check key change factors such as a change of CEO, mergers and acquisitions or major downsizing.
● Managerial Aid	Understand the individual patterns of staff motivation with a view to taking the most appropriate action.
● Selection/Promotion	Ensure that motivational energy is maximized in the match of person–job–culture.
● Training and Development	Channelling staff towards areas that suit their motivational profile and finding development methods that suit their motivational preferences.
● Counselling	Pinpointing areas of individual dissension and dissatisfaction. The motivational analysis provides a structure and a basis for depersonalizing issues.
● Organizational Development	Audit motivation in order to restructure, redefine jobs, change basis of reward, shift values and culture.

- rewards in terms of remuneration and recognition are commensurate with output;
- ideas and new ways of working are valued by management;
- team work is valued perhaps in a context of healthy internal competition;
- bosses are seen to understand and value their subordinates.

Summary

Motivation is a critical factor in occupational performance. We are talking here of an individual's source of energy and what directs and sustains it. If organizations are to learn, adapt, change and innovate in order to achieve competitive success, then they need a strong element of dynamism in their workforce. This is held to be particularly true at the top of the organization.

There is an important link between motivation and leadership. Models of transformational leadership concentrate on the leadership characteristics which can encourage followers to work beyond any normal levels of expectation. Relevant characteristics include the importance of being able to read subordinates well and to know how to develop them to best effect. This is similar to Gardner's concept of 'Interpersonal Intelligence' which nowadays has been built into the broader notion of 'Emotional Intelligence'. We are learning to recognize the importance of understanding and managing the more emotionally based aspects of our lives.

In this chapter we recognize the complexity of motivational analysis in the world of work. We describe the eclectic but innovative work of researchers at SHL in building an occupational model of motivation covering 18 separate dimensions. The model sees motivation as an interaction of the personal characteristics of the individual, the nature of the job and the prevailing culture of the organization. It provides managers with a basis for understanding an individual's pattern of motivation. Linked with job and culture analysis, it helps us to answer the key question – 'Will this individual be motivated by this particular job in this particular culture?' It also provides the basis for enhancing motivation in the future or for counselling those with a current problem.

Like personality assessment, motivational analysis can be complex but management cannot afford to ignore it. We simply make better leaders, managers, sellers and the like if we think about and understand those that we are leading, managing or to whom we are selling. This may appear a truism but is nonetheless important. What is more, without motivation, individuals are unlikely to drive a programme of self-development. We also note the important case for monitoring the level of motivation in the organization as a whole. This can provide a means to taking early action against a potential productivity decline.

Note

1. For more detailed summaries refer to 'The Motivation Questionnaire: Manual & User's Guide', Saville & Holdsworth (UK) Ltd.

9

Leadership

Background

There are two distinct approaches to leadership. The first is about observing leadership behaviour so that we can deduce and encourage those actions that are positive in the value-adding process which is at the root of all leaders' endeavours. When optimal, these observable actions will help to get the best from the people at all levels in an organization. Because of this we look at the nature of leadership and the distinction between leadership and management, before looking from the viewpoint of followers. While still in this observation mode, we briefly touch on inspirational and perspirational leadership because both elements must be in evidence.

The second approach deals with the underlying attributes of leaders so that one can do better in identifying, selecting and developing leaders for the future. This is the approach adopted in the second part of this chapter. Leadership is an essential competence for those managers who would be successful in their chosen place of work. This then is at the heart of our central message that 'putting the right people into the right job and encouraging the right development activity will enhance organizational efficiency, productivity and where appropriate, profitability'.

What is leadership?

When a group of managers are asked to rank the most important characteristics of those who are successful in their role, leadership comes either at the top or near the top of the list. This was the case in the comparison of attributes of professional managers, first by the managers themselves, and then by those who are professionals in the field of recruitment and selection. In the survey reported in *Successful Management* (Bain, 1995) leadership was at the top of the list of both groups. Today, most people would see that the quality of leadership is a key requisite for any person in a position of authority, but many remain unclear as to what is really involved. The search for clarity is not really helped by definitions, which tend to define some aspect yet do not give the help that is needed by those aspiring to improve their leadership capability.

A number of organizations that have in place management development programmes have tried to spell out the managerial competencies that they require in their managers. Such a company was Coats Viyella plc which included the following as a description of the competencies required by a good leader:

- has the ability to motivate individuals and teams to reach the agreed business objectives;
- delegates tasks appropriately and effectively;
- inspires a shared vision or a common set of goals;
- provides stability and direction;
- leaves specifics to others;
- constructively challenges the status quo.

Leadership and management

Before looking in more detail at the characteristics of leadership, it is worth looking by way of contrast at the management tasks. Of course management and leadership are not mutually exclusive, and a general manager in almost any setting will need to have both. There are tasks of management that have been identified over time and which are quite specific, usually fact related. It is convenient to group these into five categories:

1. *Planning.* This is the forward thinking that is needed to deal with issues and opportunities, consider the alternatives, and map out the preferred way forward.
2. *Budgeting.* Usually this will be at least an annual event perhaps coupled with regular forecast updates for an agreed time forward. This of course is a largely financial exercise but is closely linked to strategy and the other annual plans, such as marketing or information technology.

3. *Organizing*, by putting in place a formal structure to achieve the results that are envisaged. Individual objectives that are linked to the budget will be set for individuals in the organization.
4. *Creating incentive programmes* that support the central thrusts of the business.
5. *Controlling*, by measuring progress against the right things that depict the health of the business. This will usually come first to mind in many managers who have been brought up in a performance culture.

Now compare this list with the main behavioural components of leadership. These are shown in summary form in Figure 9.1. First is defining the vision which gives the team a common goal. While the input for this will arise from various sources, some internal and some external to the company, the commitment and ownership must be the leader's. The best leaders are capable of thinking the unthinkable and of championing innovations that have not necessarily originated from them. They will have a high curiosity level and will be well informed from their networks of knowledge and their wide reading.

The second requirement of leadership is commitment to success. The leader typically shows energy and drive, and the will to win. The will to win by itself is not enough, for this desire and enthusiasm is for nought unless adequate preparation has taken place.

Third is the need to communicate openly and freely. There is a requirement to share information on goals, any adjustments being taken from the agreed route to achieve these, and any new initiatives that are being pursued. There are many cases of leaders having changed direction, yet not having advised their troops of this, and they may well be marching towards a precipice that the leader had seen and was avoiding.

Fourth is challenging the status quo. The challenge is to have the right environment where the 'not invented here syndrome' is not permitted and where new more productive ways are sought. Once the decision has been made then all in the team are expected to play their part in getting the

---

Figure 9.1   Five dimensions of leadership[1]

- Defining the vision
- Commitment to success
- Communicate freely (sharing goals, insights, and approaches)
- Challenging the status quo
- Develop personal characteristics of leadership (learn the skills)

---

deliverables for the benefit of the organization. This is especially important for young managers to grow and develop who still, today, are turned off too often by the culture that says, 'We don't do things that way around here.'

Finally, there are a number of specific behavioural characteristics frequently highlighted in successful leaders. These include:

- flexibility
- ability to inspire others
- enthusiasm
- ability to build relationships
- ability to inspire trust
- ability to communicate
- ability to delegate
- willingness to experiment
- frankness
- integrity.

Although not covered in this list, there is the prerequisite that the leader must have the intellect and conceptual capacity to handle successfully the scope of his or her job. As the commercial arena becomes both more complex and rapid in change, this broader issue of having the required intellect is becoming increasingly important.

At the start of this chapter we observed that it is not easy to paint a picture of leadership through definition. Rather like a good work of art, you know that it is good when you see it, you can describe the physical characteristics under observation, but this is highly likely to miss the essence of the work. This is also true of leadership, and for this reason it is helpful to draw together a contrasting list of words that distinguish between leadership and management. A good example of these word pictures is found in some material of the specialist consulting firm PCO[2]. This is included as Figure 9.2.

Without managers the visions of leaders become dreams. Leaders need managers to convert vision into realities. For continuous success organizations need both managers and leaders.

Followers' perspective

Reviewing the above list of characteristics of a leader, we are reminded that there is a constituent's view that needs to be considered if the leader

Figure 9.2   Leadership and management in word pictures

Management	Leadership
Not emotional	Passionate visionary
Tell	Ask
Talk	Listen
Expect less	Encourage more
Trust is difficult	Trust is easy
Calming	Enthusiasm
Knows the answers	Open to suggestions
Tells how	Shares why
Directs	Points the way
Has subordinates	Has followers
Sees detail	Sees the overall view
Systems centred	People centred
How and why	What and why
Maintains	Originates
Controls	Inspires
Stands apart	Seeks company
Goals/plans	Identity/values
Doing the job right	Doing the right job
Good soldier	Own person
Eyes on the bottom line	Eyes on the horizon
Aims for security	Enjoys change
Structured	Flexible
Accepts the status quo	Challenges the status quo

(Reproduced with permission of PCO)

is to develop the full potential of the organization that he or she leads. Not a great deal of work has been done on reviewing the characteristics of good leaders, as viewed from the followers' perspective. Common sense tells us that those who follow will do so more readily and more enthusiastically if they have loyalty and a clear sense of direction. Loyalty cannot be commanded; it must be earned, and can only be retained by continually building on the bond of trust between leader and follower.

In a study by Kouzes and Posner conducted amongst 15 000 people from around the world, which focused on those at the receiving end of leadership, they found that the ten most used words of how the followers felt when led by a good leader were:

1. valued
2. motivated
3. enthusiastic
4. challenged
5. inspired
6. capable
7. supported
8. powerful
9. respected
10. proud.

In order to maintain the high level of motivation that is a characteristic of a well-led organization, the thinking leader is constantly helping the constituents to top up their skill base with new experiences and new formal learning. They need to feel involved, believe in the goals and their ability to deliver them. The more confident the organization, the greater their ability to achieve and to see and deliver the really big step change.

Inspirational and perspirational leadership

A number of works on leadership refer to different types as charismatic and technocratic leadership. The former is the visionary and inspirational, while the latter tends to deal with the technical basis of achievement. Although this is a valid division, the trade-off is that people have a preconceived notion of charismatic leadership. This will usually evolve around a high profile individual who has achieved prominence in his or her chosen field. It is sometimes synonymous with heroic leadership, where the emphasis is on the individual and his or her achievements, rather than those of the team. This approach may also suggest that leadership is something that one is born with and is only applicable in really high profile roles occupied by very prominent people. Our experience is contrary to this. We see ample evidence that leadership skills can be learned, improved and mastered, provided there is the time and resource applied to this objective.

It is largely for this reason that we have opted for the more descriptive approach of inspirational and perspirational leadership. To gain a greater understanding of these we list below some of the key features of both.

Inspirational leadership

1. The leader is seen around the company and is very visible. He or she

uses opportunities through questions and answers and statements to reinforce values, the culture and the objectives.

2. The leader is the role model for other leaders in the organization, is transparent in decision making and uses symbolic behaviour.
3. The leader is the living ethical standard, aware that his or her actions are always under scrutiny.
4. The leader is agent provocateur, a non-conformist and an agent for change.
5. Every leader has apostles who are equally energized and committed to the same cause. The leader needs feedback.
6. The leader recognizes the importance of excellent internal and external communication that is designed for the specific audience.
7. The leader is able to fight bureaucracy without destroying essential control.

Perspirational leadership

This is equally as important as inspirational leadership, if we want action. The perspirational aspect is the practical steps that must be put in place to deliver the vision, or else there will be a psyched-up organization without the ability to deliver. Standards of achievement are the currency of the vision. Tools are needed to achieve this and will include:

1. clarity of objectives and organizational clarity;
2. reward systems that are aligned with the goals;
3. compatibility of resource allocation and deployment;
4. controls that will enable the business to be measured correctly against suitable and predetermined goals.

Successful leadership in practice

Successful leaders do not just lead – they also need to manage. They discern the difference between the twin aspects of their role. They are not solely great inspiring charismatic people, but link their vision to the practical, mundane tools of achievement. The leader achieves success through team building, using a spirit of openness, and seeking out feedback from the followers. Much time will of necessity be spent in communication within and outside of the organization. A generous allocation of time will be committed to the development of the members of the organization, and additionally the leader will be aware of the constant need to improve his or her own capability and performance. The style of leadership will reflect the individual's own aptitudes and strengths, and will not require a major transformation to a 'new personality' that would be unrecognized by the people being led. The leader's style may be modified to lead from individual strengths and to ameliorate any obvious negatives or weaknesses.

The cognitive approach

So far in our examination of leadership, we have drawn heavily on the experiences of leaders in practice, and on the tenets of what is judged to be best practice. Little attention has been paid to trying to understand the minds of the great leaders to try to establish if there are generic lessons of practical application for leaders. Most of the work that has been completed to date in this area has been in the category of interesting reading, but with no universally applicable message. In our experience there are numerous individual lessons, many insights, but perhaps as expected, no panacea of a role model for the aspiring leader. Much of the published work that attempts to find the answer to lessons from great minds is neither deep enough nor rigorous enough to draw conclusions.

However, one of the best studies of recent times is the work of Howard Gardner, published in his book with Emma Larkin, *Leading Minds*. The author has taken a cognitive approach by studying the mountain of material available, and examining the minds of 11 great leaders from very diverse areas and backgrounds. The subjects of his study are diverse and range from Pope John XXIII to Robert Oppenheimer, Margaret Thatcher to Martin Luther King, and Mahatma Gandhi to Jean Monnet. With 11 subjects one cannot claim quantitative significance, but the richness of the work is its value!

Gardner claims that 'our understanding of the nature and processes of leadership is most likely to be enhanced as we come to understand better the arena in which leadership necessarily occurs – namely the human mind'. Gardner, reflecting on the lessons from the past and applying this to the future, saw six constants of leadership, which are summarized below:

1. The story. A leader must have a central story or message. The evidence from the leaders in his sample was that most of those messages were inclusive of the participants, in that they could see the implications for themselves as constituents.

2. The audience. No matter how great or important the message it will be stillborn if the audience is not ready to hear it.

3. The organization. There is a limit to what one leader can do on his or her own. Leadership will be much more effective in an organization that helps promulgate and reinforce the message.

4. The embodiment. There must be a form of embodiment of the central message in the actions of the leader and those that have been enlisted to support. This congruity of actions and words is well recognized in business and political circles, and phrases such as 'walking the talk' have been coined to emphasize this very point.

5. Direct and indirect leadership. There are two types, and leaders may mix the two approaches or operate in mainly one of these. Gardner observed that Churchill exerted his influence mainly in a direct way through the stories or messages that he communicated directly to his audience. On the other hand, Einstein used the indirect way, through the ideas that he developed and the ways that these ideas were communicated to his audience through, for example, treatises.

6. Expertise. In almost every domain there is a body of necessary technical knowledge that must be absorbed if credibility is to be won and maintained. This highlights the need for all leaders, of whatever type, to spend the time that is needed in staying up to date and maintaining their power base of knowledge.

There is, especially in the case of a field of expert knowledge, a great need for communication, as this body of knowledge needs to be communicated in practical, non-specialist terms to the general audience. As we have seen earlier in this chapter, the need to communicate effectively is a very necessary trait of the effective leader.

In the examination of the guidelines for effective leadership, Gardner concludes with three lessons that are relevant for the training of leaders and for the successful prosecution of their enterprises. We have summarized these as follows:

1. Appreciate the enduring features of leadership. The essential point here is that to be effective a leader must construct a clear story, and communicate this clearly to a well-prepared and motivated audience. The message needs to be embodied in actions, in the values and the very culture of the organization. The leader needs to find the time needed to build his or her own skills, as well as those of the team to maintain effectiveness. Leadership is a state that must be renewed, and this includes the renewal of relevant technical knowledge. These

considerations should be fully taken into account in the training of leaders and the enhancement of the skills of existing leaders.

2. Anticipate, and deal with new trends. This is fully compatible with our experience too and, throughout this book, there is a strong message 'to look outward' and to scan the environment for trends that will have an impact on the industry or the business where the manager is employed. Trends that will affect leadership today include the need to operate in a fast changing, often unstable world, where communication is instant even to the so-called under-developed economies. Most leaders will need to take a global view, as issues increasingly transcend national boundaries. This brings with it the need of the modern leader to be aware of, and empathetic to, cultural diversity. This is beyond 'learning a second language', and encapsulates an understanding of the essence of different ethnic groups and national characteristics.

3. Encourage recognition of the problems, paradoxes, and possibilities of leadership. We can only enhance and add to the stock of leaders if we are able to communicate the widespread appreciation of the central issues that surround effective leadership. Society must have a better understanding of this, and be able to see why quality leadership is important and what is needed to make leaders more effective. Gardner observes, 'society remains ignorant about leadership'. Even if we believe this to be an over-statement, there remains much work to be done to educate society as a whole on leadership, its value to society, and the expectations that it is reasonable to have of good leaders.

There are many paradoxes and issues which require judgements and there is no single answer. These might include the need for a significant technical knowledge on a subject, yet also the need to communicate simply. There are many others, which all lend weight to the fact that a leader must be capable of being effective in ambiguity, and in the absence of certainty. There is usually no single answer and optimization is a skill that is very much needed.

Identifying and developing leadership potential

The implication of our focus on leadership behaviour is that we believe that leadership skills can be learned and developed. However, we also hold that some individuals have a greater aptitude than others. If we can identify leadership potential, then we can focus attention on developing it, at an early stage, to the benefit of the organization.

A particular model that has focused on the underlying personal attributes of leaders is that of 'Transformational Leadership'. This asserts that true leaders can encourage subordinates to perform beyond normal levels of expectation by shifting their priorities from self-interest to the good of the group or organization. The model proposes four key attributes of the Transformational Leader – charisma, intellectual stimulation, individual consideration and inspirational motivation. This model reflects many of the characteristics covered above and we have referred to it in Chapter 8 on the specific issue of motivation analysis.

There is a danger here of trying to write a long specification of desirable personal attributes to cope with the many facets of leadership behaviour. We need to find the essential underlying attributes and we need a manageable number or the process of measurement will become a barrier in its own right. In effect, the Transformational model is saying that if an individual is intellectually bright, has a heightened awareness of people and how to develop them, exudes a certain charisma and has the ability to inspire motivation in others – then he or she has the potential to be a strong and effective leader. The charisma attribute is particularly relevant to our differentiation of 'inspirational' as opposed to 'perspirational' leadership.

When it comes to measurement for assessment, we would break these attributes down into a set of underlying traits of ability and personality. Figure 9.3 uses the ability and personality models of Chapter 7.

In terms of assessment, the abilities and traits shown in the figure can be measured by tests and questionnaires. This should then be combined with behavioural assessment through simulation exercises of the kind used in development centres. In particular, group- or committee-based exercises offer the potential to watch the individual in interaction with others. Leadership action can be observed and the inclination of others to follow can be noted. In these exercises, there are options to assign leadership roles or to leave them unassigned to see who emerges to take the lead. However, we do have two strong preferences. First, the exercises should be occupationally relevant, for example budgeting issues or marketing strategy, in the interest of demonstrating the justifiability of any related career decisions. Second, they should be intellectually demanding so that effective leadership requires a good grasp in a short time of some quite complex information inputs – so that the group is not dominated by an individual who offers only a strong assertiveness.

In Chapter 5 we argued the case for running developing centres at three career levels – new graduates, young managers and senior managers. It is appropriate to look at the leadership competency at all three levels but the

Figure 9.3 Core ability and personality traits of leadership

Leadership attribute	Relevant ability/Personality traits*
Intellectual stimulation	The ability to reason with complex verbal and numerical information. The ability to think laterally and see new perspectives.
Individual consideration	This is dependent on the ability to read people well. Relevant personality traits include: • 'Behavioural' orientation • Empathy traits of 'Caring' and 'Democratic'
Charisma	This is a complex concept but at its heart lies self-confidence and an apparent conviction that a chosen course of action is right. Relevant traits include: • 'Social confidence' • Low 'Worrying' • 'Tough minded'
Inspirational motivation	This links with charisma and central components are an extraordinary determination and generally high levels of activity and energy. Personality traits would include: • 'Achieving' • 'Controlling' • 'Vigorous'

*See Chapter 7 for trait definitions

focus early on would be more towards underlying potential, while at senior management level there would be more focus on current actual behaviour and performance. At this latter level, the career-based interview would be an important development-centre component of the leadership judgement.

Where potential is identified amongst younger and trainee managers, the development programme should be designed to ensure a good all-round level of knowledge and competencies to lead within that particular organization. This clearly ties in with the development of management competencies covered earlier in this book. It also requires a culture to be created that is positive towards the development of leadership. This might include the preparedness to devolve responsibility, tolerance of errors in the interest of encouraging new leads, creating time to give feedback and advice, and putting an emphasis on continuous learning and innovation.

Summary

Any book that is examining the benefit from the optimal use of its people resource must have a focus on leadership. In this chapter we have taken two approaches. First, we have tried to describe how leaders behave – what they do and how they think. Second, we have considered the underlying attributes of leadership in the interest of identifying potential. There is a good deal of research that indicates that leadership is near the top of the list of important characteristics found in the best, most successful organizations. This is different from management as we have shown in this chapter, yet both are important. We have highlighted the traits most often found in successful leaders, and looked at the words that best described good leaders, as seen through the eyes of the followers.

There are two different aspects of leadership that we have highlighted. The first is the charismatic, which we have termed as 'inspirational'. This is the visionary, motivating, uplifting part, and needs to be coupled with the 'perspirational' which sets out the processes for delivery. Both are important if we want the leadership to lift people to higher levels than they thought possible. While some regard the perspirational as more mundane, we are clear that the practical steps must be put in place to deliver the vision.

We have drawn attention to the importance of leadership to the effectiveness of the organization. It starts at the top, but must permeate the whole organization. Given this importance, there is a big prize if the organization can identify and develop leadership potential.

We believe that there are certain attributes which can predispose an individual towards an effective leadership role. These include an intellectual capability, the ability to read people well, strong self-confidence, an achievement drive and a high level of energy. We have proposed that these attributes can be assessed through the analysis of ability and personality coupled with the use of simulation exercises.

Notes

1. With acknowledgement to Harry White Bancorp NZ.
2. Abbreviation of People Change Organization.

10 Further Applications – Creativity, Entrepreneurship, Stress and Communication

It is not enough simply to improve our understanding of the people who work with and for us. Management has to be able to **apply** its improved knowledge in areas that are relevant to the enhancement of productivity and the well-being of the staff involved. We have dealt with applications such as selection, placement, competency development and leadership. The purpose of this chapter is to extend our view on management applications into the areas of creativity, entrepreneurship, stress and communication.

Creativity – an elusive resource

Creativity in the corporate world is a prize that most firms would seek. Indeed, one would observe that this is true of any organization, commercial or not-for-profit. Creativity is needed in the strategy process if the organization is to achieve a sustainable competitive advantage. It not only requires that organizations examine their internal processes and procedures in order that they can drop those activities that do not add value, but it also requires managers to look outwards. However, the paradox is that, in practice, managers confess to spending too much time on fire-fighting or dealing with short-term issues and insufficient time on the longer term, or the wider environment.

Yet creativity is elusive. We can define it and observe it in individuals, but when we turn to organizations to try to find a model that is more conducive to creativity, we are disappointed. While there is some evidence that loose organizations, where freedom of the individual is paramount, may produce superior creativity, there is no clear evidence that this is so; at least not in the sense of converting that creativity into commercial benefit. In attempts to provide pockets of innovation and creativity in

161

larger organizations, a number have followed the American example of creating free-standing 'skunk works' where managers can pursue activities they believe in. Even in these cases, ideas are taken and tested for commerciality within the organization, before they become projects seen as good in their own right.

The big spenders like the pharmaceutical companies have a disciplined framework set in commercial reality that becomes the template against which projects are supported or aborted. Arthur D Little, the management consultants, conducted a study of significant breakthrough in the world-wide commercial arena to see if there were any lessons to be learned. Their findings can be summarized as follows:

- They found no corporate culture that facilitates breakthroughs more than any other.
- Creativity exists in almost all organizations and is more prevalent than first thought.
- Breakthroughs resulted from creativity that made incremental product improvements, as well as more revolutionary thinking.
- Emotion is a key element in every breakthrough. The individual attached to the innovation needs to feel totally committed, and part of the notion he or she is pursuing.

It is clear then that the organization that wishes to grow, that wishes to reach its full potential over the long term, needs to engender a spirit of creativity amongst its people. It needs to get its managers to be aware of the wider environment in which they operate so that they can see the opportunities, avoid the worst of the threats and continue to develop. One of the greatest inhibitors to this may well be the organization's current success. There is much evidence that, over time, nothing fails like success because there is no real imperative for change. 'Why fix the wheel when it isn't broken' seems to be the approach. Yet many good, well-executed strategies are taken that step too far, and the companies decline. Most management groups spend the great proportion of their time trying to squeeze more out of the existing business model, perfecting and squeezing. Richard Pascale, in his book *Managing on the Edge*, suggests that managers spend 99 per cent of their time on this, and the remainder of their time searching for new ways to compete, new ways to add value and totally new approaches to competitive challenge.

If this mould is to be broken, the organization needs to have a culture that encourages the wider view, that promotes curiosity in its managers and ensures that they are widely aware. Challenging the status quo needs to be encouraged, and destroying the red tape but without losing essential controls should be a highly valued activity. Yet this is not enough. We also need within the team of players those people who have the essential elements of creativity as a part of their preferred style, and as an important element in their string of competencies.

Identifying creative potential

The above thoughts raise the question as to how we can identify creative thinking potential within new or existing staff. This is yet another difficult question because while organizations may recognize the need for creative thinking they are not precise when it comes to its definition. They can hardly be blamed. Researchers in the field are still striving to clarify and explain the cognitive process of creative thinking. It has been clear for some time that measures of creativity do not correlate highly with other measures of intelligence. It has also been clear that there are various ways of assessing different components of creativity and that they do not correlate highly with each other. In talking above of the need to encourage creativity in organizations we might reflect on the view of some researchers that creative intuition is enhanced by an adequate period of incubation. In other words, there is a need for ideas to develop – perhaps at a sub-conscious level – in a context of low stress and pressure, before the creative insight occurs. Many notable breakthroughs in science and the arts are reported to have occurred in such a way and yet it is counter to most organizations' cultures to allow time and space for the incubation of ideas.

In our experience of trying to assess for creative thinking potential we have taken a limited view of the concept. We have been guided principally by Guilford's distinction between 'convergent thinking' which involves logical thinking, towards 'one right answer', and 'divergent thinking' in which a lateral process of searching around is undertaken and in which 'a number of answers will do'. In occupational studies therefore, we have tended to define creative thinking competencies in terms of a potential to think laterally; to be unconstrained in approaching problems; to have the confidence to look at issues from a new perspective; and to be highly productive in generating new ideas.

This brings us to the method of assessment and we have in the past opted for a dual approach. We have looked at creativity as an ability to be measured by some kind of structured test and as a personality trait reflecting an underlying predisposition to think divergently. In short, we have tried to find people who fundamentally enjoy the process of lateral thinking and who, in a controlled assessment, show that they can do it.

Conventional assessment and development centres have not found it easy to measure creative potential as an area of competency. If it occurs within a normal management simulation exercise, then it can be assessed and scored. The problem occurs if creativity is not observed in that pressured situation. Does it mean that the individual is not creative or that a creative thinking potential was not seen in that situation? For this reason we have tended to favour exercises with work-relevant content in which creative thinking is the goal. SHL's Test of Productive Thinking is an example of such an approach and is based on Guilford's attempt to break down creative thinking into various constituent parts.

The SHL Test of Productive Thinking presents candidates with a series of occupational scenarios and in each case the individual is required to produce as many explanations or solutions as he or she can within a defined period of time. The exercise is scored against relevant norm groups in terms of the fluency, dimensionality and originality of the answers. 'Fluency' is based on Guilford's 'ideational fluency' and is the total number of appropriate answers. 'Dimensionality' is Guilford's concept of 'spontaneous flexibility' and reflects the individual's ability to jump from one category of response to another. 'Originality' reflects the degree of unusualness in the answers based on a statistical evaluation of the frequency of occurrence of each category of response. The test is carefully named as a test of 'productive thinking' and appears able to differentiate those who can think quickly along a number of different avenues of thought in reviewing a problem. We believe that its occupational relevance gives it an edge over the more conventional tests of creativity such as thinking of uses for a cup or a brick.

The personality measurement route to assessing for creativity requires the identification of traits that are related to creative thinking. Validation work carried out at SHL with its Occupational Personality Questionnaire has given good support to the following three traits as relevant to rated performance in thinking creatively:

- 'Independent' – having strong views; being prepared to speak up and take a position in an argument.
- 'Innovative' – enjoys the process of generating ideas; likes to show ingenuity and think up solutions.
- 'Not Traditional' – less conventional, prefers radical, less orthodox thinking.

Other studies using Cattell's 16PF questionnaire have also shown that less rule-bound (Scale G) and more radical thinking (Scale Q1) individuals have met occupational performance criteria of creative success. While there is more research to be done in this area, we would hypothesize that energy and low anxiety may also turn out to be relevant personality-related attributes. They should facilitate perseverance in the face of difficult problems and encourage less conventional and constrained thinking.

We believe it is possible for competency in creative thinking to be developed. At one extreme this can be an issue of specific training in which individuals are taught to break down constraints in their thinking and are encouraged to use devices to keep an open mind and take a lateral view. Even more important is the point referred to at the start of this chapter. That is, the need to create a culture that positively encourages creative thinking. It is a culture that creates the resources, space and time for original thinking to occur. It is one that encourages so-called 'out of the box' thinking. It will also encourage experimentation and tolerate failures in the interest of learning and making the next step significantly better. It is a culture that is ready to break assumptions and supports new perspectives in the interest of finding a competitive edge.

Science has advanced on the basis of a hypothetico-deductive approach. Hypotheses are put forward – that is the creative bit – and then they are tested. Organizations do not need all their people to be creatively inclined. But someone has to be thinking that way and the culture has to encourage them. We believe we have the means to identify those with creative potential with a reasonable degree of reliability and validity. The rest is up to those leading the organization.

Entrepreneurship – the management paradox

We live in an age where global competitiveness is set to increase. We can expect to see top management use a repertoire of devices including mergers, acquisitions and alliances as well as restructuring and resizing with greater use of technological advances in order to grow and maximize the generation of profit. Alongside this mix of options lies the role of the entrepreneur who will be able to see and develop new opportunities to the commercial advantage of his or her organization.

We have put the focus on entrepreneurship in this chapter because of the challenge it poses from a human resource management perspective. This challenge derives from the fact that the characteristics of the entrepreneur do not sit comfortably with the requirements of many organizations for management to be structured, systematized and rule-bound. The question is how this paradox can be reconciled.

Our own experience of successful entrepreneurs would suggest the following four components of entrepreneurship:

- **Commercial Orientation** – a strong sense of profit/loss and cash generation that provides a clear context for operational decision making;
- **Vision** – derived from a capability to think laterally to identify trends and to see large new opportunities;
- **Sense of Purpose** – a goal orientation; a clear motivation towards achieving results;
- **Need for Control** – derived from an independence of mind and a requirement to be able to move quickly in a direction of one's own choice.

An analysis of the UK's top entrepreneurs (as defined by their achieved net worth) tends to suggest that they are not high educational attainers and we would speculate that the potential for logical analytical reasoning with complex information is not a key discriminator of their common strength. However, personality is another matter and although our sample size is admittedly small, we have seen some common ground in terms of entrepreneurs being:

- assertive
- independent minded
- innovative
- relatively unstructured in terms of planning and detail
- achievement driven.

It is interesting to reflect on how these characteristics might manifest themselves in a young employee at an early stage of career progression. They may well not fit neatly into a school leaver or graduate recruitment profile – particularly for larger organizations. Later on in life, there is a good chance that they will have worked for themselves or built their own businesses. A potential danger occurs when such an individual tries to fit and is constrained by a large and systematized organizational culture.

Take the case of one successful entrepreneur in the leisure industry who was bought out by a major organization in the same field but was retained to run the business post-acquisition. In this well-publicized case, there was a clash of entrepreneur and prevailing culture. The individual felt constrained by the bureaucracy and the need to comply with internal systems. In particular, the freedom to make decisions was limited and the process perceived to be too slow. After a relatively short and difficult period, the relationship ended.

This is not to say that there is no room in a major corporation for a big entrepreneurial player but it makes the point that the relationship needs to be thought through most carefully. For the entrepreneur to remain motivated, there will need to be scope for independence of action, for tolerance of mistakes, for a minimum of systematized bureaucracy. This is not to say that the organization should abandon standards or conformance requirements. Limits will need to be set and agreed within which the entrepreneur can operate and the structure and discipline will need to come from others within a supporting team. In the final analysis the true entrepreneur will certainly be results focused and will put in a great deal of energy to achieve success.

It is yet another of the paradoxes of human resource management that people who tend to deliver the best results are often not the easiest of people with whom to deal. Their focus is frequently towards the task or the goal for which they strive and creating comfortable working relationships may not be top of their agenda. The danger lies in the failure to manage this discomfort while the organization is manifestly benefiting from the achievement of results.

Entrepreneurship as a competency

Another way of looking at entrepreneurship is to treat it as a continuum – a competency variable on which some individuals score higher than others. From the organization's point of view, the objective is not to identify top-flight entrepreneurs, but rather to find those individuals who can bring a relative degree of entrepreneurship to the normal process of management and, in particular, in the marketing area. In this respect, an 'entrepreneurial' competency may have a definition along the following lines:

> **Entrepreneurial** – maintains a commercial orientation with a clear awareness of profit/loss and cash generation; thinks laterally and identifies new opportunities; has the confidence to define and propose a new line of action with commercial benefit; has the achievement drive to push for success.

As part of an SHL major survey of personality within the UK, respondents were asked to rate themselves as suited or not to entrepreneurial activities. Those suited to entrepreneurial activities were different in personality terms in a good number of respects from the population at large but the main differences were in line with the picture drawn above. The self-rated entrepreneurs were:

- more assertive (persuasive, controlling and independent)
- more change orientated
- more innovative
- more achievement driven.

In reporting the survey, SHL compared the self-rated entrepreneurs with those who rated themselves as good managers of others. SHL found that compared to those suited to management, entrepreneurs consider themselves to be less modest and less controlling (although more controlling than the majority of the UK population), more artistic, less traditional and less concerned with detail. They are even more conceptual, forward thinking and achieving than the 'good managers', suggesting a stronger future vision in potential entrepreneurs as opposed to managers.

In a separate study of management competence at Lucas Aerospace, one of the competencies measured was labelled 'Entrepreneurial'. The definition was given to Dr Meredith Belbin (designer of the Belbin Team Type model) who hypothesized that the best predicting team types would be 'Shaper' (the task leader who brings competitive drive to the task; the person who makes things happen but may be thought abrasive) and 'Resource Investigator' (the sales person, diplomat, resource seeker; good at improvising and with many external contacts; may be easily diverted from the task at hand). The analysis showed that, as hypothesized, both these team types correlated significantly with the competency ratings. Interestingly, 'Plant' was seen as a less relevant team type: perhaps a function of it being a rather pure creative thinking role.

In yet another UK study (UMIST/SHL, 1995), the management competency 'Commercial' was correlated with personality dimensions from the OPQ®. 'Commercial' was defined as 'understands and applies commercial and financial principles; views issues in terms of costs, profits, markets and added value'. Four dimensions were pre-hypothesized as likely to correlate with 'Commercial'. These were 'Achieving', 'Persuasive', 'Competitive' and 'Innovative'. In the data analysis, all four were found to correlate significantly.

There is no self-evident requirement for organizations to load themselves with entrepreneurial resource staff and as we have seen, there is plenty of associated risk that such people may not remain motivated. However, if the organization chooses to develop an entrepreneurial culture and wishes to ensure that an element of its management is orientated this way, then we are now in quite a strong position to write a specification and to measure the appropriate individual attributes. The organization will need to be aware of the motivational aspects and to ensure that its systems have an appropriate level of flexibility to take benefit from the entrepreneurs' flair and energy.

It is not unusual these days to hear the cri-de-coeur that managers are afraid of making mistakes and, at times of downsizing, are more concerned to play it safe and protect their positions. If organizations are to win in the more competitive world markets, perhaps it is time to ease our tolerance of non-conformist thinking and encourage the entrepreneurial element.

Stress – a costly problem

The underlying theme of this book is the enhancement of productivity and this would not be complete without a consideration of the organizational impact of stress-related problems and how these can be overcome. Recent estimates put the annual cost of stress-related illness in the USA alone at tens of billions of dollars with more than half being the cost of absenteeism and lost productivity. Charlesworth (1996) has a UK estimate of 270 000 people per day taking time off as a result of work-related stress. The cumulative cost is put at around £7 billion annually. Terry Beehr in his book *Psychological Stress in the Workplace* makes the point that it is hard to cost the effect of stress in the workplace. This is partly because of the differing definitions of occupational stress and when a definition is agreed there is no clear research to allow accurate estimates. There remains a general consensus that it is a costly problem.

The changing economic and commercial context within which jobs exist is frequently reported and well understood at a macro level. There is an ever-increasing emphasis on global competitiveness leading to a drive to achieve more and better at less cost. We have seen downsizing, delayering and the introduction of new work practices involving new and more complex technology as well as an increase in more isolated home-working. We are continuing to see a growing demand for accountability at all levels of the organization and particularly at the top. The overriding theme is 'change' and change can be uncomfortable particularly when it is towards leaner structures with less time and resource to support the consequent stress on people. Clare Huffington has referred to this effect as feeling 'psychologically naked' with people being thrown 'onto their own resources with no-one telling them what to do, how to do it or protecting them from the outside world'.

This is yet another area which is not easy for the manager to understand and yet we should be able to give some guidance as to how stress-related problems can be managed within normal working environments. The danger lies in closing one's eyes to the potential of stress to create problems somewhere within our area of management responsibility. In cases of stress, the management solution may well require some specialist input but the solution is extremely likely to require action from the organization as well as the individual affected.

The management of stress

SHL – through Dr Sue Henley – has worked on the development of a practical approach to the management of stress which can be more widely applied by managers and human resource professionals, albeit on the basis of some thorough preliminary training. The SHL approach – see Figure 10.1 – emphasizes the importance of personality as a mediating mechanism between the causes of stress and the optimum coping mechanisms. The complexity of the total process is implicit in the model. There are multiple causes of stress and a wide range of coping mechanisms. In between lies the individual's persona which we have already seen to be multi-faceted in its own right. Even with identical causes of stress, no two individuals are likely to utilize the same coping mechanisms to reduce or remove its impact.

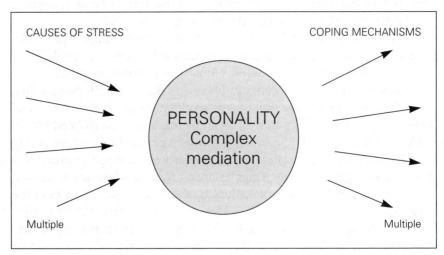

Figure 10.1 Model for stress management

The analytical process is all-important. For example, one approach to the treatment of alcoholism may be abstention but this can be completely overwhelming to a sufferer. For many, a better approach is to break the problem down into its component parts and create a treatment that is specific but gradual and manageable. The same is true with stress-related and other aspects of management development. The objective is to break any issues down into manageable chunks, each one specific to a development goal.

There is good evidence from SHL that managers can take effective steps to resolve stress-related problems of their own and of their staff. The belief is that most individuals will find the capacity to cope if they are pointed in the right direction and given support. Management in general has a twofold role. It needs to understand the stress-inducing context and take whatever action it can to reduce its impact. It also needs to understand more about individual coping mechanisms – probably with specialist help – so that it can take action to support an individual who is suffering from stress.

In one case dealt with by SHL, a divisional managing director had experienced coronary symptoms and suspected a stress-related cause. The individual had successfully built up the division from scratch but was under increasing 'group' pressure to expand further and under economic pressure to downsize to be cost effective. The individual was socially charming. He had a highly 'caring' personality and a preference for a flexible style of management. The analysis was complex but in brief it reinforced the need for the individual to define strategic goals; to create more structure (he had no job description!); to develop a thicker skin; and to take more time out to relax. The point is that the solutions were consistent with the individual's personality. More importantly, the analysis of the problem helped him to realize that the situation was manageable. The outcome for him was positive.

In another case a systems director was suffering symptoms of stress but was not inclined to face these as a stress issue. The problem was analyzed within the context of a more conventional and acceptable management development session. The individual in this case was highly status conscious. He set exacting standards for himself and others. In personality terms, he had maximum scores on being critical and emotionally controlled. He could destroy his staff's work without a flicker of emotion. For him the issue was his difficulty in creating positive interpersonal relationships and his own weak interpersonal skills. Again, the analysis focused the problem for the individual and created the incentive to find a solution through various brainstorming devices.

The People Advantage

The SHL model developed by Dr Henley recognizes the criticality of the individual's personality in planning stress management. The starting point is personality analysis which is used to create a profile of likely stressors. A model has been developed of 24 relatively common work stressors and Figure 10.2 shows a sample stressor profile based on this model. The profile provides the analytical structure for an objective discussion of the causes of the stress and key stressors can be developed and expanded. The underlying personality profile is then used again to identify coping mechanisms which would be particularly appropriate to the individual's personal style and characteristics. The total process makes it relatively easy to discuss and explore stress-related factors without making it seem like an unmentionable affliction.

The old adage that prevention is better than cure applies particularly to the management of stress. Organizations need to be aware of the

	Probability of being stressful*									
	Low 1	2	3	4	5	6	7	8	High 9	10
Managing others		●								
Making 'tough' decisions			●							
Selling/negotiating				●						
Delivering 'bad news'				●						
Dealing with the public					●					
Bureaucratic structures							●			
Lack of power									●	
Lack of status						●				
Lack of autonomy								●		
Lack of consultation					●					
Lack of clear objectives									●	
Poor promotion prospects								●		
Thwarted ambition								●		
Working in isolation		●								
Lack of social support			●							
Interpersonal conflict		●								
Team work									●	
Change and uncertainty				●						
'Reactive' environments					●					
Complex problem solving						●				
Few intellectual demands					●					
Repetitive routine work									●	
No creative opportunity								●		
Severe time constraints								●		

*Based on personality (OPQ®) analysis
© SHL Group plc 1999 – reproduced with permission
SOURCE: SHL Expert System Report

Figure 10.2 Sample profile of potential work stressors

development of potential stressors where the cost may not be immediately apparent but could hit hard in the future. It is a matter of maintaining a high level of awareness and monitoring on an ongoing basis how people are feeling about their working environment and their particular goals and objectives. Regular staff attitude surveys have an important role to play here. Structured quantitative surveys enable benchmarks to be set and trends in attitudes to be followed over time. However, structured surveys are not so good for in-depth analysis and there is a good case for more qualitative, exploratory interviews carried out on a one-to-one basis or with small groups. Topics for such quantitative and qualitative survey work might include:

- The effect of change and uncertainty
- Management style/credibility
- Impact of technology
- Pressures of work – supervision, teams, variety, autonomy, and so on
- Industry/sector prospects
- Opportunity to discuss personal issues
- Sports/leisure options
- Pay and conditions
- Prevailing culture
- Potential to influence management
- Potential for self-development
- Personal sense of well-being

As the above topic list would suggest, organizations whose employees feel satisfied and personally fulfilled in their jobs are not simply those that manage stress well. They are the organizations that understand the criticality of people and take them into account in all aspects of strategic and operational planning.

A further consideration in terms of taking action to prevent the effects of stress is whether it is possible to identify individuals who have a fundamental tendency to be stress prone. In a major survey of the personality of the UK adult population (SHL UK, 1997), SHL asked respondents about their proneness to stress. About one in three UK adults claimed that stress and personal problems significantly affect the tasks they perform. SHL's personality analysis concluded that 'those affected are less assertive, slightly less extroverted, less happy with practical or numerical problem solving and are more reserved about change and variety. They are also less structured, more tense and emotionally sensitive. Optimism is low, with lower participation in activities requiring physical exercise. Despite the fact that they are affected by stress and personal problems, their emotional control is not significantly reduced, suggesting that their work colleagues may not always be aware of their problems.'

Of all the above personality characteristics, the most substantial individual predictor by far was the **ongoing** tension that makes it difficult for individuals to wind down and relax. This is sometimes referred to as 'Trait Anxiety' and is differentiated from the shorter-term 'State Anxiety' which may cause someone to become anxious and worked up over a specific event or issue but dissipates afterwards. The evidence would suggest that self-assessed characteristics and, in particular, Trait Anxiety can be used as a warning signal of a proneness to stress.

Finally, it should be remembered that anxiety can also have a beneficial effect on work performance in that it is a source of energy in its own right. As a general observation, people who worry about things tend to get things done. The issue is to be able to recognize when anxiety is getting out of hand or becoming 'dysfunctional' so that appropriate action can be taken as we have indicated above. This is not an easy matter and some specialist medical advice may well be necessary. Broadly speaking, there are three main categories of indicator. 'Cognitive' indicators cover elements such as faulty memory, tunnel vision, concentration problems or unprecedented errors of judgement. The 'behavioural' indicators focus on changes in normal behaviour patterns such as feeling more anxious, depressed or irritable. The 'physical' indicators include symptoms such as headaches, digestive problems and other unusual symptoms with no physical cause. The line between positive and negative impact anxiety can be a fine one and we reiterate the need for specialist guidance.

The need for skill in communication

Since the earliest moments in one's career, whether this be in business, the public sector, or in other not-for-profit areas, there has been instilled in us the importance of communication. Those attending a business school know that the need to communicate in the written and spoken word is a critical factor in determining their grades. There seems little opposition to the notion that communicating is a key activity and that proficiency with this skill will enhance one's performance. Incidentally, even in home or social life this observation holds true. Given such universal recognition of this competency, it is surprising in our view that more attention is not given to improving performance in this key area. Formal training in communicating at universities or business schools is in our experience lacking or inadequate, and the same is largely true for those employed in the private and public sectors.

In the survey of successful managers that has been previously referred to, we found that the managers themselves, and the human resource and search firm professionals, saw communication as a key competence for future managers. Indeed both of these groups put the ability to communicate within the top three competencies required for success in the new millennium. This is not just a task for top managers, or those in public relations or marketing; the need to have this ability is important for the whole organization.

There is a body of opinion that believes that one is born with the ability to communicate and in support of this contention will point to the extrovert type that seems to find this an easy task. While there may be some correlation between an individual's style and the ability to communicate orally, the skills are ones that can and must be learned, in order to improve their influence and effectiveness.

Critical role in management

Within any organization the specific needs will determine the amount of time that especially senior management will need to devote to communicating. For example, the needs of a stable organization on a path of 'steady state' will have a lower need than where a major change programme is being effected. How much time should be spent communicating to ensure that the manager is oiling the wheels effectively? While the old adage that one can never communicate enough is a truism, this is not much help when a manager is trying to allocate time behind his or her priorities. The real answer is that the time allocated will certainly differ in organizations that are at differing stages. We noted from the research amongst senior managers that they claim to spend anything from 10 to 50 per cent of their time communicating. The great majority spend around 20 per cent of their time in this area. Communication, both internally and externally, has a high priority. It is not our intention to give a comprehensive coverage of the elements and channels of communication or how individuals can become more effective in building this competency. This has already been well covered in existing literature. We wish to emphasize the general importance of communication but to focus our attention on the assessment and development of personal influencing skills. We see this as one of the most complex aspects of communication and we believe that an understanding of the process of influence is important to the development of the skill.

Personal influencing skills

Communication is seen as a critical core competence for the manager today and especially tomorrow.

The requirement for communication skills across the breadth and depth of management tasks and in reinforcing leadership qualities is clear. Whether the subject be the motivation of a team, getting the best from a change programme, or reinforcing strategy, values and culture, the need is there. In addition to all of these practical benefits, the individual will lift his or her personal influencing skills perhaps more through the role of communication than in any other way. This will lift self-confidence which in itself enhances performance through the virtuous circle of confidence, self-belief, more experimentation, greater success, in turn enhancing confidence again.

Personal influencing skills are of vital importance to managers who are striving to reach their full potential, especially as they are thinking about their own future potential. In Figure 10.3 we therefore identify the key areas where excellence is needed if the manager is to have the greatest possible influence.

Figure 10.3   Key areas for personal influencing skills

Area	Description
Knowledge	• Technical, appropriate to the current role • Organizational knowledge • Industry, competitors, customers, suppliers
Communication style	• Uses facts and figures to persuade • Technically competent in relevant forms of communication • Listens, evaluates and responds
Widely aware	• Alert to new trends that may have relevance (curiosity) • Has visibility in the organization
Avoids the use of hierarchical power	• Breaks down barriers across layers, teams and functions • Operates with ease at different levels of management, and with the workforce
Appearance	• Appropriate to the occasion in both style and dress

The process of influence

The process of personal influence is a complex one to understand. Undoubtedly some people come across as more influential than others and it raises the question as to whether there is some fundamental personality type that is well suited to influencing. If we can understand the personal basis of influence, then we can use this knowledge in assessing managers for specific roles and in deciding whether development is possible.

Researchers at SHL looked at these issues during the 1980s with a view to developing a model of 'Influencing and Selling'. In brief, they found no single 'influencing' type. On the contrary, there were many ways in which one individual could influence another. For example, some influenced by the sheer quality of their thinking; some by their self-confidence; some by the easy way they established rapport; some by their infectious enthusiasm; some by their dogged persistence on an issue; some by their preparedness to take an independent view and so on. SHL opted for a multi-type model as a means to characterizing an individual's style of influence so that this could be used to match a seller or an influencer to suit a recipient's own personal style or needs. The SHL model is summarized in Figure 10.4.

While emphasizing the complexity of the influencer–recipient interaction/relationship, there are some dimensions of personality which have emerged as particularly important and should be considered when planning an individual's personal development. The personality traits referred to below are taken from the occupational model of personality (OPQ®) referred to in Chapter 7.

- **Persuasiveness** is concerned with whether an individual fundamentally enjoys the process of selling or changing others' opinions. People who are low on this scale are likely to be less assertive and will prefer not to have to influence others by persuasion. Such people may well need a strong external motivator to take on such a role.
- **Socially Confident** is concerned with how comfortable an individual feels in social interaction. The low scorer may feel ill at ease in less familiar social situations. If this is communicated to a recipient, it will reduce the influential impact. Social confidence is open to development, particularly if sources of anxiety can be identified and moderated.

Figure 10.4　Model of influencing and selling style

---

1. CONFIDENT COMMUNICATOR – A behavioural style reflected in social confidence and low anxiety; performs particularly well in more formal situations; will appear poised and in control of the situation; firm and clear oral presentation.

2. RAPPORT CREATOR – Influences by building warm, friendly relationships; seen as approachable and reasonable and concerned to understand the personal needs of a client; interested in people and enjoys working in teams.

3. CULTURE FITTER – Identifies a prevailing culture and modifies own behaviour to fit in; creates trust and confidence through an apparent sharing of opinions, values etc. Tends not to push attitudes and values of their own.

4. CULTURE BREAKER – Influences by pitching him or herself at odds with the prevailing culture; creates an image of independent views and radical thinking; seen as new thinking and a breath of fresh air but needs to be seen as having integrity and relevant 'know how'.

5. ENTHUSIAST – Demonstrates an infectious energy and enthusiasm; a driving energy complemented with the optimism of a cheerful disposition; influence derived from an emotional impact.

6. PERSEVERER – Manifests a determined persistence to make a case; doggedly pursues leads and opportunities and disregards put-offs. Emotionally tough-minded in moving steadily towards personal objectives.

7. BUSINESS WINNER – Influencing style is marked by high competitiveness, social confidence and a preparedness to take a risk and bend the rules; tends to be energetic, always seeking opportunities and quick to make a decision.

8. TECHNICIAN – Uses a cerebral style of influencing; enjoys analysing information and dealing with more complex issues and products; good at using logic to unravel complex situations; usually bright, easy to train and has a good command of words and numbers.

Note: The above eight influencing styles are supplemented in the model by two team roles appropriate to sales teams. 'Admin Supporter' ensures proper administrative follow-up. 'Team Manager' understands the optimum client allocation of sales resources as well as how to motivate and develop the team.

SOURCE: SHL Expert System Report

© SHL Group plc 1999 – Reproduced with permission

- **Behavioural** is concerned with the individual's inclination to analyze the thoughts and behaviour of other people as part of trying to understand them. The assumption here is that we are more likely to influence someone else if we have succeeded in understanding what are that individual's own preferences, concerns, motivations and the like. Some people have a natural inclination to do this and some do not. It follows that one should be able to adapt one's style accordingly.

From an assessment point of view, these three factors are all well worth considering if there is a need to know whether an individual is likely to make a good influencer.

When considering the development of the capability to influence, it is the last area – behavioural – which we believe to be particularly important and worthy of developmental focus. In achieving a successful process of influence, the emphasis first is on watching and listening. The need is to achieve a first stage of analysis in which the recipient is considered carefully. The outcome of this stage is a decision on the best way to influence the particular individual in the particular circumstances. This is not to say that a fixed style of influence – say energetic and enthusiastic – cannot be effective; but we do believe that careful consideration of the particular context is likely to optimize the process. We have proposed a development emphasis here because we believe that this aspect of the process is open to learning and long-term behaviour change.

Personal influencing skills are commonly included in development centre programmes. They allow specific facets of influence to be examined and this leads to a tailored and more cost-effective use of development resources. The case study from New Zealand is illustrative of this point.

CASE STUDY 10.1
Insurance sales – New Zealand

A New Zealand insurance firm wanted to increase the sales orientation of their staff. Accounts Underwriters and Branch Managers within the company had traditionally adopted a 'relationship building' approach rather than a more direct 'sales' approach when liaising with Insurance Brokers to market/sell insurance. Development centres were conducted by SHL to increase the incumbents' awareness of their sales function and to identify potential development needs in areas associated with a sales role, such as persuasiveness, negotiation and presentation skills. The assessment was used to target specific areas which were the focus for tailored development plans. This was seen by the insurance firm to be more cost effective than running general development workshops for all incumbents when this may not have been beneficial. The incumbents found the assessments pinpointed specific areas which needed development and provided a clear action plan by which to gain improvements.

Summary

In this chapter we have focused on four aspects of work performance which can have a significant effect on organizational productivity but which need to be managed proactively as part of a total human resource strategy.

We have argued that organizations need to do more to identify their creative talent; to develop it and to promote a culture which is seen to value the creative process. Paradoxically, current success can be a disincentive to seeking new options. However, for those organizations who wish to encourage new perspectives on their markets and the way they operate, there are options available. We argue that individuals with the potential to think laterally can be identified through a mix of simulation tests and personality assessment. We also believe that this potential can be developed and that cultures can be shifted to become more accepting of creative input.

The substantial financial impact of stress on organizations is noted. We take the position that prevention is better than cure and that management needs to think carefully about the potential to create stress in the workforce from its ongoing operational decisions. When stress occurs for an individual, the danger is that performance may be adversely affected before clear danger signals are picked up by others and acted upon. In stress cases we have noted the importance of an analytical process which breaks the problem down into bite-sized chunks, which encourages the individual to believe that something can realistically be done and focuses their action. As with other aspects of human performance, the individual's personality is a key mediator of the correct coping solution and needs to be well understood.

We have chosen entrepreneurship for special attention because it offers an opportunity to identify new commercial opportunities and the will to drive them to success. The problem is that entrepreneurs do not fit neatly into organizational structures which emphasize correct procedures and systematized approaches. There needs to be careful planning if major entrepreneurs are to be brought into senior positions in which a balance is struck between freedom to act and compliance with necessary procedures. We also argue that it is possible to think of entrepreneurship as one part of a set of more general management competencies. This would be appropriate for organizations who want to encourage more independent-minded and commercial thinking on a broader managerial front. We offer a definition of this competency and describe the personality traits that will help it to be identified.

We have also dwelt on communicating because this is seen as a critical core competence for successful managers. There is clear evidence that the need is there and that communication skills can be developed. Although the process of influence is a complex one to understand, it is well worth reviewing the key determinants that enhance influence. It is for this reason that we have reviewed personal influencing skills and the process of influence. The OPQ® instrument has three factors well worth considering if one is considering whether a particular individual is likely to make a good influencer. These are 'persuasiveness', 'social confidence' and a 'behavioural' orientation which focuses on the inclination to analyze the thoughts and behaviours of others.

Thinking carefully about those we wish to influence is seen as a fundamental prerequisite for success. There is danger in standardizing our style of influence for all recipients.

11 Further Applications – Strategic Thinking and Knowledge

Strategic thinking

The emphasis here is on strategic thinking rather than the more comprehensive topic of strategic planning. The reason for this is that we wish to draw attention to the people aspects, and that strategic thinking is a key requirement for most managers today, especially for those in a general management role. This concept of strategic management thinking focuses on delivering long-term value to an enterprise while at the same time ensuring that predetermined short-term goals are met.

In order to see the important role that strategic thinking plays, it is helpful to look at the key elements of the strategy process. These have been summarized in Figure 11.1, but a word or two of explanation may be helpful at this stage.

1. Mission

The mission is an inspirational statement that endeavours to set the broad expression of the purpose of the business. It explains how it expects to achieve excellence and the competitive advantage that is required. The very best mission statements start with where the business is today and where it wishes to be in the future. The scope will normally include the geography in which the company operates, its markets and the products or services. An important role of the mission statement is to inspire. People are more likely to receive inspiration if the statement is short, clear, and is a rallying call to those employed in the company.

2. Environmental and internal reviews

These usually take place at the same time, providing an objective, analytical review of external factors as well as those that are internal to the firm. It is from this data gathering and the assessment of the application of its importance to the firm that the opportunities and threats are considered, having had regard for the firm's strengths and weaknesses. It is following this analysis that the 'big idea' hopefully will emerge so that the company can consider a step change in performance. This is important even for companies that are pursuing a winning strategy, for they must be alert to the changes that are occurring around them and decide when to change emphasis or direction.

3. Key issues

This is the distillation stage where there is an action list that will need to be fully addressed in the various strategies that may be available. They will be the big issues that will influence strategy. The list will vary by business, but may include the unexpected entry of a new competitor, or market factors such as the implications of changes to tariffs and quotas under GATT that, for example, have had such a major impact on the textile industry. The list may also include industry alliances as we have seen in the airline industry, new technology and new supply arrangements that have a significant impact on the market. An example of this latter point can be seen with coal supply to the privatized UK power industry.

4. Alternative strategies

There are always strategic choices facing a firm and never just one alternative. When a strategy that is already in place is working well and there are not perceived to be any nearby threats to this, then the time spent on finding alternatives can be restricted. This need not be an annual event in these circumstances, although the prudent firm will have a review to see if there is a better way perhaps every third year or so.

5. Resources required

People with the right skills, motivation and drive in the numbers required will be needed to deliver the chosen strategy. Equally the chosen strategy must be manageable within the culture of the company. It may well be that strategy shifts are being used as the initiating source of a needed culture change. As an example, in a production-led company, where the financial imperative had been to fill the factory, the needs of the customer took second place. Closure of marginal manufacturing units was seen as a useful value-adding role in its own right, but also as an essential step in changing the culture to one where it is customer led. One should never underestimate the time that is required to achieve this, as well as the need for communication, to get the workforce on side with the painful way forward.

An objective appraisal of the people requirements of the plan is critical, yet is often either overlooked or hurriedly prepared almost as a free-standing document. In many cases the speed of implementation may well have to be constrained until the right people are identified, put into place and receive the necessary training.

On the other hand, most strategic plans address the cash resource required much more effectively, perhaps in part due to the more precise and homogeneous nature of this compared with the human resource.

6. The preferred strategy

This is the working document that will guide the executive in their execution of the key planks of the strategy. The main elements are:

- A description of the key elements of the plan;
- Details of the resources required;
- The expected outturn of the plan, appropriately quantified. This will include the financial outturn, using headline numbers for sales, operating profits, operational cash flow, capital spend, and special development expenditure on people, marketing or new technology. The forward balance sheet would also be prepared, backed up with ratios that are relevant to the particular business;
- The key strategic benchmarks that must be achieved if the plan is to be successful.

7. Implementation

Clearly the delivery element is critical. The best strategy process will integrate this into the total business processes of the company and the information system will reflect this. The strategy becomes the precursor to the annual plan or the budget and other annual plans such as the marketing plans are derived from this too.

It will be seen from this brief analysis that the plans will be of limited value if the firms involved do not have the capability for strategic thinking. The right sort of people are required with the right sort of skills to turn data into information and information into knowledge. They need to be capable of looking outwards to see the trends that will have an impact, and then to use creativity to understand the alternatives and the best way forward.

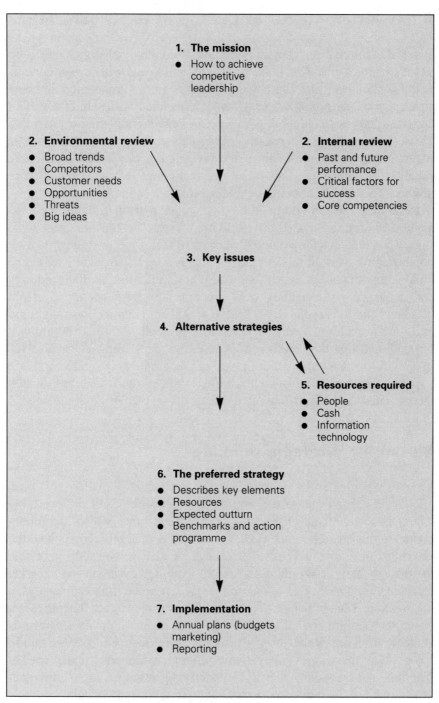

Figure 11.1 Seven elements of strategy

A key differentiator at the top of the organization

Given the competitive pressures that drive commercial organizations to adopt strategies that are capable of differentiation and will deliver benefits to the owners over time, strategic thinking is a key competence for those at the top of the organization. Closely associated with this is a sort of curiosity that resides in those who have strategy high on their priority list. This is manifest in the outward-looking nature of the individuals, and is so important in the selection of the preferred strategy. These traits are capable of being identified in relevant assessment, and perhaps more importantly capable of being developed through training.

Returning for the moment to the evidence from the research for *Successful Management* (Bain, 1995), we observe that the managers in the survey believed that they spent 23 per cent of their time on strategy in their organizations. Most of this sample felt that they wished to spend more time on looking outward at trends that would have an impact on their industry and company, but that they were precluded by the constant short-run pressures and the urgent issues that flew at them at an increasingly rapid rate. In a few cases, it was observed that strategic ability at the top was missing, and that the incumbents would invariably immerse themselves in activity, as an alternative to thinking. The simple point is that both are required. Further, looking to the future, strategic understanding, which incorporates thinking, is high on the list of competencies that are needed in a successful manager.

Measuring strategic thinking

In our experience the measurement of strategic thinking has been effectively carried out with a mix of two approaches. On the one hand assessors focus on the underlying personal attributes which are fundamental to this area of competence. For example, in ability terms, the issue is whether the individual has sufficient analytical reasoning skills to be able to analyze and draw inferences from complex written (say, market segmentation reports) or numerical (say, corporate financial analysis) information. Then in personality terms, the issue is whether the individual possesses the right kind of traits which will predispose him or her towards strategic thinking. Relevant traits here include 'independence of mind', 'conceptual thinking', 'innovative', 'critical evaluation' and 'forward planning'. Possession of the right underlying attributes is an important determinant of the individual's motivation to think strategically.

The second approach is concerned more with whether the individual is able to use his or her fundamental attributes to manifest high quality strategic thinking. The interview has a role here in that past strategic thinking can be probed and explored. There is an issue of the genuine origination of any historical examples and for that reason there is a good case for a management simulation exercise. This may take the form of a strategic planning objective given some quite complex background information or it may be part of a high-level 'in-tray' exercise in which the candidate takes on the role of a business leader. Such exercises are usually set against time limits and have scoring processes designed to maximize objectivity of evaluation.

Organizations utilizing internal assessment and development centres as part of succession planning and management development would commonly include a strategic thinking competency in their assessment model. This helps the organization to identify where its strategic thinking talent lies and this in turn has a developmental benefit for other, more junior managers who are interested in developing this skill and need a resource for mentoring, tutoring or general advice. This provides a valuable and organizationally relevant supplement to the more conventional training and self-learning options. Given that the ability to think strategically is high on the required list of competencies, more attention needs to be given to assessing capability in a pragmatic way and in developing that capability.

While it is not uncommon for strategic thinking to be assessed as a total competency, it may be helpful to break it down into several components, each of which may require rather different personal attributes. We have worked with one financial institution which made a point of differentiating at the top of the organization between 'strategic conceptualization' and 'strategic implementation'. Board-level candidates showed quite different profiles against these differentiated elements. Our own experience across the seven elements of strategy defined above is that there are probably four relatively independent attribute sets to be considered:

- Idea Formulation: lateral thinking; use of imagination; retaining an open mind; more conceptual thinking
- Critical Evaluation/ Review: logical review; critical evaluation; high-level analytical reasoning
- Implementation: planning skills; seeing implications; optimizing the allocation of resources
- Decision Making: balancing options; weighing probabilities; tolerance of risk and the confidence to make a radical proposition

We made the point in Chapter 2 that organizations may work with hierarchical models of competencies. There are often practical constraints on the number of competencies that can enter a broadly based management assessment and an overall measure of strategic thinking may be all that is realistically manageable. However, it is a concept with several facets and, therefore, the issue of definition becomes critical for reliable measurement. In an assessment which is more narrowly focused on strategic thinking – for example, in more senior-level jobs – we would recommend a more finely differentiated set of competencies.

Knowledge

Today and tomorrow, the greatest sources of competitive advantage will reside with the knowledge of the people within the organizations. This has led people like Nonaka and Takeuchi to talk of 'The Knowledge Creating Company', where the organization's total capabilities exceed the sum of the parts. In *The Fifth Discipline* Peter Senge describes the five parts of a learning organization. Each plays an essential part in developing the right atmosphere for success:

1. Systems thinking: adopting a way of thinking about and a language to describe those things that shape the behaviour of organizations.
2. Personal mastery: encouraging individuals to take control of their own lives, to understand themselves and, from this base, to develop a plan of self-improvement, thus expanding one's personal capacity. The organizational culture must support this.
3. Mental models: within any organization there are assumptions, generalizations, patterns or images that influence behaviour. These must be brought to the surface, to be challenged and reflected upon, so that they improve our understanding of the world. This is the precursor to action.
4. Building shared visions: this will help to lock in the commitment of the people and is a key element of leadership within a group. The vision is the picture which we wish to create and is shared across the organization.
5. Team learning: this takes the individual skills and lessons and embeds them in groups of people so that the organization's ability is much greater than the sum of the individual parts.

Knowledge, just like people skills, needs to be upgraded constantly. This requires investment which regrettably is not uniformly applied or directed for greatest impact, in many organizations with which we have contact.

Indeed, the concept of developing knowledge, as a competitive weapon, is not universally practised either. The UK Post Office is an organization that has regularly invested in its people skills and is now making a conscious effort to understand the knowledge that exists, to bring this together, share it, and utilize it to improve performance. Mike Hall, a senior Post Office manager, has summarized that experience which we have included as a case study.

CASE STUDY 11.1
Knowledge and The Post Office (UK)

Several years ago, Royal Mail set up an organization to provide an internal consultancy and project management capability mainly for the British Post Office but, increasingly, for other post offices across the world, where such capabilities could be used strategically to improve the quality of the international mail services. Uniquely, in order to create centres of excellence in the appropriate areas of knowledge, many of the former functional departments of Royal Mail were dismantled and integrated into the new organization so that, by using the consultancy concept (including contracts, timesheets and customer satisfaction indices), the members of the new organization became more customer responsive and willing to share work and knowledge across the previous functional fiefdoms.

RM Consulting – as it became known – realized that its core competence was its ability to leverage and deploy the knowledge of its people to the benefit of the Post Office as a whole and recognized that its only asset was intellectual capital in the form of the knowledge of those people. To maximize the development and application of that knowledge and to change the culture still further, a large-scale change management initiative was developed based around organizational development. This involved the deployment of a number of tools, techniques and approaches to improve both the capability of individuals and the ability of the organization to learn from assignments and deploy that learning across the organization quickly and efficiently. The vision was to deploy the right knowledge to the right people at the right time and in the right format.

From this vision a programme for knowledge management was born. This programme includes various elements designed to encourage the development of personal knowledge and capability, the deployment of learning points across the organization and the creation of understanding through discussion and dialogue and organizational alignment. These elements support various stages of the knowledge process, including converting tacit knowledge (in the minds of individuals) to explicit knowledge (in the form of information), tacit to tacit and explicit to explicit. The programme will take until 2001 to complete and consists of over 25 individual projects and initiatives designed to support knowledge capture, deployment, utilization and review, including:

- the creation of 21 practitioner groups to be centres of knowledge in both core operational areas such as postal delivery or distribution and also in areas, such as operational and marketing research, where RM Consulting interprets the work of outside agents into the knowledge required by the postal industry;
- the flattening of the organizational structure and the phasing out of line management;
- a CV and skills database which helps identify those within the organization with the relevant skills and experience to resource assignments;
- an assignment database to capture knowledge created from individual projects as they progress;
- after action reviews – a technique developed by the US Army and used by a number of companies to identify the learning resulting from a specific activity;
- expert panels which provide a safe environment to assess the degree to which learning can be deployed across the organization;
- a virtual library based on an intranet using information-pull technologies;
- development counselling where over 10 per cent of the organization has been trained and designated as support counsellors to assist people in understanding their opportunities for development;
- the development of Communities of Practice including an Association of Royal Mail Project Management with over 700 members, both in RM Consulting and throughout the Post Office;
- the *RM Consulting Journal* which is designed to encourage knowledge sharing through referenced articles on all aspects of the organization's work.

In this way, over 1000 members of functional hierarchies in the former headquarters of Royal Mail are being changed into 'knowledge workers' who gather, share and deploy their knowledge for the benefit of the Post Office as a whole and use their Post Office knowledge to spearhead change both at home and abroad.

SOURCE: Mike Hall, The Post Office (UK)

Some companies go to great lengths to record the lessons from major events or projects and to ensure that this knowledge is shared across the organization. Others just don't bother and go on repeating those mistakes or, at least, not improving the process in the future. Managers have few tools with which to capture institutional experience and to share the lesson and develop remedial action plans for the future. To alleviate this, new tools are being developed such as 'learning history'. (See, for example, Art Kleiner and George Roth, 'How to Make Experience The Company's Best Teacher'.) This requires trust and openness within the organization.

Professional intellect

Within any organization, the true professional commands a body of knowledge, according to Quinn, Anderson and Finkelstein (1996). There are four levels of professional intellect in an organization, listed here in order of increasing importance.

1. *Cognitive knowledge* (know what): this is the basic mastery of a discipline that professionals achieve through extensive training and certification.
2. *Advanced skills* (know how): this takes book learning into practice in real-life situations. This is the value-adding part that is essential in managers and consultants alike.
3. *Systems understanding* (know why): a deep understanding of the web of cause and effect in real-life situations. It helps people solve larger, more complex problems and may result in a highly honed sense of intuition.
4. *Self-motivated creativity* (care why): this is the will, the motivation, the adaptability for success. It explains why highly motivated and creative groups outperform their peers. Without this, the dread of complacency can filter in with a resultant loss of motivation.

The challenge for organizations is to recognize the value of knowledge, to develop professional intellect to the fourth level and to ensure that the culture is supportive of this. This will require new skills for individuals, a new orientation in many commercial enterprises and systems to share this information widely and quickly.

Reflecting on this, there are lessons for those that would develop the most effective knowledge-based organizations. These have been gleaned from our own observations but supplemented with the experience of others such as Quinn, Anderson and Finkelstein. We summarize these lessons as follows:

1. *Recruit the best:* the most able people who have the pre-agreed skills and personalities to fit them to the role.
2. *Rapid early development:* set demanding standards, exposing them to real complex problems at a very early stage but under the guidance of a well-chosen mentor. Immerse them in the organization and encourage a challenging, questioning approach.
3. *Set clear stretching objectives:* objectives must be prioritized and set out clearly. Performance needs to be monitored against them. Training needs to be given to enable the individual to perform to the standards set.
4. *Provide wider opportunities:* there will be stretching new areas, usually as a team member, that will broaden horizons, provide challenge and development.
5. *Encourage self-development:* the support must be from the employer but the initiative should be from the individual.
6. *Evaluate and weed:* an objective evaluation will be welcomed and, if people are misplaced, they need to be weeded out from that role.

The employer should be clear if there is a mismatch of skills to the job requirement or if motivation is missing. The solution will be retraining, internal redeployment, or encouraging the person to further their career outside.

In addition to these people issues, the employer will need to provide the environment that allows the benefits from knowledge to be maximized. To achieve this, the following will need to be in place:

- problem-solving tools to assist the decision-making process;
- encouragement of movement of individuals across different areas which are not discipline dependent;
- systems for widely sharing information and knowledge;
- a culture of openness where lessons learned do not result in judgemental behaviour;
- communication channels that work and communication skills as an embedded competence in the individuals.

The need to create the right culture has a particular relevance because there is a human factor that can work against the dissemination of knowledge. The maxim that 'knowledge is power' reflects a part of the value system of more senior managers and the consequent motivation is to restrict the outward flow of acquired knowledge. The important issue here is whether there is a clear sense of team participation in order to meet a genuinely shared vision or a set of goals. In our experience, if an individual really buys in to the team's objectives, then everything will be contributed to achieve success. However, if there is a personal agenda or a private career-related goal, then this will interfere with optimal performance.

We use the analogy of a professional football team playing for a championship trophy. If an individual player genuinely wants the trophy – the team goal – then personal needs will be subordinated to those of the team as a whole. But if individuals are concerned with their own performance and their dollar value in the transfer market, then the danger is that the team goal becomes subordinated to the demonstration of individual excellence.

The need to share knowledge brings us back to the criticality of leadership. A strong and inspiring leader creates the buy-in to the team goal and is able to communicate the binding vision that motivates the individuals in the organization to want to share their knowledge. Of course, the personality of the individual is also a factor and this reinforces the need to help managers to develop a deeper understanding of their subordinates.

Summary

In this chapter, we have drawn attention to the fundamental importance of strategy to the commercial success of a business. We do not endeavour to set out a full treatise of strategy for this has been well covered in other publications. Given our emphasis on people as the key to unlocking enterprise value or in achieving other goals in the not-for-profit sector, our focus here has been on the value of strategic thinking. As we have seen throughout this book, there is a case for objective assessment. This is certainly true of strategic thinking where, in ability terms, we can see if the individual has sufficient analytical reasoning. Equally, from a personality viewpoint, we can measure if a person has the relevant traits that would predispose him or her towards strategic thinking. We suggest that strategic thinking can be broken down into constituent parts for more thorough and focused assessment.

Knowledge sits comfortably with strategic thinking, for we have shown that the source of competitive advantage is increasingly to be found in the knowledge that exists, is shared and is acted upon. In many organizations, there is no cohesive way to mine the knowledge for it is spread in many different corners. There is a need to value knowledge and to see that it is effectively retained and maintained. It needs to be freely and easily available to all those who can use it, improve it and use it again.

As we reviewed the four levels of professional intellect or the body of knowledge in the organization, we highlighted that the value increases as we go up the scale from cognitive knowledge to self-motivated creativity. We also concluded that there are important lessons for those who would develop the most effective knowledge-based organizations. Above all else, the leadership must be committed, openly supportive of this and the importance of growing and using the knowledge base must permeate all levels.

12

Improving the Performance of the Board

The critical role of the board

It goes without saying that the board has a pivotal role in ensuring that long-term value is created and maintained for the benefit of all shareholders. The board is accountable to the shareholders who have appointed the directors to act in their collective best interests. It has an amalgam of functions which can be summarized as follows:

● It is the representative of shareholders and it must ensure that the company has clear goals and measures the progress against those goals.
● The board needs to agree the strategy and the resources needed to achieve it.
● The chief executive is appointed by the board which will monitor his or her performance, along with the rest of the executive directors.
● Reflecting the absolute importance of the human resources needed to deliver the strategy, the board must annually review succession management development plans.

The board will need to set down and monitor the operating climate in the company through a statement of values that describes the character of the company and the policies that reflect those values. However, the position is a little more complex than this, as the board has its legal obligations and conduct codes to look to, in order to ensure that the company is in compliance with these. Additionally the community at large has expectations of the commercial sector in which the company operates. It needs to operate within the community, winning if possible its support, or at very least its understanding. Other stakeholders will also have legitimate claims which will need to be recognized within the hierarchy of values. In the end though, the board must add real value to the company over the long term. This is the ultimate goal which needs to be kept at the forefront of the board's mind.

Before we look at the different ways that the board can and must add value, it is instructive to look into the wide variety of expectations of a board of directors. In the research undertaken by Bain and Band in 1996, there was a great diversity of expectations from within the community. This research was based in the United Kingdom but is mirrored by the earlier European-wide research of Demb and Neubauer. If we try to summarize the various views, we find an array of expectations, broadly as follows:

- Shareholders expect the board to act in their best interests.
- Employees have an historic expectation of job preservation that is still strong in a number of industries, and different countries.
- Customers and suppliers expect that the company will continue and that resources will be adequate for that purpose.
- Government and the community expect to see their wider interests supported, and often, and increasingly, government is transferring social and administrative burdens to the private sector.
- The board is expected to monitor the executive, its progress and its remuneration.
- The board should also protect the environment in its decision-making process.

Unfortunately, it is unlikely that all of these tasks can be delivered by a board of directors, and there must therefore be a focus both on the critical issues for the board and the important issue of how the board will prioritize and manage itself. The determining role of the board is the same in almost all free enterprise economies. It must consistently act in the best long-term interests of all shareholders. This is the guiding principle that must be constantly followed.

The management of the board

Any top body, if it is to be fully effective, must have rules of governance that are clear, communicated, and supported. The board must therefore have broad agreement on the following matters:

- It must agree how to manage itself. This will include the composition, its agenda, process and performance. However, we have observed with some considerable disappointment that there remains in many companies a lack of professionalism in the selection of directors. Often, this process relies heavily or even solely on an interview process of dubious quality. Little effort is given to getting real balance on the board, in the sense of setting out the key competencies that are required to deliver the forward agenda, or to look at the balance of styles that might deliver synergistic benefits. Agendas, too, are often unchanged from meeting to meeting and this stereotyped approach usually has insufficient time for quality debate on the really important issues such as the strategy, or the management development and succession plans.

- It will need to be clear about the directors' terms and tenure and how the new appointees are chosen.
- There will need to be a process that monitors the chief executive as well as his or her colleagues which will involve the chairman and the non-executive directors alone. This is a challenge to the unity of the board which need not be divisive given adequate leadership from the chairman.
- The chairman will ensure that there is a periodic review of the functioning of the board. An appraisal of the board is a very useful two-way communication which regrettably is not common practice today.
- There must be freedom of the outside directors to meet individually or collectively with members of the executive, including non-board members.
- Either through the special committees or through direct involvement, there must be an appropriate opportunity to review compensation plans, succession plans, strategy, and issues of internal control.

Information needed by the board must be agreed in advance, then provided in good time and in sufficient depth to deal effectively with the issues before it. Within this information pack, there needs to be clear measures that focus on the growth of value for the benefit of shareholders, together with an array of non-accounting measures that give a balanced view of the health of the business.

The role of the chairman

The performance of any board will depend quite heavily on the effectiveness of the chairman. The role that the chairman takes will vary in differing countries and with the needs of the individual business. The scope of the chairman's role needs to be pre-agreed, and seen alongside that of the chief executive to ensure efficiency of effort and clarity of leadership. There really does need to be a clear understanding of whether the chairman or the chief executive is directly accountable for the formulation and implementation of strategy and also directly accountable for the results.

The chairman is the leader of the board and therefore must set the standards required from board colleagues. He or she must provide the required leadership by following an appropriate agenda. The contribution of the chairman will ultimately determine the board's effectiveness. Style may vary, but standards must remain high. The choice of chairman is therefore of primary importance, and this needs to be reflected in the professionalism of the selection process. Careful consideration must be given to the immediate and future needs of the business so that the right choice can be made with the matching of skills against the key tasks. Although there are well-proven methods to achieve a better match, and to establish the profile of candidates for the role of chairman, these are usually ignored. The typical appointment will be made after a professional search, from candidates in the search firm's database, and will be heavily reliant upon a review of the candidate's curriculum vitae and the interview process. This is sub-optimal and in our experience the probability of getting the best fit for a defined role can increase materially when some basic tests are applied on top of a thorough and structured interview process.

It is of course obvious that there is no single model of defined characteristics that will prove to have universal application for all chairmen. There are, in our experience, some common traits that are relevant. A chairman must:

● be a strong leader;
● have the intellectual capacity to deal with complexity and multi-dimensional issues;
● be an able communicator;
● have the energy, time and inclination to get around the company and see the executives in action on their own turf.

The non-executive or independent director

The non-executive director has been the butt of derogatory jokes and inadequate remuneration for a long period of time. The derogatory jokes are becoming far less frequent as companies are seeing that the best people are adding real value. While in some quarters it is still popular to think of the non-executive as a rubber stamp in the business process, or as 'decorations on the Christmas tree', this is neither the reality nor the view of most people in the commercial sector today. Unfortunately the question of inadequate remuneration remains, which in turn is a barrier to an adequate supply of top-level people prepared to undertake this role as a profession. As is the case with the selection of company chairmen, we find that the selection of the non-executive director is heavily reliant on the interview alongside the review of his or her career. Little effort is made in terms of balance on the board save for the experience or initial training of the candidate. Many of the briefs given to the specialist search firms will state that the board is looking for a new director with experience at main board level and a background in, say, finance for example. Where an attempt at balance on the board is sought, this is usually seen in terms of background experience such as finance, legal, human relations, sales and marketing, or general management.

Many countries prefer the title independent director to that of the non-executive, as this reflects an important, desirable trait, in that the person has no connections with the firm save for that reflected in the role of independent director. This also helps all the directors to understand the schizophrenic role of the independent director. On the one hand, he or she has the same responsibilities as every other director, and is therefore part of the top team. On the other hand, there is also a role of monitoring the executive, and ensuring that the company is on track to achieving the agreed goals. The ability to be effective in both of these roles is clearly an important competence.

Survey after survey of chief executives reveals that the characteristics rated most highly in independent directors by chief executives are business experience and their knowledge base. This is understandable and there is a value-adding role that can be played here. We would also suggest that it is also a little limiting when compared with the full potential of contribution that is possible from a balanced group at the top of the company. It is our view that applying some simple tests will get a team that has more capability as a group than the sum of the parts of that group.

Director selection

It is now accepted as good practice that the adoption of more formal and rigorous director selection procedures is essential. Many boards are now planning their own composition with the company's strategic goals in mind. As a part of the strategic planning process, when consideration is being given to the human resource implications of the plan, the chairman will ask the question, 'What are the implications for the composition of the board, and the competencies needed to deliver the strategy?' From this starting point, the specifications of the most appropriate mix are drawn up. These serve as guidelines for the director selection process. Unfortunately, too few of these forward-thinking companies go to the next step of formally evaluating candidates against these specifications.

Given that around the world it is accepted as good practice to have finite periods for independent directors' tenure, many companies will pre-plan to ensure a staggering of ages and retirement dates so that the core of experience is retained over time. Given that the selection process is well founded and selects the best available people, the company needs to set about implementing a formal induction process, and then to tackle the task of ensuring that ongoing training is applied across all of the members of the board. These are topics that we will pick up later in this chapter.

The board in interaction as a team

Jon Katzenbach is probably the best known business writer on the effective use of teams, and how they can be used more productively in any organization. He has observed that teams work best when they have a tangible goal, a limited life span, mutual accountability, and when multi-discipline skills are needed to deliver the best solution. Teams in this context exist for a defined purpose and a finite time. In recent work published in the *Harvard Business Review*, he argues that the idea of a team at the top is a mistaken one, because the concept does not apply in practice at the top of an organization. Most businesses have a clearly defined hierarchy of power, where the final authority rests with the leader of the organization. In this sense the concept of the team at the top is a myth, for they do not have the responsibility or the authority to take charge in the way that a single leader does. One of the most telling observations that he makes, in support of his observation that teams at the top are a rarity, is that the right mix of skills in the team is often absent. Membership of the 'top teams' observed by Katzenbach has been primarily driven by the members' formal position in an organization rather than any team skills that the member may bring. Looking behind this, the incumbent will have usually been appointed to the role as a result of past success in previous roles. The great pity of this is that it is possible to put in place selection procedures that will help understand the wider skills of the individuals, so that it is possible to get balance in the top team, gaining the extra benefits of synergy of the directors of the board.

This concept of interaction between board members is often overlooked but can be critical to the board's output. A board member may have the potential to bring laterality to the board's strategic thinking, but this will only be effective if the capability is recognized and encouraged by the chair. A chairman who is assertive and autocratic – not necessarily inappropriate characteristics – may constrain the critical evaluation of proposals and demotivate those for whom this is a strength. Board members who are too self-interested may find mutual support affected at key decision points. Too much independence of mind without empathy in the personal make-up of board members may lead to clashes. The list of possible implications goes on and on. The conclusion is that if board members can understand the capabilities, the motivation, the personalities and the potential of their board colleagues, then they are more likely to adapt their behaviour to better effect. This is a particularly important consideration for the chairman who is best placed to influence the agenda, the time allocation and the overall process of board interaction.

We have worked with organizations who have been prepared to put board interaction and relationships under scrutiny. The process assumes that issues will only be resolved if they are first understood and brought to the surface. We have begun with an interactive analysis of the board personalities looking for potential issues of the kind noted above. This has been supplemented by 360° analysis in which board members use questionnaires to make specific observations of board relationships on structured scales. The analysis identifies the issues which are then discussed in individual and group sessions. We have found the use of questionnaires to be valuable because they help to depersonalize any problems and reduce sensitivity. The meetings focus on what the 'analysis is saying' and not on what one person is saying about another. As with most management interventions related to people, motivation is a key factor. If there is a genuine interest and concern to build a more productive team interaction – often driven by the chair – then the means exist to bring issues to the surface and resolve them.

The assessment of new board candidates

As we have indicated above, there has been a lack of professionalism in this area in recent years although we are beginning to see signs of change. Many of the principles and practices outlined throughout this book apply to the assessment of new board candidates. A clear position description should be written that is based on a thorough position analysis. This should lead to a person specification which defines the required personal competencies. Assessment should be relevant and specifically related to these competencies. However, there is an important point of difference for board members.

In the case of new executive board members, there is a good argument for a duality of assessment. On the one hand, there should be a clear specification related to the executive function. This would cover the tasks and context factors relevant to the individual's specialized line or staff role. This would be much as for any senior management role and we would recommend a thorough assessment procedure covering interviews and high-level simulation exercises, as well as the standardized assessment of abilities, personality and motivation. On the other hand, we believe that the board role should be examined separately. The issue is how well the individual fits the particular requirement of that specific board given its current composition and likely style of operation going forward. We are arguing, for example, that an individual may make an excellent divisional leader but be inappropriate to contribute productively to an existing board. Of course, the reverse may also be true and may have implications for supporting roles in the executive function.

The requirement is to get the dual specification right and, because so much board assessment is focused on historical roles, it is the second part that is often overlooked. SHL has created a 'Board Fit Inventory' to try to bring some discipline to the process. It is designed for use with a chairman or a chief executive and can be used as a structure for a briefing interview or as a preliminary questionnaire. Figure 12.1 summarizes the structure but in effect the respondent is being asked to consider the board role by answering questions about the board's style of operation, the preferred personal style of new entrants to the board and the values, knowledge and experience that they should bring to the board.

This second part of the candidate's evaluation is unlikely to require assessment inputs other than those utilized for the executive function. However, it may affect the structure of the interview and it will affect the analysis and interpretation of the total data. The final report should clearly differentiate the dual objectives of the assessment.

We would normally expect the executive board chairman or chief executive to be closely involved with the definition of the dual specification as well as with the nomination and the review of candidates. However, for reasons of impartiality, the final sign-off should sit with a thoroughly informed non-executive director – the chair of the nomination committee if one exists.

Figure 12.1 Summary of SHL Board Fit Inventory structure

Section	Examples
A. Background	Organization size, board composition
B. Board style of operation	Critical questioning/creativity encouraged, entrepreneurial emphasis, participative decision making, frequency of disagreements, risk aversion
C. Required personal style	Assertiveness, independence of mind, emotional resilience, analytical skills
D. Required values, knowledge, experience	Entrepreneurial flair, customer orientation, high ethical values, handle critical media well, effective ambassador
E. Respondents' own words	Style of the chair, current factors inhibiting board interaction

In theory, a similar process should exist for non-executive directors. As Sir Adrian Cadbury has commented, in noting the trend toward nomination committees:

> Word of mouth is still a far too common way to find non-executive directors, yet no company would appoint a senior manager in a similar fashion. Nominations to the board are gradually being made more professionally in Britain but there is still a long way to go ...

In the short term, we are unlikely to see non-executive director candidates undergoing intensive multiple assessment. However, it is perfectly reasonable to expect to see more rigorous person and job specifications and a process of structured competency interviewing against that specification.

Survey findings

In its 1997/98 Personnel Practices Survey, SHL asked a sample of 301 personnel managers in large and medium-sized UK organizations about board assessment and development. Figure 12.2 indicates the relative strength of the interview, although a solid minority of more than a quarter of large organizations frequently use psychometric tests.

Formal appraisal of board incumbents was also found to be a majority practice. Three-fifths of the organizations surveyed had a process of formal appraisal for board members and a similar proportion used a process of

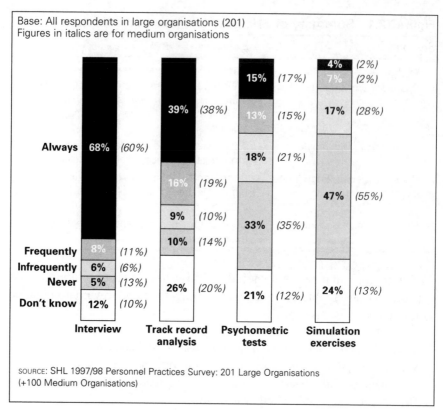

Base: All respondents in large organisations (201)
Figures in italics are for medium organisations

SOURCE: SHL 1997/98 Personnel Practices Survey: 201 Large Organisations
(+100 Medium Organisations)

Figure 12.2 Assessment methods of candidates for board positions

development planning for the board. Much less common is formal training for a board role. When asked about the last board appointee, 19 per cent said there had been formal training, while 55 per cent said there had not and 26 per cent did not know. It was more encouraging that half the interviewees said that the MD of their organization actively supported the 'development centre' concept although one in ten thought their MD was not aware of the concept and 17 per cent could not give a view.

On a more general issue, respondents were asked who represented human resource issues at board meetings; 54 per cent of large organiza-tions named the HR director or director of personnel and 13 per cent named the personnel or HR manager. However, in about one-third of cases, the respondent did not name an HR specialist – with the finance/ admin manager and managing director being most frequently mentioned in this group. In medium-sized organizations, HR was represented by an even wider variety of different job roles and functions.

Director development

Given the criticality of their input, board members should plan their ongoing development using the principles and procedures described throughout this book. Nowadays, we are seeing an increasing availability of training programmes aimed specifically at board members.[1] There is also much more scope for directors to manage their own development. The UK Institute of Management has collaborated with SHL to produce a 360° director competency assessment questionnaire (entitled 'Director Development Audit') which links directly to a large portfolio of director development options (entitled 'Check-A-Board'). Systems such as these provide a positive and practical context for the ongoing appraisal of board members.

The ongoing appraisal of board members

It is commonly accepted practice that individual executives have clearly defined objectives and that they are regularly appraised against these in a formal process. The appraisal process is seen as a valuable two-way communication exercise. Typically the appraisal process is applied to all of the executive directors, but often the formal appraisal stops short of the chief executive. There is every good reason for the chairman to sit down formally with the chief executive once or twice a year, formally to review progress against pre-agreed objectives and personal goals.

Very few chairmen attempt to review the individual performance of the non-executive directors. In many ways this is easily understood, as they are not in the same clearly defined area as their executive counterparts. They do not have formal objectives, and therefore any discussion is likely to dwell on the quality of their contribution which is less easily measured in a precise way. Indeed, we would argue that a formal evaluation process is likely to be less effective for non-executive or independent directors. This is just as true in the USA where according to a 1996 Korn/Ferry study, only 16 per cent of the Fortune 1000 companies appraised individual directors on the board. In our view the most effective way of sharing in the two-way communication of the contribution from this category of director is in the less threatening environment of reviewing the effectiveness of the board as an annual event. Here messages can be imparted and received without the need to appear to put the individual director into a subordinate role, and perhaps cause offence rather than improvement. However, the chairman will have a checklist that he or she will at least mentally use in assessing the effectiveness of an individual director of the board. The areas covered would normally be as follows:

1. Independence. Is the director confident, courageous, of a free-standing posture, and without conflicts of interest?
2. Preparedness. Does the director brief him or herself well and where necessary talk informally to key staff to get greater detail? Is time given to have a wider view of the company and the industry?
3. Practice as a director. Are the individuals thoroughly prepared, do they ask probing questions, while avoiding surprises or avoidable conflicts?
4. Committee activity. Does the director understand the meat of the committee issues, work with enthusiasm and do the necessary home-work? Does the director work equally well with the management where appropriate and the board members?
5. Development of the organization. Does the director make penetrating suggestions on innovations, strategic direction and planning?

The director's checklist

Equally the thoughtful director will have his or her own checklist that will serve as a reminder of key areas where judgements can be made about the effectiveness of the board. The six areas that we have found most helpful are as follows:

1. Is the balance on the board right? We think of balance in terms of independent directors to the total number on the board, and in terms of experience and styles that individuals bring.
2. Does the board give the required leadership to the business? As we have seen, the chairman is key both in setting the tone within which business is conducted (the standards adopted), and in ensuring the board provides the clear consistent leads that the business needs.
3. Is the agenda appropriate? Does it provide the right balance to address the important issues, and is there sufficient time for quality debate?
4. Is the information appropriate in sufficient, but not excessive, detail? Is it current and does it monitor the right things?
5. Are informal meetings and contacts encouraged? Meetings between the independent directors and members of the executive team should be encouraged so that there can be an informal exchange of information, and access to the executive on his or her own turf.
6. Does the board have its own governance in place? This includes the rules of engagement and very importantly a regular, probably annual, appraisal process.

Evaluation of the board

It is becoming increasingly clear that major investors, and active investors, are concerned about the effectiveness of the board. This is seen as a key area of differentiation between the really highly performing companies and those that are 'also rans'. This outside scrutiny will examine the board structure, the members of it, and how well it performs in practice. This in itself is a cogent reason for the board to appraise itself, but there are other reasons too. These include:

- clarifying the individual and collective roles and responsibilities of directors;
- improving the total effectiveness of the board;
- improving relations between the executive and the independent directors.

What is performance evaluation? It is a flexible, dynamic process that includes the act of setting goals and standards of performance. These goals need to be measurable and achievable. This is then followed by a formal process that measures actual performance against the pre-decided goals. The purpose of the exercise is to ensure that the board operates in the most effective way, adding real value to the decision-making process. It is not a negative or critical role, and certainly should be non-confrontational. Elements of the process may in some circumstances be undertaken on an individual basis between the chairman and a director. This may be especially helpful a short time after a director has been recently appointed, or if there is evidence of interpersonal skills being unsatisfactory. Perhaps the most universally useful evaluation work is done when the board on a regular, say annual, basis reviews the effectiveness of the board, and includes a review of the goals for the year ahead. The chairman will typically lead this item on the agenda and the following areas will be covered:

- A review of the agendas over the period under review to see that adequate time has been allowed for the important items.
- Ensuring that key processes have been fully addressed at the board, including strategy, management development and succession plans, the budgetary process, and key investment decisions.
- Examining the information provided on a regular basis as well as for ad hoc decisions to ensure that it is received in good time, is relevant, in appropriate depth, and in a form that imparts information readily to the reader.

- Checking that individual directors are satisfied with the conduct of the meetings, in that they feel that they can always make their points and that their opinions are sought out.
- Considering the number of meetings on the annual calendar to ensure that they are adequate but not so often that they become routine and concerned more with form than effectiveness.
- Ensuring that the legal and code requirements are fully met.
- Importantly, considering the key objectives for the company over the next year, considering if changes are needed to the agendas or the information provided that will be more appropriate to the future.

Demb and Neubauer have adopted a three-way approach of looking at the evaluation process. They look at the directors, their role, and the board's working style. Their main points are summarized as follows.

The directors themselves

- Intent: The chairman and the chief executive set the context and lead the board to the performance level. They should ensure that the board is a forum in which the wisdom and expertise of the members can be tapped.
- Selection, nomination and departure: Choose directors who will have as their central focus the interests of the shareholders in general. Ensure that there is an orientation process for new appointees. Departures must be handled with sensitivity, and carefully.
- Competence and balance: In choosing directors, consider stature, integrity, courage, enthusiasm, experience and expertise. Ensure that there is a skill balance. On the question of board size, there is no universal rule. The precise number should reflect the personalities involved.

The role: doing the right thing

Define a role – a set of functions and activities – that adds value.

- Agreeing on the board's mission. Evaluating the board's role asks the question, 'Is the board doing the right thing?'
- Defining the portfolio. Identify areas where the board can add value, and how it should best allocate its time. The board should ensure that default agendas are not set by the management.
- Setting priorities.
- The board–management balance. Address the board–management

power issue explicitly. Ensure that there is a clear understanding of issues reserved for the board and those items explicitly delegated to the management.

- Legal requirements. These will set minimum standards and the board may also require wider more comprehensive ones embodied in a formal statement of values.

The working style: doing things right

- Size/Structure/Committees
- Meeting schedules
- Information
- Climate: this must support constructive criticism. Key words are frank, open, courteous, critical, interested, involved, direct and helpful.

Once these features are accepted as positive standards then the evaluation process can measure performance against these.[2]

Where the board can add value

This chapter has been devoted to improving the performance of the board. We have spent time looking at the way the board functions with an eye to improving its effectiveness. We have also looked at the individual director and how a board can maximize their effectiveness through good selection procedures, a quality induction for new members, and through ongoing training. Balance on the board is more than making up the numbers according to some preconceived, usually historic pattern. Real value can be added through having a board where there are complementary styles amongst the individuals and an array of differing experiences and skills. We have made a number of practical suggestions on how to achieve this.

In addition to all of this, there are some key areas where the board can, and must, add real value. While for individual firms there will be additional specific areas, we would suggest that there are five areas which have more universal application. These are as follows:

1. The appointment of the chief executive. More than anything else this will determine the future direction and performance of the company. Finding the right match of executive skills against agreed strategic and operational priorities is very important, and worthy of the required investment of time and specialist help. The skill that he or she brings

is important in its own right, but it also must be seen against the team skills and needs. With this decision the board expresses its vision of the company's future potential through the selection of the executive leader.

2. The board's interface with corporate strategy. Primarily through the involvement in the strategy process, the board can play an important, forward role as it shares in the strategy process. In most cases, quite appropriately, the executive is charged with strategy creation and execution. This does not minimize the board's contribution. It has a crucial role in considering, modifying, and approving the way forward. Here, the wider experience of the individual, especially independent, directors is especially valuable.

3. The board as a monitor of management. To acquit itself of this role, which is both important and sensitive, it must have access to timely information that measures the right things. This will include non-accounting measures of the general health of the business, and measures of shareholder value.

4. Corporate accountability. The board must choose the external standards to which the corporation must respond and be held accountable. It must clearly act in the best interests of all shareholders, but must maintain its 'community licence' to continue to operate, by recognizing the legitimate claims of the other stakeholders. This requires good judgement and the implementation of ethical standards.

5. There must be agreed areas reserved specifically for the board. These will cover the important control, approval, legal and code areas.

The board is a key to improved performance and maximizing value for the shareholders. The winning companies are spending the time and resource in continuously improving the effectiveness of the board.

Summary

The board's key role is to ensure that long-term value is created and maintained for all of the shareholders. This is a most supportable statement but it is too general to give effective guidance on how to improve the effectiveness of the board. It needs to think about how it can best achieve this in practice and to have the processes that support this ideal. The task is a demanding one, which is not helped by the fuzzy and mixed expectations of the community at large, who often have their own unrelated agenda.

However, there are some guidelines that, if pursued, will improve the performance of the board. First there are the governance things – how the board will manage itself, how it will alter the composition, and how it will monitor the progress of the executive. Second, we have reviewed the roles of the chairman and the non-executive or independent directors, noting the traits that are found in the most successful people in these roles. This then leads on to the third point that more rigour and thought needs to be applied to the selection process. This will then assist in appointing people to these roles that are a better fit for the requirements pre-specified. The thoughtful consideration of the personalities and profiles of different people is helpful in building a more effective team at board level. To illustrate this, we outlined the principles of the SHL Board Fit Inventory which is a helpful tool to assist with the effective selection process.

The disappointment for us is that, although there is now clear evidence that objective assessment using a combination of interview, tests and simulation exercises improves candidate selection, these methods are rarely used at board level. For example, we estimate that only about one in four large/medium organizations are regularly using tests for board assessment while they are much more frequently used for other staff members. Although there is evidence that nomination committees and professional search firms are now much more widely used, there is also the continuing practice of getting candidates at the top of the list through 'word of mouth'.

We commend the director's checklist of six areas where judgements can be made about the effectiveness of a board. These are:

- Balance
- Leadership
- Agenda
- Information access
- Informal contact
- Own governance in place.

It is our strong belief that through the leadership of the chairman, the board needs to evaluate itself in a formal way on a regular basis. This also applies to board members. Our final thought is to underscore that the board is key to improved performance of any enterprise.

Notes

1. See, for example, the range of programmes designed specifically for board member development by organizations such as the UK Institute of Directors.
2. For a detailed review of a form for a director's check-up, see pages 68–77, Neville Bain and David Band, *Winning Ways Through Corporate Governance*, Macmillan, 1996.

13 Looking into the Future

Imprecise but valuable

There will be those that argue that looking into the future is imprecise, at best, and akin to crystal ball gazing at worst. They suggest that in a rapidly changing world where the speed of change cannot be accurately envisaged and where occasional major leaps cause discontinuities, there is little point in spending too long thinking about the future. The secret in these circumstances is to be alert to the first signs of change and to be able to react rapidly. Managers from this school will argue that it is better to be totally focused in the here and now, maximizing the current opportunities for the firm. As one senior director of an international manufacturing company put it, there is only one imperative: 'just get the goods out of the door'!

While there is certainly a strong element of truth in the observation that 'any future prediction will be inaccurate', it is our experience that the most successful managers, from our studies, were those that were naturally curious – those that were aware of the outside trends and thoughtfully considered the opportunities as well as the threats presented to their organizations. This breed of manager is well aware that they cannot prescribe the future with total accuracy, but they can take into account observable trends which will affect the business. Indeed, we can see in modern strategic planning systems, adopted in most countries today, that there is an environmental analysis that has regard for external factors that will affect the business. The strategy that they adopt will need to be robust when evaluated against the expected scenario.

It is also clear from our work with managers over many organizations that the most successful managers not only recognize this, but actively plan to reflect this in their own personal development programmes. An approach that we have seen work well in practice is where the manager systematically reviews trends and seriously thinks about the impact of these on his or her future environment and then considers the implications on his or her personal style or skill-base. Each individual undertaking this exercise will be thoughtfully reflecting upon the changes that flow through to him or her in new skills that will be needed. It is a competitive world and this applies to success amongst managers. While we would not pretend that there is only one blueprint in approaching this exercise, we suggest in Figure 13.1 how the exercise might well be summarized for an individual prior to preparing his or her own personal development plan.

Changing job demands

Manufacturing has steadily moved away from the monolithic production bases producing endless quantities of the same product utilizing the principles of intense specialization to reduce labour costs. The world of breaking down manufacturing tasks into the smallest specialized factors

Figure 13.1 Future trends and implications for managers

Trends

- Speed of change is increasing
- More global planning
- Growing importance and greater volatility of emerging economies
- Fundamental role of knowledge and importance of knowledge workers
- Continuing and accelerating consumer demand for value
- Greater demand for individuality both by customers and the workforce
- Shorter life cycles of technology and products
- Service is increasingly a source of differentiation
- Greater complexity
- Important demographic changes impact differently in different countries. Labour will become scarce in many developed countries and unemployment will remain high in high growth populations
- Mergers, acquisitions and disposals will increase
- Regulation will grow in some areas and deregulation will continue in others

Implications for Managers

- Need for strategic understanding, judgement and speed of action
- Need to cope with complexity
- International outlook is essential
- Must be able to deal with diversity
- Should be curious, widely aware, forward thinking
- Value broad experience
- Communication is key
- Knowledge of technology, especially information technology, will be increasingly important

performed at ever-increasing output per worker, envisaged by Adam Smith in his 'Wealth of Nations' in 1776, is no longer a model for success. Modern manufacturing practice reflects the benefits of self-controlled teams with multi-skilled talents, responsible for their own standards and their own outputs, who win the day. This arises because the motivation, commitment and enthusiasm of the team are enhanced when they can see elements of the big picture and are given both the skills and the freedom to enhance their own performance.

The manager in this more modern environment is no longer an authority figure who issues and dictates instructions that workers are expected to follow to the letter. The modern manager in this situation is more an enabler and a mentor who is there to guide and advise, not to dictate. This requires a flexible approach where it is readily acknowledged that the mindset changes from 'I know best' to one that acknowledges that no one person knows best. The successful leader knows that people are the critical resource, not to be exploited, and that they must be the key drivers to delivering competitive advantage to the firm.

Sharing knowledge

There are many management writers and truly successful companies that recognize from the current trends, which we have summarized above, that the key to success is about building up the knowledge base and sharing this across the organization. In almost all of the companies we have seen where there are different business streams or where they operate in more than one country, we observe that the best of these find ways of working to share best practice and share their knowledge.

John Browne, the innovative Chief Executive of British Petroleum, in his interview in the *Harvard Business Review* (Prokesch, 1997), observed:

> Knowledge, ideas and innovative solutions are being diffused throughout the world today at a speed that would have been unimaginable 10 or 20 years ago. Companies are only now learning how to go beyond seeing that movement as a threat, to seeing it as an opportunity ... Learning is at the heart of a company's ability to adapt to a rapidly changing environment.

Browne goes on to say:

> That anyone in the company not accountable for making a profit should be involved in creating and distributing knowledge.

The same theme is reinforced by Bob Garratt in describing the 'Learning Organization' in his book *The Fish Rots from the Head*:

> There must be systems for comparing regularly what is happening outside the organization by monitoring the external environment, benchmarking and competitor analysis, and what is happening internally, through comparing customer satisfaction, productivity and financial ratios with policies, strategies, plans, budgets and projects. Comparison, reflection and action help to build people's experience and show them the benefits of continuing to learn.

Communicating

In a diverse, spread organization, it is critical to ensure that there is good communication. Some firms tackle this by having sophisticated IT solutions that have the capability of instantly sharing valuable data around the world and allowing the information to be updated by others, interrogated by all, and used for different modelling exercises. This, coupled with video conferencing facilities, allows multi-site involvement. There is always the addition of face-to-face meetings on a regular basis to ensure that where more time together is needed, the physical interaction is provided.

The culture of the organization must be such that new ideas and new thinking are valued. The 'not invented here' syndrome has no place in the enterprise that strives for continual improvement and the wide sharing of knowledge.

We have seen in Chapter 10 that the importance of communication is very high on the agenda of the successful firm or manager. Within the context of looking to the future, the need for excellent communication is even more important. The ability to communicate is one of the top competencies of the leader of today and tomorrow.

Retaining top talent

A review of current articles and research literature shows an emerging theme that will increasingly occupy management in the years to come. Cyclical periods of economic growth squeeze the labour market. This, coupled with intensifying global competition and the shorter-term nature of work roles, increases the risk that an organization's top talent will become harder to hold. In some parts of the world, this trend has begun and there are worrying signs that management is not capable of dealing with the problem as well as it might.

The *Harvard Business Review* (September–October 1998) reported a worrying survey completed by McKinsey & Company with assistance from the human resource consultancy Sibson & Company. In the survey corporate officers and other top-level executives in 77 US companies were asked to rate their own organization's skills in managing top talent. Among the findings reported in the *Harvard Business Review* were the following:

● Only 16 per cent of senior managers were confident that their company could identify its high and low performers.
● Few companies track the progress of their high potential employees after their second years – even though the loss in those years is high.
● Only 11 per cent said they believe that high potential people are given the best development opportunities or that job assignments are used effectively for development.
● Only one-third of top executives strongly believe that their companies attract highly talented people and only 10 per cent strongly believe their companies retain most of the high performers they do hire.

One of the interesting McKinsey suggestions is that companies should develop a brand positioning strategy aimed at employees and designed to differentiate the employer in consistent and compelling terms. This is referred to as an 'employee value proposition'.

For us, the significance of this research is that it confirms many of the points made in this book and in particular in our chapter on 'motivation'. Organizations will need to work much harder to understand their key players and to ensure that development plans are in line with both competencies and motivational needs. The future will be less forgiving of organizations who do not identify and nurture their top talent or who assume that remuneration alone is the key to healthy retention. It is time for management to strengthen its appreciation of key players as 'people' rather than as units of employment.

Assessment and development practice

In the SHL Personnel Practices Survey, respondents were presented with a number of issues and asked for each whether their organization was facing it now, would face it in the future, both or neither. The results for large organizations are shown in Figure 13.2.

The largest issue for both the present and the future is seen to be the growing emphasis on the development of senior managers and directors.

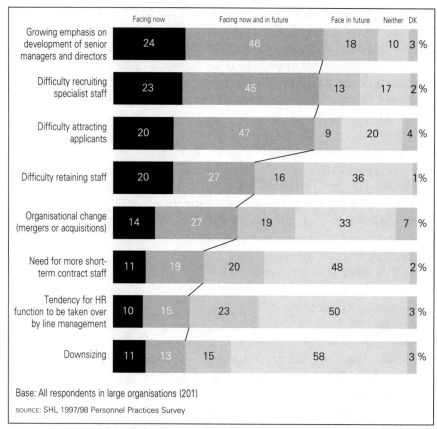

	Facing now	Facing now and in future	Face in future	Neither	DK
Growing emphasis on development of senior managers and directors	24	46	18	10	3 %
Difficulty recruiting specialist staff	23	45	13	17	2 %
Difficulty attracting applicants	20	47	9	20	4 %
Difficulty retaining staff	20	27	16	36	1 %
Organisational change (mergers or acquisitions)	14	27	19	33	7 %
Need for more short-term contract staff	11	19	20	48	2 %
Tendency for HR function to be taken over by line management	10	15	23	50	3 %
Downsizing	11	13	15	58	3 %

Base: All respondents in large organisations (201)

SOURCE: SHL 1997/98 Personnel Practices Survey

Figure 13.2 Past and future people issues

It has been a recurrent theme of this book that the development of people is not simply something that senior management does to or organizes for other people in the organization. It is even more critical at the top and we can expect to see the highest levels of management accepting this proposition in increasing numbers and ensuring that development bites where it matters most.

Although not currently a major concern, the most frequently mentioned issue for the future is the perceived tendency for HR functions to be taken over by line management. We have been through a number of years of organizational downsizing and a reduction in the size of the HR function has occurred in many cases. Line managers have had to take on roles that would previously have been the domain of specialized staff.

There are important assessment and development implications here for assessment and development technology. Line managers generally do not have the time or the inclination to undertake the level of training required for a full appreciation of all the technical issues related to the assessment and development of people. They often do not have an implicit interest in the measurement process or indeed the theory and structure of personal attribute models. But they do have important questions to answer – and they want them answered with maximum efficiency. For example, they need to know:

- Will this person be competent in that job?
- Will they be able to work with that boss?
- Will they fit the operational team?
- Will they fit the organization or divisional culture?
- How will I best motivate them?
- What development needs do they have?
- Can they sell effectively for me?
- Do they have leadership potential?
- How will they cope with devolved responsibility?
- Are there any stress issues?

And many more.

In our view, the future will bring thorough computer-based procedures to the line manager's desk to enable these judgements to be made on a sound basis.

The technology is already emerging in what are called 'Decision Support Systems'. Rigorous assessment data are fed into a computer which holds complex expert knowledge and allows decisions to be made in a justifiable way. The HR role remains but it is much more a specialist advisory one as we point out below. The computer will never be able to replace a trained and experienced specialist in balancing complex human information but it will bring enormous discipline and standardization to bear and is likely to be a long way ahead of the alternative of untrained intuitive 'feel'.

The computer is likely to bring us other benefits as its technology advances and its reach into homes increases. The Internet is already providing a basis for providing information about jobs, receiving and filtering applications and sending information for final stages of selection. We can expect this to increase and to improve in years to come. The computer itself is being used for the administration, scoring and interpretation of tests and other assessment procedures. We can expect to see more use being made of multimedia options with the potential for candidates to interact in much more realistic simulations of jobs than has been possible with pencil and paper options.

We have emphasized the need for more rigorous assessment and development at the top of the organization. Further down the organization, we expect to see an ongoing realization of the importance of customer service and support, as markets become tougher. Organizations will focus more carefully on ensuring that they have the right people for these roles and that they are given the right training and development. Other staff will also come under pressure to add value to the organization and we expect to see a continuing growth in measures of 'dependability' covering areas such as personal integrity and motivation. It is noticeable that the USA is taking strong strides in these directions.

Finally, we expect to see more 'pure development centres' where there is an assessment component but it is utilized totally in the interest of helping an individual to come to terms with their relative strengths and limitations and to plan development accordingly. The usage of 360° assessment instruments will also increase as part of this process and we would like to think that sensitivity to all-round assessment will decline as its developmental benefits are recognized.

The HR management role

As organizations have striven to operate from leaner bases, the number of HR practitioners may have declined but the good news is that the importance of the HR management role must inevitably increase in the years to come. If this book has any validity then we are right to argue for more time and attention to be given to the management of the people resource. An increasing part of this job will shift to line management. The HR managers of the future will be increasingly specialized in their knowledge of how human attributes interact with jobs. They will become much more involved with internal consultancy, the creation of computer-based systems and the determination of best practice. Their role, quite rightly, will have less to do with HR administration. They will be required to demonstrate added value through people initiatives and they should be able to do it.

International development of HR management

Our own experience leads us to believe that there are four broad stages in the evolution of the HR function within organizations (Figure 13.3).

At stage 1, the HR role has more to do with administrative needs than

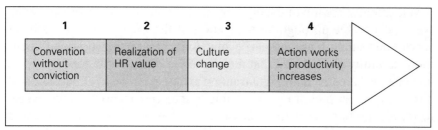

Figure 13.3 Evolution of the HR function

productivity concerns. Even where the latest assessment and development technology is utilized there is still an element of this being the right thing to do rather than a belief – particularly at the top of the organization – that it is a vital ingredient of longer-term success. If this were not the case, then it would be hard to explain why tests of proven predictive value are overruled in selection decisions; why assessment, appraisal and development are relatively rare at the top of the organization; and why HR budgets are cut at times when their impact could be most beneficial.

It is true that organizations that practise the latest methods and technology increase the probability that they will establish the real benefit to be derived from people. However, this realization alone is not enough and there needs to be a serious culture shift in which the value of people is recognized at all levels of the organization before the vital fourth stage is reached and management action leads to real productivity growth.

In the developed economies HR management practice varies considerably with organization but in general large pools of experience and knowledge have been developed and some organizations are taking a lead in shaping productive policies and practice. Publications, conferences and seminars abound as opportunities for learning and sharing experiences. In the developing countries, the degree of HR management sophistication is less advanced but there is an enormous motivation to seek out and establish the world's best practice. These countries are moving fast and they operate with a high degree of pragmatism. They will research carefully, identify the best practice and then implement it ruthlessly. They will expect it to work and will change tack quickly if they have to. They will not take as long to evolve to a position of optimum performance as their counterparts in the developed world.

In the assessment area, for example, we have seen Asian companies developing the concept of computer-based decision support systems ahead of Western companies. This is based on a realization that it would take too long to train and develop staff to understand attribute models of human performance. Their alternative is to build the knowledge into computer systems and focus on the management applications of that knowledge. Their emphasis is on the usage of the information rather than the rationale for it.

Our perception of the future is one in which organizations world-wide – having realized the criticality of their people – become much more competitive in developing and utilizing that resource. As we have seen in other professional areas such as advertising and marketing research, differences in international standards of practice will decline and performance will sharpen up all round.

CASE STUDY 13.1
Hyundai – Selecting sales representatives

In terms of global competitiveness, a pertinent issue for the future is how the more recently developed and developing economies will respond to changes in assessment and development practice.

South Korea is not a country that would readily be thought of in terms of having sophisticated HR management practices. At the time of writing, the South Korean economy is in bad shape but certain companies will come through this period more strongly than others and the quality of HR management should have a part to play.

Hyundai – the car manufacturer – has been reviewing the way it assesses its car sales staff in order to see whether measures of personality could enhance the effectiveness of its selection. This is an important issue. At the time of the research, Hyundai had approximately 3300 sales representatives in Seoul City alone. These were classified into categories of high, middle and low sales performance with the high category estimated to be selling an average of 82 cars per annum.

A sample of 116 sales representatives was selected for a research study – 45 in the high sales category, 36 in the medium category and 35 in the low category. These were given a Korean language version of the Occupational Personality Questionnaire. The results were then correlated with sales performance.

In the analysis, nine competencies had been pre-hypothesized as potentially relevant to sales performance. Each competency was defined in terms of a particular mix of personality scales. Five of these competencies turned out to have significant correlations with sales performance. These were:

- Achievement orientated/Energetic
- Good at interpersonal relations
- Less change orientated
- More emotionally expressive
- Confidence in communication

The sales representatives were then given a total score on these five predictors and were divided into three groups of high, medium and low scorers. As expected, there was a strong tendency for the high personality scorers to be in the high sales category. More precisely, it was found that the chances of correctly identifying top performers increased by 38 per cent and the chances of identifying and rejecting poor performers went up by 50 per cent over existing interview and experience-based selection techniques. More detailed utility analysis based on the profit generated from each car sale led to an estimated potential increase in annual profitability of 14 per cent if the new procedures were used.

This is one of numerous examples in the countries of Asia Pacific of large organizations becoming increasingly aware of and experienced in assessment methods that have tended to be associated with the West. When the current economic turmoil is past, we can expect to see new disciplines emerging in this aspect of people management.

Bringing the human barriers down

Our final observation in considering the future is that the increasingly competitive market context will force organizations to lower current barriers to improving HR management practice. We already have available many assessment and development techniques and procedures which can improve the critical fit of people to jobs. However, these will only deliver benefit if they are used with integrity by the managers for whom they have been designed.

There is no point in designing new and more valid test procedures if a senior manager's subjective judgement is going to take precedence. There is no point in implementing thorough appraisal procedures if managers lack the honesty to confront areas of limitation and discuss appropriate action. It is ultimately futile to design an expensive 'development centre' if there is no serious organizational commitment to developmental follow-up. We cannot allow politics and self-interest to deter us from objective evaluation and decision making. Most of all we have to encourage our very best technology to be applied at the top of our organizations and not be deterred from confronting the mismatch of senior person and senior role.

These are all human factors which stand as barriers to best practice. They have been tolerated while organizations have grown and prospered in favourable market conditions. We believe that a tougher future will favour those organizations who demand maximum objectivity and bring these barriers down.

Summary

In this chapter, we have emphasized the need for managers to be alert to trends and changes in their business environments and to plan their personal development accordingly. In an increasingly competitive world, there will be a premium on optimizing the management process through the better use of people. The sharing of knowledge and the development of the mentality of the 'learning organization' are both important in this respect. We will further facilitate the process of learning by enhancing the means of communication within an organization.

In terms of assessment and development practice, we can expect to see more rigorous procedures brought in at the top of the organization. We also anticipate fast growth in the use of computer-based 'decision support systems' and much more sophisticated 'multimedia' assessment methods. Despite downsizing, we expect to see the HR management role strengthen but much more as an internal specialist consultancy than as an administrative support function.

On the international front we are already seeing signs of the emerging economies realizing the power of objective assessment and we expect this trend to continue.

14

Lessons Learned

A review of the main messages

The overriding message of this book has been that people have the potential to make a big difference to the performance of the organization. However, people are complex and so are jobs and managing this interaction successfully is no easy matter. There are some current paradoxes that need to be resolved. Human Resource departments are being slimmed down; managers are spending tiny fractions of their time on the development of themselves and others; boards are only slowly recognizing the need for objective assessment and development at their own level and people are still not figuring strongly enough in the valuation of the assets of a business.

The first lesson of the book has been to recognize the difficulty of thorough Human Resource management but to teach us not to be frightened by it. We have tried to show how both jobs and people can be broken down into constituent parts in the interest of maximizing the person–job match. We have voted in favour of competency models because they provide a behavioural framework for managers to understand capabilities in non-technical terms. However, we have also argued for parallel models of human attributes for those with specialist training to use because they help us to understand why competencies have or have not been developed and how development should best be applied. The ultimate goal is to be able to take complex job and people information and turn it into straightforward management actions to help objectives to be met. Our maxim is 'complex inputs – simple outputs'. The danger for us all is that we allow the complexity to overwhelm us so that we shut our eyes to it and revert to an over-simplified and possibly prejudiced intuitive 'feel'.

We have tried to show that where organizations improve the fit between people and jobs, productivity gains of between 10 and 15 per cent are realistically attainable. This is an important message and has implications for a country's economy as a whole. We encourage the idea that management should demand accountability from those providing assessment and development services. We are comfortable that the most professional providers will welcome this and the opportunity to show how productivity can seriously be enhanced. We also note in passing that it is often easier to shape a job than it is to shape a person but this aspect of 'fit' is all too often missed by management.

At the start of the book, we identified the preparation and implementation of a sound **strategy** and the release of the power of **people** as the two main challenges facing management. We used these two challenges as a means to covering a number of themes and specific issues. We emphasized the importance of defining objectives and of creating thorough systems of appraisal. We reinforced the need for excellent communication both in terms of informing staff of mission and objectives and as a general management competence. We differentiated leadership from management and went into some detail to explore the characteristics of both 'inspirational' and 'perspirational' leadership. We noted the importance of identifying external trends and then developing the competencies and attributes that will be suitable for both today's and tomorrow's environment. We favoured the early identification of high flyers in the interest of ensuring that they are properly developed in good time to deliver tomorrow's benefit – and to keep them within the organization.

We have strongly recommended the use of management assessment programmes with a development focus and we have referred to these as 'development centres'. We have offered advice as to how these should be best implemented and in particular we have extolled the benefit of creating a development culture. If development is to occur within the organization then individuals must believe that it really matters to top management and that time and resources will be made available to ensure that it works. This links into the concept of personal motivation which is essential to all new learning.

Part I of this book concluded with a focus on international assessment and development. These are vital ingredients if the organization is to be successful in the new and ever more competitive global markets of tomorrow. The goal is to be able to strike a balance between the standardization of international practice and the need to take account of cultural differences in everyday practice. We also support the careful identification of managers who are suited to operate on an international basis. We offer a specification of which cross-cultural adaptability is a key component.

In Part II of this book we concentrated on a number of specific assessment-related themes. In terms of the assessment of both new and existing staff, we argued that no single procedure is to be preferred to any other. The optimum approach is to use a multiple of different methods with the emphasis on **relevance** to the content of jobs to be undertaken by successful candidates. However, testing for abilities and personality has grown on a world-wide basis over the past decade and we can now see good evidence to support the validity of these methods. These remain somewhat technical areas for managers to understand and utilize but they have the potential to facilitate many aspects of management decision making.

A related area concerns the assessment of motivation which is a major contributor to an individual's success in a job and an important determinant of the level of organizational output. We argue that no single theory of motivation is satisfactory in accounting for the entirety of this complex feature of people. We describe an eclectic model which can be used to increase our understanding of the links between the individual, the job and the prevailing culture.

An individual's personality is clearly an important part of his or her motivational mix. We saw further evidence of the importance of under-standing personality in examining creativity, stress and entrepreneurship. We need to be able to encourage creative talent, to foresee areas of impending stress and to be able to adapt the organization to cope with the particular characteristics of the entrepreneur. Most of the issues here lie in the personality domain and managers in general need to sharpen their perceptiveness of the personalities of those with whom they work. We believe that the concept of 'emotional intelligence' will become increasingly important in our definition of effective management.

In recognizing the importance of strategic thinking, we have described seven main elements of strategy. In particular, we have emphasized the need to ensure that the right people are in place and properly developed to deliver the required strategy. As well as experience, there are ability and personality attributes which can be defined in this respect. We have also put the spotlight on the performance of the board and emphasized the need for the board to add value to the organization. We expect to see more attention on the process of board interaction and an increasing tendency for the board members to be objectively selected; appraised individually for their annual contributions; developed as required and evaluated in total for their performance. The role of the chairman is critical and we have offered guidelines for the effective management of the board.

We recognize, as others have, that there is a team issue at board level in that the kinds of people who make it to this level of operation are unlikely to make a balanced team. Individual ingredients for success may include single-mindedness, a strong task orientation, independence of mind and a narrow achievement-driven focus. Successful team interaction at board level is likely to require strong leadership, a binding common purpose and a realization of the different personal make-up of team members and the implications for interaction. This final point allows at least some potential for the management of relationships.

If we are right about the power of people, then there are many things that can be done to help to release it. Organizations may not reach perfection but they can go a long way towards taking more value from the people they employ. If these actions are taken then the **value** of the organization should be enhanced but how would we recognize this and how should we measure it? Is it time to start rethinking the basis on which we judge the true assets of a business?

What is value?

Think about the following comments which purport to look at the value of a company.

- 'The company's value is the difference between the recorded assets and liabilities on the Balance Sheet.'
- 'The company's value is the market capitalization at any particular time.'
- 'The value is ultimately found in the break-up or price that could be achieved in the open market.'
- 'The theoretical value is the sum of the future cashflows discounted for the company's cost of capital.'
- 'The true value of a company is found in the quality and competence of its people.'

This array of quotations shows that there is a different perception of value. Accountants, steeped in the principles of 'double entry', follow convenient conventions that give them a Balance Sheet produced in a consistent way. The Balance Sheet seldom shows the value of an enterprise and it is not unusual for the market value of a quoted company to be double the shareholders' funds recorded in the Balance Sheet. However, even the market capitalization is not in itself a firm foundation of value. This is because the rating a company receives depends upon the perception of potential buyers and sellers of the relative value of a particular company, compared with other investment opportunities. Indeed, in the case of a take-over sale, it is usual to achieve a premium over market price of between 20 and 30 per cent.

The theoretical value, calculated by discounting future cashflows by the cost of capital, is a more appropriate measure for a business as a going concern. However, the assessment of future cashflows is far from certain. We need to look behind this to get a more complete answer. The future cashflows will be driven to one level or another depending upon the quality and competence of the human resource. We believe that there is, therefore, a real challenge to today's management in finding ways to focus on this and to measure it, despite the lack of accounting accuracy.

Latent assets

The difference between the value of an enterprise as shown in the Balance Sheet and the true value is due to latent assets which are those additional to the physical assets. They are centred on knowledge and competencies:

- Knowledge retained by the management and the workforce
- Knowledge of customers and suppliers
- Knowledge of brands or trademarks which drive value
- Knowledge of the industry or market-place
- Technical expertise
- Competencies to add value to the existing business.

These provide the additional value that will lift the profitability and cashflows to higher levels to sustain higher ratings than those derived from the physical assets. Importantly, these are the source of competitive advantage. Some of this knowledge is recorded in accessible records but much of it resides with the management and workforce.

Unsurprisingly, these assets, like physical ones, do not retain their value in perpetuity. They need to be provided with adequate funds to maintain their value. As an example, 'brands' need to be sustained with advertising if they are to retain value and remain relevant to the needs of their customers over time.

As investment in brands is seen as essential in maintaining their value, a number of measures have been established to assess the adequacy and

value of the spend. Some of the more common measures include:
- Share of advertising voice compared to the brand share
- Awareness measures, both prompted and unprompted, sometimes referred to as share of mind
- Advertising tracking studies to measure how perception changes
- Focus groups to give qualitative feedback
- Advertising effectiveness, measuring the value received per unit of advertising spend, and how this influences consumers' spending.

Managers need to find a way that measures the most important of all these latent assets, the competence of its people. The great challenge is to find a way that is meaningful and focuses managers' attention on their most important task – on how they can improve human performance.

Measures

Over time, the inadequacy of financial reporting has been recognized. It really looks at the past in financial terms, making appropriate comparisons against a plan and explaining differences. This has moved on to enrich the database to include the strategic dimension, so that information and comparisons can help managers make strategic decisions.

In the mid-1990s, the concept of the 'balanced score card' as a strategic management system was introduced. The concept here was to have financial as well as non-financial reporting. The enterprise would determine what are the critical factors to sustain shareholder value and would then regularly measure them. It was recognized that, with some of these measures, precision was not possible, although direction was. We support the concept of the balanced score card and the inclusion of people-related measures.

Measuring the capability of the people resource

Turning now to the measurement of the people resource, we have some interesting challenges. There are three inter-related dimensions. First are the transactions involving people which we can record with varying degrees of accuracy in each accounting period. These may be gathered through the financial reporting system, or they may need to be captured separately. This group would include:

- the spend on training and development by classification of the various groups of people and including per capita measures;
- productivity indices;
- labour turnover, absenteeism, cost of recruiting and percentage of new staff by category retained for more than 12 months;
- employee attitudes on key development issues.

Second is an annual assessment of competence that would include:

- an audit of staff and management competencies against the job requirements using objective assessment methods;
- percentage of performance appraisals by category of workforce, completed by the required time;
- percentage by category of the workforce who have personal development plans agreed and being pursued;
- capability in key areas, such as information technology, communicating ability, customer service;
- if succession plans identify emergency cover for around 75–80 per cent of key jobs, and on a planned basis, what is the cover for key roles in three to five years' time?

Third is the culture of the enterprise. The fundamental question is 'Are people supported in the development of their competencies?' Are they well motivated, valued by the organization and likely to outperform their peers employed by competitors? This normally requires some annual qualitative and quantitative research to provide answers to the following:

- The degree to which sharing of best practice and networking is positively encouraged and, where appropriate, supported by IT systems.
- Is management seen to be committed to the development of its people?
- Is there a climate of learning and thirst for knowledge, where experimentation is welcomed?
- Do members' incentive reward systems support such behaviour?
- What do external benchmarking studies show in relation to best practice with people?

The latter two categories together provide a 'snapshot' in time, which is usually annual, and which is in a form that can be compared with previous periods. The measures are not precise and not universal for each employer.

Those who are serious about improving human performance will find answers that provide a lead for them in their special circumstances. There is no universal panacea but the effort and the focus will add real value, as well as reinforce the culture of 'people first because they are the greatest source of competitive value'.

People Advantage Health Check

We think that it is helpful to have a health check that can be used across different businesses to help the appraiser to take a view about the real focus on important human resource related areas, to establish if people are effectively utilized. To facilitate this we have prepared 30 big questions that call for observations or sometimes independent research on the board, the management, the workforce, business processes and culture, as well as some more general issues (see Figure 14.1).

This shows something of the broad scope that affects the ability to derive the maximum benefit from the total people resource. There is an added benefit. Organizations that see the importance of utilizing the people resource create a productive environment that leads to higher levels of attainment, and attracts new entrants who see value in belonging to a truly exciting, great place to work.

Figure 14.1 People Advantage Health Check

Question	*Answer*		
	A definite yes	It's satisfactory now	No
The Board			
1. Is the balance on the board right, that is, both for independent/executive skills and experience required?			
2. Does the board provide leadership?			
3. Is the agenda appropriate for the business context?			
4. Is there sufficient information?			
5. Does the board have its own governance in place, including its own appraisal?			

Question	Answer		
	A definite yes	It's satisfactory now	No
The Management			
6. Are clear objectives in place and is progress against them monitored?			
7. Are appraisals open, two-way and valuable?			
8. Are career reviews available and helpful?			
9. Are managers selected objectively using relevant and justifiable methods?			
10. Is there an objective fast track system to identify and develop managers of potential?			
11. Is training routinely available to improve skills?			
12. Does the employer identify and communicate key competencies to meet future needs?			
13. Is there clear communication of key messages to all management levels?			
The Workforce			
14. Does the workforce feel involved?			
15. Is there communication and consultation before key decisions are taken that affect the workforce?			
16. Do all staff have an appraisal and the opportunity for training?			
17. Is selection completed using relevant and justifiable methods?			
Business Processes: Human Resources			
18. Is there a quality formal management development and succession plan?			
19. Does the data bank of individuals' attributes allow for speedy identification of people to match specific job specifications?			
20. Is the investment in people development measured and compared against the benefits?			
21. Is the graduate recruitment programme pitched to identify the best fit of candidates with organization requirements?			
22. Is the HR department seen as value adding where views are sought out because of their value to the business?			

Question	Answer		
	A definite yes	It's satisfactory now	No
Culture			
23. Is there an open culture where challenge, improvement and seeking of better ways is the norm?			
24. Is there a climate of continuous learning where knowledge is truly valued?			
25. Is there commitment to the real importance of people as a major source of competitive advantage?			
General			
26. Does the organization free people to deliver their full potential and allow speedy decisions to be taken?			
27. Is there a clear understanding of the purpose, directions and values?			
28. Is the strategy understood and clearly communicated to the appropriate level of detail through the business?			
29. Is management alert to external trends and knowledgeable about the impact of these on the business?			
30. Is the organization seen as an exciting, great place to work?			
Total			

Scoring

Mark one of the three choices and add up the ticks in each column.

Score +3 for definitely
Score +1 for satisfactory
Score −2 for no

Evaluation

60 and above	Exceptional
51–59	Excellent
41–50	Good but some areas for attention
31–40	Attention clearly required in a number of areas
21–30	A major investment in people is needed
20 or less	Unsatisfactory

A final thought

In past ages, competitive advantage was derived from physical assets or some special advantage such as mineral rights, or derived from being in protected markets, that make the cost of entry high for would-be competitors. Economies of scale are no longer as important as they were and superior service is often a differentiator that can be utilized. Today and tomorrow the success of businesses will be derived more from the building up of knowledge, sharing it, renewing it and exploiting it in the marketplace. This requires management with new skills and new ways of working in a supportive environment.

More than ever before, employers must find the right people with the right skills and place them where they are most effective – doing the right job. Tackling this task with the rigour needed is essential and will pay off. Developing these people so that they are 'fit for the job' as it is today and will be tomorrow and motivating them to perform will also pay big dividends. This applies at all levels, including the most senior, a lesson still to be picked up by many enterprises today.

Human Resource directors and those that provide consulting help in the HR field should willingly hold themselves accountable to the bottom line for the expenditure that they make in pursuit of these goals. Accountants need to find a way more appropriately to record the value created from this spend and general managers should demand no less. Managers' behaviour will readily be altered when reward systems reflect the items that are 'top of the agenda'. There is then a good case for ensuring that reward systems reflect the value created from people, despite the difficulties this may bring. The ultimate advantage of unleashing the power of all of the people will only be achieved when this pursuit is genuinely seen as the source of greatest competitive advantage.

Appendix A

Calculating the Financial Return of an Improved Selection Method

In Chapter 1, we gave an example of an organization having taken a sample of current job holders and then tested them with a relevant method on a 'personal attribute' while at the same time measuring their job performance. Figure A.1 shows the correlation of the two measures, a test cut-off score for future selection and the expected gain in average level of job performance.

Using the distribution in Figure A.1, we can take a future selected group and estimate the **job performance** of the average member of that group in terms of the **personal attribute scores**. This can then be multiplied by the total number in the future selected group to provide a total estimate of

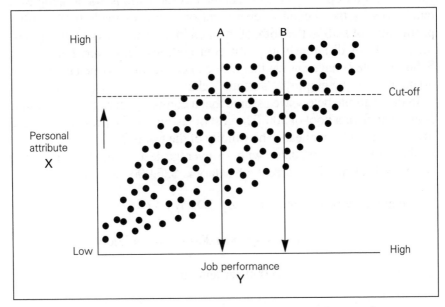

Figure A.1 Productivity gain when an attribute predicts performance

job performance to be compared with the current level of job performance. The basic formula here is:

$$\text{Annual \$ gain in profit} = (r_v . \bar{Z}_x . SD_y . N) - C$$

where

r_v　　= validity coefficient for the test of the attribute

$\bar{Z}_x$　　= the average Z score on the test of the selected group

SD_y　= standard deviation of profit per annum on the job performance measure in dollar terms

N　　= number in the selected group

C　　= cost of the testing programme

This is a basic model for which there are a number of refinements depending on assumptions about the existing selection procedures and the financial modelling of profit over time. A complex central problem is the estimate of the standard deviation of job performance in dollar terms (SD_y). Various options include detailed computations for a sample of employees by the accounts department or estimates made of the dollar profit value of staff at the 16th, 50th and 84th percentiles (which approximate 1 SD of difference in profit contribution). However, Hunter and Schmidt (1982) have shown that SD_y can conservatively be estimated at 40 per cent of the employee's annual salary.

In the example below, we assume that a company recruits 50 sales staff from an applicant pool of 500. The cost of testing for the personal attribute in question is $10 per head. The validity of the test is 0.4 and the company is able to recruit candidates with an average test score at 1 SD above current sales staff. The current job salary is $25,000.

$$\text{The annual \$ profit gain} = (r_v . \bar{Z}_x . SD_y . N) - C$$

$$= (0.4 \times 1 \times \$10,000 \times 50) - \$5,000$$

$$= \$195,000 \text{ per annum}$$

It can be noted in this example:

- The cost of the testing is small against the potential gain.
- The more valid the test and the higher the cut-off on the test, the greater the pay-off.
- The pay-off is linear to the validity coefficient.
- The more people recruited, the higher the potential pay-off.
- In this case, SD_y has been estimated at 40 per cent of salary. SD_y can be thought of as the difference in profit contribution between a very good (84th percentile) and average (50th percentile) salesperson. This is a good check of the credibility of SD_y. For very senior jobs in an organization, the 40 per cent of salary guideline is likely to be over-cautious as an estimate of SD_y.

The converse of the above points is that even a valid procedure will offer little return on investment if the difference between good and average job performers is minimal or there is very little choice of applicants such that $\bar{Z}_x$ approaches zero.

The main implications for management of models of this kind are to ensure that valid assessment procedures are being used for jobs where performance really matters and to ensure that there is a sufficiently large applicant pool for the assessment procedure to be able to filter out high scorers.

Glossary of Terms

Abilities – Specifically defined capabilities such as numerical reasoning, diagrammatic reasoning, clerical checking and so on. To be distinguished from general intellgence.

Adverse impact – see 'Disparate impact'.

Aptitudes – Areas of potential to acquire new skills or knowledge in the future.

Assessment centre – An assessment approach usually involving a variety of specific methods with a strong component of simulation exercises. It is also likely to have several assessors and a multiple of applications such as recruitment and development planning.

Balance sheet – Statement of assets and liabilities of an enterprise or organization at a particular time.

Biodata – Biographical information – such as age, length of past job tenure – about a candidate usually collected via a questionnaire or application form. The concept has been extended to cover interest, attitude and even personality questions collected at the same time.

Bottom line (of the profit and loss account) – The residual profit (usually net profit before tax).

Business Plan – Sometimes called a strategic plan. This is a short document that describes the goals and how the business will get there. Typically the plan is for three or four years ahead.

Capital spend – Sometimes referred to as Capex or capital expenditure. Payment for investments not charged against current income.

Career development review – The planning of steps in an individual's career.

Cash flow – Cash receipts less cash payments before any financing or dividends.

Competencies – Definitions vary but the term is used here to refer to more broadly based behavioural capabilities such as planning and organizing, making formal presentations, formulating strategy and so on.

Competency mapping – The drawing of distinctive profiles of sets of competencies to reflect a current state of organizational development and culture.

Corporate culture – An organization's dominant system of beliefs, values and practices.

Corporate governance – The rules and procedures put in place to see that a company is properly run.

Correlation- The relationship between two variables or sets of data. Usually expressed as a coefficient ranging from 0 (no relationship) to 1 (a perfect relationship allowing perfect prediction).

Cost of capital – The cost to the company of servicing its total capital base including equity and debt.

Creativity – A complex concept describing new thinking including elements of speed of association, the ability to think laterally to related areas, the origination of new ideas as well as others.

Critical incidents method – A method in which incidents which are relatively important to an area of study are explored and categorised. Quite commonly used in job analysis to explore important incidents in terms of job outcomes.

Cut-off score – The score on an assessment method which separates those accepted from those rejected.

Decision support systems – Computerized systems designed to facilitate management decisions on the assessment and development of people and utilizing well researched knowledge bases concerning performance in the world of work.

Depreciation – The amount provided for the diminution of an asset over the year. This is not a cash cost but is a charge against the Profit and Loss account.

Development centre – An assessment centre approach with a particular orientation towards developmental applications for each participant.

Differential model of abilities – A model which emphasizes the differentiation of specific abilities as opposed to focussing on a more generalized concept of intelligence.

Direct discrimination – Treating a person less favourably because of their membership of a defined population sub group (for example, ethnic, religious, gender).

Disparate impact – The effect of setting a selection criterion where proportionately fewer members of a defined population sub group (for example ethnic, religious, gender) can meet the criterion.

Emotional intelligence (EQ) – Quite a complex social capability at the heart of which are several important elements including the ability to read one's own emotions; the ability to read the emotions of others and the broad capability to manage one's own and others' emotions to best effect.

Emotions – A general term used to describe feelings such as anger, fear, love, pride etc. Based on the Latin 'Motere' – to move, the term suggests an impulse to act and is an important aspect of motivation.

Equal opportunity legislation – Legislation designed to promote fairness in employment practice for defined population sub groups. It commonly attempts to prevent both direct and indirect discrimination.

Error of measurement – A statistical measurement – which reflects the accuracy of an assessment method's scores.

Extrinsic job factors – Used in motivation theory to describe elements of motivation which are external to the nature of the job tasks. For example – remuneration or benefits.

Faking – Usually denotes an intentional distortion of a self-description questionnaire. It should be distinguished from self-deception in which an individual may genuinely hold a view which is at odds with reality.

Fast track development – Special development programme for high potential individuals to bring them quickly to an appropriate job level with the necessary knowledge and experience.

Graphology – More commonly known as handwriting analysis.

Group exercise – An exercise that simulates working in a group in a work environment. It is common for the number of participants to be around six. In some cases, specific roles are assigned to participants.

Human resource (HR) management – The management of people as an organizational resource covering, for example, recruitment, working conditions, pay and benefits, training and development.

Humanistic approach – A theory of personality which emphasizes higher human motives and the development/improvement of the 'self' concept.

Hygiene factors – Used in motivation theory to describe job context factors such as working conditions which are pre-requisites of satisfaction but not positive motivators in their own right.

Indirect discrimination – An unjustifiable requirement or condition which has disparate impact on those from a defined population sub group (for example, ethnic, religious, gender) to their detriment.

Intelligence (IQ) – A broad, generalized mental capability.

In-tray exercise – A simulation exercise in which a candidate takes over a manager's in-tray or in-basket and completes one or more exercises concerning the contents.

Intrinsic job factors – Used in motivation theory to describe elements of motivation which are derived from the nature of the job tasks themselves. For example, interest in creative thinking.

Job analysis – A systematic approach to gathering and analyzing information about a job. Thorough job analysis is usually based on several methods and an intensive process of inferring job requirements. It should be distinguished from a cursory consideration of a job.

Job description – A structured description of the purpose and objectives of a job together with the principal tasks, responsibilities and other contextual factors.

Management development committee – A committee set up with the broad objective of ensuring that succession planning is in place and that individuals have been correctly identified for future roles with appropriate development planned.

Market capitalization or value – Generally used to indicate the total value of the company on the stock exchange at a particular time. It is calculated by multiplying the share price by the total number of shares in issue.

Mentoring – Where a senior experienced manager in an organization guides and advises a younger developing manager. The mentor is usually not the individual's direct boss.

Mission – The major purpose for which the company exists.

Motivation – Something which acts as a source of human energy as well as directing and sustaining it.

Nomination committee – A sub-committee of the board of directors commonly charged with ensuring sound senior level succession planning and appropriate levels of director remuneration. Likely to have a strong representation of non-executive directors.

Non-executive director (NED) – A director appointed to the board of directors of a company who does not have a specific executive function. This is an independent individual who acts both as a governance control and as a source of independent advice.

Normative data (Norms) – Standard distributions of assessment method scores based on the performance of a representative sample of a given group. Used as a basis for comparison in interpreting psychometric test scores.

Operating profits – Profits before interest and tax and before dividend distributions.

Performance appraisal – Regular retrospective evaluation of an individual's performance against defined job objectives. A common basis for developmental planning as well as an important input to remuneration decisions.

Person specification – A detailed statement of the personal requirements of an individual to meet the demands of a particular job.

Personal attribute – A characteristic of an individual. The term is used in this book to differentiate underpinning characteristics of an individual from broader categories of overt behaviour.

Personal development plan (PDP) – A document which utilizes career, competencies and aspirations analysis to plan the on-going development of an individual to both their own and the organization's benefit. The process may be referred to as a career development review.

Personality – A complex concept with definitions rooted in specific theories. In this book it refers to how an individual typically thinks, feels and relates to other people.

Personality questionnaire/inventory – A questionnaire which looks at the way that an individual typically thinks, feels and relates to other people.

Position – Used in job analysis to denote the specific position held by an individual. An organization has as many positions as employees. Homogeneous sets of positions are classified as jobs in an organization.

Positive (affirmative) action – Setting a criterion for selection which is to the advantage of a particular population sub-group. Usually applied where that group has been disadvantaged in the past.

Psychoanalytic approach – A theory of personality which among other facets emphasizes the role of the sub-conscious on the personality and behaviour of the individual.

Psychometric tests – Measures of psychological constructs which are characterized by acceptable levels of reliability and validity.

Reinforcement – A concept taken from learning theory describing the rewards or consequences associated with behaviour.

Reliability of an assessment method – Concerned with the consistency of the method as a measuring instrument. For example, when a person is tested on two separate occasions.

Repertory grid – A method which is used to map how an individual construes or thinks of part of his or her environment. Quite commonly used in job analysis to understand how individuals construe jobs familiar to them.

Shareholder value – In a general sense this focuses on improving the long run net wealth created for shareholders. Shareholder value is positive when there is a surplus over the cost of the use of the capital in the business. The cost of capital, often referred to as the weighted average cost of capital, is based on the after tax cost of debt and equity.

Simulation exercises – Exercises which simulate part of a job. Common examples include group or committee exercises; the taking over of a manager's in-tray; fact finding exercises; decision making exercises, and so on.

Social learning approach – A theory of personality which emphasizes the role of observation and imitation in the development of personality.

Standardized tests – Tests designed and used so as to maximize standardization in terms of the content, the environment, the administration, the scoring and the interpretation.

Stress – An emotional pressure resulting from a situation where the perceived demands on an individual exceed their perceived ability to cope.

Succession planning – The process of preparing succession for key executives in an organization.

Team building – The process of putting together or developing teams in the interest of maximizing their productivity and personal satisfaction.

Three sixty degree (360°) evaluation – Evaluation of an individual by self, boss, direct reports, peers or colleagues. Usually in the form of a questionnaire and based on a competency model.

Top-down selection – A basis of selection in which candidates are rank ordered on a criterion and the required number are taken off the top.

Traits – Relatively long-lasting and habitual characteristics of an individual. They should be differentiated from shorter term moods or states.

Transformational leadership – A theory of leadership which emphasizes the power of leaders to inspire followers to perform beyond normal expectations by emphasizing higher levels of need fulfilment.

Types – A model of personality which contrasts with trait theory and emphasizes the division of people into groups or types which share preferred ways of behaving.

Utility of an assessment method – The pay-off to the organization from using a particular assessment method. For example, this may be expressed as the annual increase in profit derived from selecting people with a new method as opposed to an existing method.

Validity of an assessment method – The extent to which the method is measuring what it claims to be measuring. The extent to which appropriate inferences can be made.

References

Adair, John, *Great Leaders*, Talbot Adair Press, 1989.

Adams, J S, 'Towards an Understanding of Inequity', *Journal of Abnormal and Social Psychology*, 67, pp. 422–435, 1963.

Anderson, Neil, and Peter Herriott (Eds), *International Handbook of Selection and Assessment*, John Wiley & Sons, 1997

Bain, Neville, and David Band, *Winning Ways through Corporate Governance*, Macmillan, 1996.

Bain, Neville, *Successful Management*, Macmillan, 1995.

Banks, Paul, and Bob Waisfisz, *Managing Inter-cultural Teams: a Practical Approach to Cultural Problems*, Chapter 3 in H Shaughnessy (Ed.) *Collaboration Management – Inter-cultural Working: New Issues and Priorities*, John Wiley & Sons, 1994

Bartram, Dave, Distance Assessment: Psychological Assessment Through The Internet, *Selection and Development Review*, British Psychological Society, 1997

Bass, Bernard M, *Leadership and Performance Beyond Expectations*, Free Press, 1985

Beehr, Terry A, *Psychological Stress in the Workplace*, Routledge, 1995

Belbin, Meredith R, *Team Roles at Work*, Butterworth-Heinemann, 1997.

Belbin, Meredith R, *Management Teams: Why They Survive or Fall*, Heinemann, 1990

Bennis, Warren, *On Becoming a Leader*, Hutchinson Business Books, 1990.

Benson, Herbert, with William Proctor, *Your Maximum Mind*, the Aquarius Press, 1998.

Bowman, Lee, with Andrew Crofts, *High Impact Business Presentations: How to Speak Like an Expert and Sound Like a Statesman*, Business Books, 1991.

Boyatzis, R, *The Competent Manager*, New York: John Wiley, 1982

Bray, D W, and D L Grant, *The Assessment Centre in the Measurement of Potential for Business Management*, Psychological Monographs, American Psychological Association, 1966

Cadbury, Sir Adrian, *The Company Chairman*, Director Books, Simon & Schuster International Group, 1990.

Cattell, R B, *The Scientific Analysis of Personality*, Penguin, Hammondsworth, 1965

Charlesworth, V, *Are Managers Under Stress?*, A Survey of Management Morale, London, Institute of Management, 1996

Cliffe, Sarah, 'Human Resources: Winning the War for Talent', *Harvard Business Review*, September–October, 1998.

Cronbach, Lee J, *Essentials of Psychological Testing*, 5th Edition, Harper and Row, 1990

De Bono, Edward, *Lateral Thinking for Management*, Penguin Books, 1982.

De Bono, Edward, *Sur/Petition, Creating Value Monopolies when Everyone Else is Merely Competing*, Harper, 1992.

De Bono, Edward. *Opportunities*, Penguin Books, 1983.

De Pree, Max, 'The Leadership Quest: Three Things Necessary', *Business Strategy Review*, Spring, 1993.

Deci, EL, 'The Effects of Contingent and Non-contingent Rewards and Controls on Intrinsic Motivation', *Organisational and Human Performance*, 8, pp. 217–229, 1972.

Demb, Ada, and F Friedrick Neubauer, *The Corporate Board: Confronting the Paradoxes*, Oxford, 1992.

Drucker, Peter F, *Managing the Future: The 1990s and Beyond*, Dutton, 1992.

Finck, Günther, Johanna Timmers, and Menno Mennes, *Measuring and Managing Employee Motivation*, The Conference Board Council Report, 1998.

Flanagan, J C, 'The Critical Incident Technique', *Psychological Bulletin*, Vol 51 1954.

Gabarro, John J, and P Kotter, 'Managing Your Boss', *Harvard Business Review*, January–February 1980.

Gabarro, John J, *The Dynamics of Taking Charge*, Harvard Business School Press, 1987.

Gardner, Howard, *Multiple Intelligence: The Theory in Practice*, New York, Basic Books, 1993

Gardner, Howard, with Emma Larkin, *Leading minds: An anatomy of Leadership*, Harper Collins, 1996.

Garratt, Bob, *The Fish Rots from the Head*, Harper Collins Business, 1996.

Goleman, Daniel, *Emotional Intelligence*, Bloomsbury, 1996

Gross, Richard D, Psychology, *The Science of Mind and Behaviour*, Hodder & Stoughton, 1992, 2nd edn.

Guilford, J P, *Traits of Creativity* in H H Anderson (Ed), *Creativity and its Cultivation*, Harper, 1959.

Hamel, Gary, and C. K. Prahalad, *Competing for the Future*, Harvard Business School Press, 1994.

Handy, Charles, *The Empty Raincoat*, Hutchinson, 1994.

Handy, Charles, *The Hungry Spirit*, Hutchinson, 1997.

Herzberg, F, *Work and the Nature of Man*, Cleveland: World Publishing, 1966.

Hofstede, Geert, *Culture's Consequences*, Sage, 1980.

Hogan, G W, and J R Godson, 'The Key to Expatriate Success', *Training and Development Journal*, Vol 44, 1990.

Hough, Leaetta M, and Robert J Schneider, *Personality Traits, Taxonomies and Applications in Organisations*, in K R Murphy (Ed) *Individual Differences and Behaviour in Organisations*, Jossey-Bass, 1996.

Huffington, Clare, 'Stress at Work', *Organisations and People – Quarterly Journal of AMED*, Kogan Page, August 1997.

Hull, C L, *Principles of Behaviour*, New York: Appleton-Century Crofts, 1943.

Hunter, J E, and F L Schmidt, *Fitting People to Jobs: The Impact of Personnel Selection on National Productivity*, in M D Dunnette and E A Fleishman (Eds), *Human Performance and Productivity: Human Capability Assessment*, Erlbaum, 1982.

Hunt, John, *Managing People at Work*, McGraw-Hill, 1992, 3rd edn.

Jacobs, Rick R, et al., 'Selecting Bus Drivers', *Human Performance* 9 (3), 1996.

Jacobs, Rick R, Frank Landy and James Farr, 'Cost Benefit analysis of Police Personnel Programmes', *Police Chief*, June 1982.

Kaplan, Robert S., and David P Norton, 'Using the Balanced Scorecard as a Strategic Management System', *Harvard Business Review*, January–February, 1996.

Katzenbach, Jon R, 'The Myth of the Top Management Team', *Harvard Business Review*, November–December, 1997.

Kelly, George A, For practical description see Stewart, Valerie and Andrew Stewart op cit.

Kleiner, Art, and George Roth, 'How to Make Experience the Company's Best Teacher', *Harvard Business Review*, September–October, 1997.

Kotter, John P, *A Force for Change*, Free Press, 1990.

Kotter, John P, and James Hesketh, *Corporate Culture and Performance*, Free Press, 1992.

Kotter, John P., *The Leadership Factor*, Free Press, 1988.

Kotter, John P, *The New Rules: how to Succeed in Today's Post-Corporate World*, The Free Press, 1995.

Kouzes, James M, and Barry Z Posner, *Credibility: How Leaders Gain and Love It, Why People Demand It*, Jossey Bass, 1993.

Latham, Gary P, and Glen Whyte, 'The Futility of Utility Analysis', *Personnel Psychology*, 1994.

Lessem, R, and S P Palsule, *Managing in Four Worlds*, Blackwell, 1997

Lombardo, Michael M, and Robert W Eichinger, *The Leadership Architect Suite*, Lominger Limited, Inc, 1997.

Mabey, Bill and Bruce W Thompson, *Implementing a European Development and Assessment Centre*, EWOP Congress Paper, Alicante, 1993.

Maslow, A H, *Motivation and Personality*, New York: Harper and Row, 1954.

McClelland, D C, *Human Motivation*, Cambridge: Cambridge University Press, 1987.

Miller, George A, 'Psychology as a Means of Promoting Human Welfare', *American Psychologist* No 24, 1969.

Mintzberg, Henry, 'The Manager's Job: Folklore and Fact', *Harvard Business Review*, July–August 1975.

Mischel, W, *Personality and Assessment*, New York, Wiley 1968.

Morton, Clive, *Beyond World Class*, Macmillan, 1998.

Murray, H A, *Explorations in Personality*, New York: Oxford University Press, 1938.

Myers, I B, and M H McCaulley, *Manual: A Guide to the Development and Use of the Myers-Briggs Type Indicator*, Paolo Alto, Consulting Psychologists Press, 1985.

Nonaka, O, and H Takeuchi, *The Knowledge Creating Company*, Oxford University Press, 1998.

Nyfield Gill, Pat Gibbons, and Rab MacIver, *Practical Implications of Assessing International Managers*, International Assessment Conference Paper, Minneapolis, 1993.

Pascale, Richard T, *Managing on the Edge*, Viking, 1990.

Pedlar, M, J Burgoyne, and T Boydell, *The Learning Company*, McGraw Hill, 1995.

Pfeffer, Jeffrey, *Competitive Advantage through People: Unleashing the Power of the Workforce*, Harvard Business Press, 1994.

Pfeffer, Jeffrey, *Managing with Power*, Harvard Business Press, 1994.

Pfeffer, Jeffrey, *The Human Equation: Building Profits by Putting People First*, Harvard Business Press, 1998.

Porter, Michael, *Competitive Advantage: Creating and Sustaining Superior Performance*, The Free Press, 1985.

Prokesch, Steven E, 'Unleashing the Power of Learning: An Interview with British Petroleum's John Browne', *Harvard Business Review*, September–October, 1997.

Quinn, James Brean, Philip Anderson, and Sydney Finkelstein, 'Managing Professional Intellect', *Harvard Business Review*, March–April, 1996.

Rowbottom, R, and D Billis, *Organisational Design: The Work Levels Approach*, Gower, 1987.

Ryan, Anne-Marie, *Unpublished Report (to date) on an International Survey of Assessment Practice*, Michigan State University, 1998.

Saville & Holdsworth (UK) Limited, Note: This is a source of various surveys on Appraisal, 360° Instruments, Graduate Recruitment and Assessment Practices in general. The latest of these all date around the late 1990s.

Saville & Holdsworth (UK) Limited, *Occupational Personality Questionnaires – Expert System, Manual and Users' Guide*, Saville & Holdsworth (UK) Limited, 1992.

Saville & Holdworth (UK) Limited, *Motivation Questionnaire – Manual & Users Guide*, Saville & Holdsworth (UK) Limited, 1992.

Saville, Peter F et al., *Manual to the Occupational Personality Questionnaires*, Saville & Holdsworth (UK) Limited, 1993

Senge, Peter, *The Fifth Discipline: The Art and Practice of The Learning Organisation*, Currency Doubleday, 1994.

Shackleton, Viv and Sue Newell, *International Assessment and Selection* in *International Handbook of Selection and Assessment*, (Anderson, N and P Herriot Eds) op. cit., 1997.

SHL UK, 'What Does the OPQ Say About the UK Population?', *OPQ Update*, Issue 15, March 1997.

Skinner, B F, *Science and Human Behaviour*, New York: Macmillan, 1953.

Smith, Mike, and Ivan T Robertson (Eds), *Advances in Selection and Assessment*, John Wiley & Sons, 1989.

Stewart, Valerie and Andrew Stewart, *Business Applications of Repertory Grid*, McGraw-Hill, 1981.

Tesluk, Paul E and Rick R Jacobs, 'Towards an Integrated Model of Work Experience', *Personnel Psychology* 1998.

The British Psychological Society, *Graphology in Personnel Assessment*, British Psychological Society, 1993

The Conference Board, 'Strategies for Retaining Critical Talent', *HR Executive Review*, 1998.

Trompenaars, Fons, *Riding The Waves of Culture*, Nicholas Brealey, 1993.

UMIST/SHL, 'The Criterion Related Validity of the OPQ: Some Recent Findings', *OPQ Update*, Issue 9, January 1995.

Vroom, V J, *Work and Motivation*, New York: Wiley, 1964.

Index